The War against the New Deal

The War against the
NEW DEAL

World War II
and American
Democracy

Brian Waddell

NORTHERN ILLINOIS UNIVERSITY PRESS / DeKalb 2001

© 2001 by Northern Illinois University Press

Published by the Northern Illinois University Press,

DeKalb, Illinois   60115

Manufactured in the United States using acid-free paper

All Rights Reserved

Design by Julia Fauci

Library of Congress Cataloging-in-Publication Data

Waddell, Brian

The war against the New Deal: World War II and American
democracy / Brian Waddell.

    p.   cm.

Includes bibliographical references and index.

ISBN 0-87580-272-9 (acid-free paper)

1. United States—History—1933–1945. 2. United States—
Politics and government—1933–1945. 3. New Deal,

1933–1939. 4. World War, 1939–1945—United States.

5. World War, 1939–1945—Social aspects—United States.

6. War and society—United States—History—20th century.

I. Title.

E806.W17 2001

973.917—dc21   00-061681

For Sarah and Julian

Contents

Acknowledgments

- I acquired many debts in completing this project. Bill Scheuerman offered early inspiration and showed me the way to the City University of New York's Graduate Center, where I found an intellectual home like no other. Once there, Frances Fox Piven provided warm and generous assistance while demonstrating time and again her unique ability to grasp the simple ideas at the heart of my complicated formulations. John Bowman in turn provided invaluable guidance by seeing where my inquiries were leading me before I was aware of it. Both Frances and John helped give my ideas form and offered friendship along with their advice. Friends and colleagues Vito Serravallo, Bill Sites, Tom Kriger, Steve Valocchi, Colin Hay, and Howard Reiter listened to my ideas and read and commented on portions of the manuscript. They all helped me over serious hurdles and provided feedback crucial to the development of my ideas and to this manuscript. James Fesler, professor emeritus of Yale University and formerly with the War Production Board, generously rehashed controversies fifty years distant and commented on the manuscript. Harry Magdoff and Edythe First, both with the War Production Board and firsthand observers of tumultuous wartime domestic battles, also offered their insights and encouragement. Stan Luger and Garry Clifford reviewed the entire manuscript, offering suggestions and flagging problems. Garry also introduced me to the Roosevelt Library and to important matters about wartime politics and modern-day baseball, and Stan offered a sympathetic ear and coconspirator's voice to the difficulties of comprehending and conceptualizing issues of economic and political power. I also want to single out the great debt owed to Fred Pfeil, who at the end provided invaluable assistance through his careful reading and painstaking attention to the manuscript. Martin Johnson at Northern Illinois University Press and two anonymous readers also offered advice that greatly improved the presentation of my argument. Alongside my great appreciation for the generosity of these friends and colleagues, I note that final responsibility for the book lies with me.

Many institutions financially supported my research and writing, including the Robert F. Wagner Institute of Public Policy, CUNY Graduate Center, the Franklin and Eleanor Roosevelt Institute, the Harry S Truman Institute, and the Research Foundation of the University of Connecticut.

Earlier versions of some of the material presented here appeared in the following journal articles: "Economic Mobilization for World War II and the Transformation of the U.S. State," *Politics and Society* 22 (1994); "The Dimensions of the Military Ascendancy during U.S. Mobilization for World War II," *Journal of Political and Military Sociology* 23 (1995); and "Corporate Influence and World War II: Resolving the New Deal Political Stalemate," *Journal of Policy History* 11 (1999): 223–56. (Copyright 1999 by The Pennsylvania State University. Reproduced by permission of The Pennsylvania State University Press.)

Last, I would like to thank my seven siblings (Karen, Judy, Dave, Deb, Laurie, Barb, and Cherie) and their families, along with my parents, David and Millicent, who indirectly supported my work during the many years of graduate study and beyond. My greatest single debt overall, of course, is to my wife and life-partner, Sarah Raskin, for always helping me clarify my ideas and for her continual support and encouragement. She and our son, Julian, are my life's treasures.

The War against the New Deal

Introduction

War and Statebuilding

• Up to the eve of World War II, America's military institutions exercised relatively little influence within the corridors of national power. The war changed all that, and the postwar institutionalization of a national security state ensured that we would not return to our prewar ways. Yet few scholars acknowledge the central influence of World War II in shaping the contemporary American state, and those that do typically ignore the military-corporate alliance that both dominated domestic economic mobilization and formed the basis for the postwar national security state. This study focuses on the alliance between the military and corporate America in order to explain the success of World War II statebuilding—but it does not celebrate this success. Domestic wartime battles represented a continuation and even a culmination of New Deal–era struggles over the shape of national authority. The military-corporate alliance triumphed in these battles by strengthening the power of the U.S. national state at the cost of compromising and diminishing America's democratic character.[1]

Why the myopia about the war's impact on U.S. statebuilding? The scholarly drive to comprehend the exceptionalist U.S. welfare state and the inattention to the national security state's impact on domestic national governance plays a part. Scholars lavish attention upon the New Deal and domestic policy-making capabilities to explain the divergence of the United States from western Europe's path of expansive social welfare policies. Yet a focus on domestic New Deal and welfare policies leads to inadequate and misleading assessments of "feeble" U.S. national capabilities compared with the welfare states of western Europe. U.S. national governance, after all, is not only defined by its welfare state but also by a powerful and encompassing national security "warfare" state that rivals European welfare states in commitment of societal resources, in scope of authority and operations, and in isolation from popular forces. Accounting for the expansion of U.S. national governance therefore means understanding this national security state and how wartime mobilization produced the institutions and policies that created this path for American political development.[2]

Although both depression and war spurred the modern expansion and consolidation of U.S. national authority, war was more influential. Since the late 1870s, U.S. national officials had struggled to develop and strengthen national administrative capacities in order to better manage the nation's growing economic instabilities and related class tensions. National authority and administrative capacities grew during the Progressive Era, World War I, and even the 1920s. But it was during the exceptional statebuilding consolidations of the 1930s and 1940s—decades of depression and war—that U.S. national governance achieved its modern form. Still, political fragmentation, expressed especially in executive-congressional conflict, combined with deepening tensions between business and government to limit the successes of Roosevelt's New Deal.

The New Deal established the beginnings of a national welfare state and managed to absorb the disruptive impulses of the depression, but the 1930s ended in a grand political stalemate pitting New Deal activists against a conservative congressional coalition. War arrived at this crucial moment, and struggles over mobilizing the economy for war became entwined with the politics of strengthening the national state. The war did not halt New Deal–era battles, and wartime developments were neither ancillary nor in any way inconsequential to U.S. political development. Rather, war upended and reoriented both national politics and business-government relations, producing new alternatives for resolving the statebuilding impasse of the late 1930s. While the New Deal thus increased the institutional responsibilities of government and heralded the U.S. welfare state, it raised controversies that were only resolved by mobilizing for war. And the results of wartime statebuilding—a weak welfare state complemented and dominated by a far more powerful national security state—provided the essential underpinnings for postwar U.S. governance.

During the 1930s, popular mobilizations prodded activist national politicians to establish greater political control of the economy. Expanding national authority associated with the New Deal appeared threatening to most corporate class forces, especially as these forces found themselves discredited and disoriented and unable to dominate the political landscape as fully as they had in the recent past. The requirements of total war, however, revived corporate political leverage, allowing corporate executives inside and outside the national state extensive influence over wartime mobilization policies. Emboldened and empowered, these executives abetted a domestic military ascendancy within the national state because greater power for the military meant heavy reliance upon major corporations, and because the consequent shift of authority and resources from New Dealers to military and corporate personnel narrowed domestic policy alternatives. Assertive corporate executives and military officials formed a very effective wartime alliance that not only blocked any augmentation of New Dealer authority but also organized a powerful alternative to the New Deal. International activism justified by anticommunism displaced and supplanted New Deal domestic activism.

Thus, postwar international hegemony and growing tensions with the Soviet Union pulled the United States toward a national security state, but powerful state and class forces pushed in that direction as well. Influential corporate executives tipped the balance of power within national politics in favor of military and national security institutions and policies. Although the wartime role of corporate advisors and industry advisory committees is often acknowledged, corporate political influence is insufficiently analyzed as a force that shaped wartime statebuilding. Following in the steps of the dominant pluralist tradition, most scholars of modern U.S. statebuilding analytically isolate politics from class power, thereby narrowing their empirical understanding of the dynamics of statebuilding.

Research on the origins of national states has reinforced this predisposition by suggesting that total wars modify the usual relationship between state and society, allowing state officials expansive autonomy relative to economic elites. As Theda Skocpol has argued, "International military pressures and opportunities can prompt state rulers to attempt policies that conflict with, and even in extreme instances contradict, the fundamental interests of a ruling class." Fred Block, taking the argument further, observes that in "certain historical periods . . . the capitalist context changes, allowing state managers more freedom of action in relation to capitalists." During "exceptional periods" such as total war and economic depression, states are driven to expand their activities at the same time that societal pressures on state activities are relaxed. During total wars, for example, state management of the economy increases, thanks to the need for national economic controls, the prominence of military over private production, and the heightened patriotism that overwhelms potential business resistance.[3]

These are attractive arguments that substantiate attempts to downplay and even disregard the role of class forces. As a general rule, however, the assumption that total wars in particular grant state officials greater leverage over their societies does not stand close scrutiny. Despite having to take positive action, state officials continue to be constrained in various ways by privately organized production. However much the bargaining position of state officials increases during total wars in the modern era, the managerial and production expertise of corporate executives increases their own leverage as well. After all, private ownership implies exclusion not only of other classes but also of state officials. This power is legitimate (in both legal and ideological terms) and difficult to override, even in the face of a national emergency.

Wars also necessitate greater interdependence between states and their societies. States may be ultimately responsible for waging wars, but they cannot succeed without mobilizing society, which is difficult to achieve by blunt coercion. Even with the increased legitimacy granted to modern states during wars, concessions to the general public and to economic elites must be offered to facilitate full mobilization; indeed, success at war is often predicated upon such concessions. Emergency expansion of state authority over economic activities, for example, will be more effective and accepted if influential class forces are allowed to guide these initiatives. Thus, mobilizing for total war can result in gains for society as well as for the state, especially in liberal capitalist states that must, while ultimately relying upon coercion, induce cooperation from most of its citizens and classes.[4]

Wars also do not halt intragovernmental institutional conflicts. Even during total wars, state officials compete for power and influence. Deepening state interventions do not by themselves signify expanding state autonomy, because an increase in state responsibilities inevitably disperses authority among a growing number of state agencies, thereby exacerbating problems of internal state competition and central coordination. For state officials jockeying for control of an expanding state apparatus, class forces can become important allies.[5]

More generally, World War II did not supplant the debates and controversies raised by the Great Depression and the New Deal. War certainly provided a new and distinct logic to U.S. statebuilding. But state and class competitors for control of economic mobilization interpreted wartime disputes in terms of the unresolved controversies of the depression, namely, whether and to what extent governmental authority would intrude upon corporate prerogatives. Although it may be true, then, that many early modern states were built on the back of military necessity, for the United States in the 1940s military necessity existed alongside the struggles associated with the depression's economic devastation. These points suggest that total wars do not inevitably increase state autonomy over powerful class forces such as nationally prominent business interests, nor do wars necessarily supplant concerns about economic relations.[6]

Power, the State, and Statebuilding

Of course, the reluctance to consider the political impact of corporate power reflects long-standing biases within social science. To study the state is to analyze the exercise of power, and this explains the furious debates among scholars of state development and institutional change. Scholarly debates about whether the state and politics are autonomous from class forces reflect fundamental disagreements among social scientists about who exercises power and what constitutes the proper subject matter and method for analyzing the exercise of power. Many scholars studying the state analytically isolate political and economic power, arguing that it is reductionist to study politics and statebuilding in terms of class or economic power. But explaining wartime statebuilding requires a comprehension of corporate political influence over and within both wartime institutional struggles and the construction of stable postwar U.S. governance. To bring class forces into an analysis of U.S. political development we need to expand upon the dominant scholarly categories that marginalize the political impact of major corporations or other class forces. To do this, we need a theoretical perspective that sheds light on the interdependencies and interpenetration of state and class power.

Interestingly, scholars who clash over issues of power and the state do agree about the need to investigate the institutional and structural forces that shape political behavior. In general, postwar social science emphasized the study of behavior over and against the study of institutions. Inspiring a generation of scholars, political scientist David Truman defended a focus on "observable operating relationships" as a necessary corrective to the "pitfalls of a too literal" focus on the "formalized institutions of government." Critics, however, eventually charged that focusing on direct, behavioral manifestations of power ignored the indirect exercise of power expressed in institutional arrangements. Scholars began to realize that analyzing behavior alone resulted in a flawed and superficial understanding of power that could only be remedied by comprehending the interrelations of structure (institutions) and agency (behavior). Scholars interested in the state, at odds over many issues, seemed to agree that institutional arrangements provide an essential starting point for fully assessing the exercise of power.[7]

Of course, Truman's influential behavioral-pluralist explanation of U.S. politics did not so much evade the historical and institutional context of the U.S. as it assumed that existing political rules and norms maximized the ability of most if not all societal forces to participate in and influence political decision making. Much of the pluralist research of the 1950s and 1960s, in turn, assumed a benign and unobtrusive state and a wide dispersal of power resources. Critics, in response, explored the ways that the rules, norms, and institutions of U.S. politics circumscribe the political opportunities of various groups and interests. E. E. Schattschneider, for example, exposed the pluralist error of assuming freedom of play among societal forces by analyzing the exclusionary impact and class bias of political and economic institutional arrangements.

And neo-Marxist Ralph Miliband specifically focused attention on the ways that the organization and expressions of state power reflected economic and social power. Miliband argued for renewed attention to the state, stressing that "a theory of the state is also a theory of society and of the distribution of power in that society."[8]

Beginning with Miliband's celebrated retort to the dominant pluralist paradigm in *The State in Capitalist Society,* neo-Marxists debated alternative methods for understanding the political and economic constraints on democracy and the interrelationships between capitalism, class power, and the state. However, underlying disputes among neo-Marxists—focused on determining the cause-and-effect relationship of structure versus agency—distracted attention from a melange of worthy theoretical propositions and provided critics with ammunition to denounce the entire intellectual project. Hence, besides being summarily dismissed by most pluralists, neo-Marxist investigations of the modern state spawned a reaction against their supposed reductionist and functionalist, society-centered biases.[9]

In response to both pluralists and neo-Marxists, scholars inspired by Max Weber developed a competing perspective presumably more attentive to the specific institutional processes of actually existing states. Advocates of a state-centered perspective argued that neo-Marxists reduced institutional and programmatic change to external class pressures or to the functional needs of capitalism. Both pluralism and neo-Marxism, they argued, are unalterably society centered. By contrast, a Weber-inspired, state-centered perspective emphasizes that states have a more or less autonomous impact because of the independent bureaucratic and coercive institutional resources of state officials (including both politicians and bureaucrats), the distinctive self-maximizing goals of state personnel, and the channeling and feedback effect of existing state institutions and policies. State autonomy is considered sui generis because of threats arising from an international system of states and because of the need to retain order and control within a nationally defined territory. States, it is argued, cannot be reduced to societal forces or economic imperatives; they are defined by nationally specific institutions and programs forged from unique historical battles by an autonomous set of officials and personnel with distinctive strategic interests and concerns.[10]

The strength of this perspective lies in its insistence on autonomous state officials, programs, and institutions and in its emphasis on concrete historical investigations of battles for power and authority between state personnel. Critics, however, grew concerned that state-centered analyses rigidly demarcated the state from society and consequently ignored the political impact of class forces. Even a sophisticated state-centered analysis such as Stephen Skowronek's influential study of the Progressive Era assumed that power struggles associated with institutional change are autonomous from class influence.[11]

Skowronek, whose work spurred much of the current interest in American political development, outlined a state-centered framework in which state officials and the existing institutional regime are themselves the central determinants of statebuilding. Skowronek correctly recognized that the state system often becomes the battleground for resolving crises confronting the broader society, and he understood that, because of the state's distinctive authoritative position, state officials shoulder the burden for negotiating stable transitions from crisis conditions. Since state officials may be unable to accomplish this task under the routines and relationships of the existing institutional regime, institutional reconstruction may become necessary. But institutional change is problematic because of political attachments to the preexisting institutional order that itself focuses and shapes statebuilding battles; it is through institutional battles "rooted in the peculiar structure of the old regime and mediated by shifts in electoral politics" that the new institutional regime is constructed.[12]

These are important insights that do not in themselves preclude considering the political impact of class forces. But it is clear that, for Skowronek, class forces are ancillary and often incidental to statebuilding efforts. They have little influence over and within the process of institutional change, since the challenges of statebuilding are considered distinct from the struggles of private groups working to exploit governmental power on their behalf. It is, after all, state officials who independently initiate and complete the task of institutional change, because the maintenance of order is their distinctive responsibility.[13] And state officials acquire a special interest in statebuilding outcomes because institutional change threatens their existing "power relationships and official prerogatives." Skowronek recognized, of course, the likelihood that "social and economic groups" would intervene in statebuilding conflicts, but he insists that societal interventions merely serve to exacerbate statebuilding difficulties: "The pressures exerted on government officials through established channels may . . . actually intensify the problems of making an effective response [to crises]."[14]

Skowronek fears that attention to class forces will "leave the emergence of the new state overdetermined but little understood." Instead, he means to treat "institutional development as a focus for analysis rather than as a mere epiphenomenon" of external forces, meaning of course that he assumes class forces cannot influence institutional development. This troublesome formulation sets up a false dichotomy. Investigating the interactions of state and class forces during periods of institutional development does not automatically reduce institutional change to external forces, nor does it preclude comprehending the sui generis political construction of a new institutional order.

Skowronek's framework, although useful, is insufficient if we wish to comprehend the interactions between state and class forces that are part of building stable and coherent national governance. Entwined with the governmental struggle for power is a struggle over how state power affects social and economic power. To comprehend these struggles it is necessary to consider the political impact of class forces. Neo-Marxist attention to the interrelations of class and state power, while perhaps insufficient in itself, can be integrated with the Weberian frameworks to cast a wider empirical net over the statebuilding moments under examination. Yet such a course remains controversial. Although analyses that integrate categories of state and class have grown in sophistication, many scholars continue blithely to assume that they lead to reductionist or functionalist analyses that ignore the state's autonomy and evade the open-ended and indeterminate nature of politics.

Despite the undoubted relevance of statist concerns, we need to overcome the fiction that state and society are independent and fully autonomous and that statebuilding can be understood best by analytically isolating state from society. The need to bring the state back into the analysis of power was a consequence of the unwillingness of behavioralists to fully consider how structural-institutional arrangements shape behavior.[15] Critics of behavioralism sought to identify structural factors in order to properly analyze power in terms of both structure and agency. The state-centered perspective failed in this project because, while promoting a shift from the behavioral-pluralist concern with "behavior within a given set of institutional constraints to the constraints themselves," it shared with the pluralist perspective the willingness to analytically isolate political institutions from class power.[16]

The formal separation of the state from the society and its economy has often prevented scholars from analyzing politics and statebuilding in terms of the relations between state and class power. State theorist Nicos Poulantzas understood, however, that although the state and economy appear fully autonomous they nonetheless "are *from the very beginning* constituted by their mutual relation and articulation." Certainly the state and the economy are formally distinct and in this sense autonomous—each sphere embraces distinct organizations, personnel, and goals. Yet states and societies are also constructed in terms of their relations to one another. Property relations are, for instance, constituted and enshrined legally: "Property is a political artifact, created by state law and maintained by state force."[17]

If anything, then, the formal separation of the state from the economy produces overt interdependencies between state officials and class forces. The division of state and economic power embodies a structural division of labor in which state officials are under pressure to maintain order and stability while limited in their ability to do so by the prerogatives of owners and private corporate managers. State officials are legally and ideologically excluded from organizing profitable production themselves. Thus, not only do a large number of policy questions lie beyond their direct control, but state officials depend on private business forces for economic stability. Moreover, state officials do not produce their own material resources; instead they fund their activities through revenues extracted from the private economy. Because of the delimitations of state power and the dependence on private economic activity, state officials internalize a general concern that any political threat to profits or private economic prerogatives may trigger disruptive investment strikes and economic instability. Certainly, state officials must also secure a degree of general public support, but in most cases the easiest way to maintain public order and stability is to maintain the conditions for profitable growth.[18]

State officials have little choice but to accept the constraints of private ownership and managerial prerogatives as central to the rules of the political game. Accordingly, although a general level of business's leverage in politics is built into the state-economy division of labor, it is also a conscious product of how state officials are socialized into their jobs and responsibilities. Charles Lindblom, a long-time pluralist, goes even further when he observes that state officials actively participate in maintaining public acceptance of business prerogatives: "Since theirs is the task of seeing to it that business performs, [state officials] do not want the fundamentals of private enterprise to become lively political issues." As a general rule, then, state officials comprehend the public, national interest in terms of the "privileged position" of business and the need for private profit.[19]

Despite these limits on the scope of state authority and on the sensibilities of state officials, neo-Marxists and others understand that only state officials are positioned to mediate, however contingently, the intensifying conflicts and assorted instabilities occasioned by an increasingly complex economic system. Thus, political interventionism has generally increased over time as central states have developed capacities to mediate problems of destabilizing competition, economic downturns, chronic inequality, and environmental destruction. Needless to say, state officials have no perfect knowledge of what will stabilize capitalism. The constraints they operate under in no way determine the specific content of their actions. State officials are themselves often forced to calculate and make decisions based on short-term competitive or security pressures; their actions have unforeseen and unintended consequences; and certainly economic instabilities can never be entirely resolved. Thus, there is no implied guarantee that state officials will succeed in promoting stable economic growth or securing the legitimacy of their rule, although they are driven to succeed for fear of the consequences. Rather, in most cases, political attempts to resolve economic instabilities will be, virtually by definition, contingent, indeterminate, and temporary despite the tendency for such attempts to cohere and congeal into fixed grooves and ruts.[20]

Skowronek understood statebuilding strategically, but he limited his analysis to the strategic problems of overcoming the division, competition, and resistance to change within the state system. Yet highlighting the structural interdependencies of the state and the private economy suggests that statebuilding is actually more complex than this, involving issues of power within and between the private economy and the state system. To begin with, any crisis-induced institutional reconstruction does more than revamp power relations within the state system. As Shattschneider reminded us long ago, "The function of institutions is to channel conflict; [yet] institutions do not treat all forms of conflict impartially . . . for the function of institutions is to discriminate among conflicts" and so discriminate among those engaged in conflict. Any particular state organization of politics, by mapping out a specific strategic terrain (institutional, programmatic, and ideological) that shapes the exercise of power, benefits certain political class forces by facilitating the exploitation of certain issues and strategies while discouraging and obstructing others. Statebuilding, by reconstructing the state's "strategic selectivity," refashions the opportunities for and constraints upon the exercise of class power and thereby threatens the existing balance of class power within society.[21]

Moreover, by expanding the scope and effect of state power, statebuilding disrupts the balance of power between state and society (which also affects the balance of class power within society). Indeed, Schattschneider observes that expanding public authority politicizes a great variety of social and class conflicts and so *"modif[ies] private power relations."* As Jurgen Habermas adds from a neo-Marxist vantage point, such expansions may involve "re-coupling the economic system to the political—which in a way repoliticizes the relations of production" so that "the class structure can now be directly affected by political disputes." Statebuilding, then, rouses intense controversy not only because it threatens governmental power relations but also because it disrupts private power relations and entails expanding state power over society and the economy.[22]

Precisely because the state is such a key determinant of class relations and class power, the state system is in general subject to, and shaped by, a political struggle that involves class forces. Simply put, we can generally expect that states shape and potentially threaten class and other social forces, and these forces in turn seek to shape states, especially during times of institutional change.[23] Accordingly, as state officials become more overtly involved in managing economic stability, class pressures within the state system will increase. And class forces, to the extent that they comprehend these opportunities and have the capacity and knowledge to act strategically, will seek to influence the direction and content of statebuilding. In strategic terms, then, statebuilding increases the interplay of state and class forces while it increases intragovernmental competitiveness, ensuring that the support or resistance of class forces will be crucial to successfully completing and legitimizing any reconstruction of the political order.[24]

Class forces are therefore strategically important to state officials during periods of institutional change because they may present either a barrier or necessary complement to any attempts to stabilize governance. Internal governmental divisions and competitions aroused during these periods make it very difficult for national officials to gain and hold state power in the absence of supportive class allies; true bureaucratic or institutional autonomy translates into vulnerability to other state officials and antagonistic class forces. By forging an alliance with class forces, state officials gain a key base of support. Such alliances also help resolve the tensions between state officials and powerful class forces caused by expanding state power. Class forces, for their part, do not passively wait to be courted by competing state officials. Rather, whether through active obstruction of those projects they fear or through strategic engagement with those projects they support, class forces can participate in the process of institutional change. Not only do state officials have their own reasons for utilizing class forces as allies in their governmental battles, but class forces seek to impose themselves in the statebuilding process.

The state-level institutional settlement (the post-crisis institutional pattern) and the broader accommodations between society and the state that are necessary to reconstruct and stabilize political rule together constitute what are referred to here as governance projects.[25] The hope is that such projects can help unify a fragmented state system while also legitimizing expanded state power to a class-divided society and to wary social and economic elites. Such projects are political creations characterized by a distinctive institutional, programmatic, and ideological framework that reflects the autonomous strategic interests of competing state officials in active alliance with class forces. Many scholars are now aware that reformulating ideological parameters is as crucial as institution building. Just as Schattschneider grasped long ago how political institutions bias policy outcomes, Colin Hay recently stressed that any particular ideological "mapping" of the available alternatives will necessarily "distort and simplify" how particular forces understand their options. Dominant political ideologies deteriorate during crisis periods, and the resulting ideological instability and uncertainty adds to the drama of statebuilding episodes. Successful governance projects are ideological in the sense that they reconstruct and channel political allegiances and normative expectations by reconstituting the central terms and alternatives of political discourse.[26]

This understanding of statebuilding can be briefly elucidated with reference to the U.S. experience in the Great Depression. The depression disrupted an existing stable relationship between the officials of the national state and U.S. business interests (the Republican-business hegemonic bloc of the 1920s), which excluded most popular forces (workers, small and tenant farmers, the elderly, the unemployed). This exclusionary form of governance, a product of the election of 1896 and post–World War I political dynamics, rested on shaky political and economic foundations, as the onset of depression itself demonstrated. The 1930s, however, aroused an expansionary political dynamic that was both cause and consequence of growing class conflicts over and within the state system. As the national state became more overtly involved in managing the economic crisis, and as economic suffering spread, the state system became a more legitimate and eventually a more hospitable arena for popular class forces.

Franklin D. Roosevelt's desire to gain and consolidate his hold on national power and the new political and institutional dynamics unleashed by his New Deal initiatives created their own distinctive logic, to be sure; yet class conflicts intruded even at this most overt level of politics. Roosevelt's hint of populist rhetoric in the 1932 presidential race raised popular expectations and granted popular class forces legitimacy in their agitation for a more responsive and democratic political order. The New Deal thus spawned new arenas not only for political conflicts but for class conflicts as well. New policies and institutions created new opportunities and incentives and a new sense of legitimacy for an expanding realm of political conflict, which in turn affected the very trajectory of the political response to crisis. Thus, 1930s statebuilding did not proceed separately and autonomously from class forces. Rather, new political initiatives and new forms of class conflict openly interpenetrated and reinforced one another within a dynamic and contingent political and economic environment.

Corporate Power and U.S. Statebuilding

Corporate class forces are of conspicuous importance to organizing governance at the national level in the United States, if only because such forces are the most likely partners for an alliance between class forces and the state. First, state officials are especially attuned to organized corporate power, since they have internalized the "privileged position" of business. Second, corporate executives are themselves vigilant and active in relation to expansions in political authority; they do not take their privileged position for granted, they fear growth in public authority, and they are organized through their individual firms and industries to protect their interests in policy matters. The U.S. business community may be competitive and divided on many issues and thus not reliably capable of effective political action, yet they project great legitimacy and have organizational and resource advantages over other class forces. And they are especially attuned to changes in the political order. As Robert Lynd posited, "It scarcely requires saying that organized [business] power tends to be most alert and active precisely at the hinge-points of change, where new options, or loss of customary ones, impend. Such options in our type of society may involve potential social gains at the expense of losses to organized private power, or the reverse." Moreover, the absence of an enduring leftist threat and the particularly weak and fragmented political order in the United States accentuate the leverage and power corporations can muster in relation to the state system. Corporate executives are thus of particular importance in U.S. politics because of their large reservoir of power, prestige, and influence and because they view statebuilding in terms of a zero-sum competition in which the expansion of public authority may expand class conflict, result in policies detrimental to particular firms and industries, or trespass upon private corporate prerogatives.[27]

Business, of course, is not a monolithic bloc; Poulantzas himself reminded us that it is precisely business divisions that prompt state officials to politically organize a measure of business unity as a base for their attempts to secure long-term economic stability. Still, some business forces are more significant than others when it comes to influencing politics. James O'Connor differentiated business firms on the basis of their size and market control. Smaller competitive-sector firms are of less interest in the formation of national policy than the much larger monopoly-sector firms—located in capital-goods industries such as metals processing, consumer-goods industries such as automotive production and related equipment (e.g., tires), and transportation industries—that engage in large-scale production for national or international markets. Corporate concentration in the United States was well advanced even before the depression shakeout of marginal firms. Economists Adolf Berle and Gardiner Means, for example, report that by 1932 80 percent of U.S. industry was owned and operated by 200 corporations. They conclude, "Clearly such great organisms [i.e., 'the modern giant corporation'] are not to be thought of in the same terms as the average company." The distinction between business firms will emerge all the more clearly in the battles over wartime mobilization that constitute the central concern of this study, since monopoly-sector firms and representatives overwhelmingly dominated military contracting and provided, by far, the largest percentage of personnel hired by both the civilian and military mobilization agencies.[28]

My narrative also draws upon G. William Domhoff's analysis of the four segments that compose the U.S. ruling class: first, an internationalist segment that includes "the largest of American corporations"; second, a nationalist manufacturing segment "symbolized by the [National Association of Manufacturers] and similar employer organizations" that is much more conservative than its internationalist brethren; third, a southern planter elite segment that has sided with the internationalist segment on matters of foreign policy and with the nationalist segment on labor and welfare issues; fourth, a more localized segment of real estate and development forces influential in urban-growth coalitions. Domhoff notes that the conservative nationalist segment's alliance with congressional conservatives has provided a blunt barrier to many reform initiatives that could be overcome only if the internationalist segment's "sophisticated conservatives" viewed reform as necessary to coopt more radical measures or as otherwise in their interest. For Domhoff, then, corporate internationalists can play a crucial positive role in guiding political outcomes, and their role is analyzed as such here.[29]

Besides the divisions among business interests, there is also the matter of their changing relationship to the state system, or, rather, their changing power in relation to state officials due to changing contextual events. There is no simple or steady power relationship between business and state officials, as the shifting relation of business forces to 1930s and 1940s statebuilding itself suggests. Although many business leaders looked to the national state for assistance as the Great Depression dragged on, many also became increasingly antistatist as the crisis granted state officials greater autonomy from particular business interests. The national state's growing autonomy and expanding interventions politicized economic conflicts and increasingly made the national state the target of popular class forces. Historian Howell Harris reminds us that during the New Deal corporate executives "suffered much more than a loss of self-confidence and prestige. There was a real reduction in their power vis-a-vis a burgeoning interventionist state, which they could no longer control, and the labor movement it fostered. Their traditional freedom to manage their own affairs was impaired, and the political environment in which they had to operate became much less certain and secure."[30]

Thus, it is not inevitable that corporate forces easily dominate within national politics. But it is true that, as the national state gained power and the changing balance of class power magnified possibilities for a progressive reconstruction of U.S. state power, many corporate executives became politically active to safeguard their profits and prerogatives. And, although corporate political influence declined during the years of depression, it increased substantially as the shift from depression to war increased the national state's reliance upon private production expertise and managerial control. In turn, corporate antagonism to any wartime expansion of New Dealer civilian authority within the state became an important variable in explaining the ascendancy of the wartime military state and the postwar national security state.

Understanding U.S. Statebuilding during World War II

Statebuilding should be understood in terms of the interplay of state and class forces. Very simply, both state and class forces were involved in the wartime institutional battles that, in turn, contributed greatly to the establishment of a successful postwar governance project. Of course, neither a class- nor state-determinist model can capture the complex relations of power contained in these statebuilding transformations. And, certainly, we can only specify the extent and depth of the interpenetration and relative impact of state and class forces through an empirical investigation attentive to the shifting historical context, the changing balance of class forces within the state and society, the varying balance of state forces, and the evolving political context.

Statebuilding during the 1930s and 1940s was, of course, complicated by the distinct yet interconnected crises of depression and war. The cataclysmic events of both depressions and wars are often thought to allow state officials expansive authority relative to economic elites. But the turn to war altered if not reversed the political equation of the depression by increasing the dependence of state officials upon major corporations. National officials had to prepare for war mobilization during a transitional period between depression and war, when a war-induced economic recovery, accompanied by an increasingly conservative and isolationist Congress, actually diminished the national state's leverage over corporate firms. And, given business opposition to the New Deal, it is hardly surprising that many corporate executives sought to exploit this situation for their own material and political benefit.

To understand wartime statebuilding, then, we must temper expectations of state autonomy and understand that the war did not displace altogether the conflicts and issues of the Great Depression. Certainly, the trajectory of statebuilding shifted as a result of the war, as one sector of the national state in particular—the military services—experienced the most dramatic growth. And certainly the resulting postwar "warfare state" was qualitatively different from the partially constructed "welfare state." It was the democratizing elements of the New Deal that corporate executives hoped to defeat by resisting any wartime expansion of domestic civilian-state authority. Corporate executives helped to channel state power into military institutions precisely because military officials did not threaten their prerogatives and because expanding military authority did not increase class tensions. The military ascendancy therefore cannot be understood simply in terms of either intragovernmental competition or the expanding wartime state autonomy. It is explicable only in terms of the interdependencies and alliances between military-state and corporate forces formed through both the narrow institutional battles of mobilization and the broader battles over the state's expanding national authority. And the successes of this wartime military-corporate alliance transformed American democracy as it channeled national power into the national security state.

The Crisis of Modern U. S. Governance

From War to Depression

• Political developments from World War I through to the New Deal set the stage for statebuilding battles during World War II. Mobilization for World War I drew upon the Progressive Era's corporate liberalism, yet war also inspired influential new departures in business-government relations. During the 1920s and the early New Deal, prominent national officials sought to capitalize on the wartime promise of a business-dominated corporatism. But the political pressures unleashed by the Great Depression and the 1932 election of Franklin Roosevelt produced contrasting political developments. Economic collapse reduced corporate political leverage and inspired innovative departures from the Progressive Era's deference to corporate power and from World War I's corporatism. Despite its limitations, New Deal programs substantially modified market relations as they broadly expanded national interventionist capacities and the class base of the national administration. Business fear and distrust of Roosevelt grew during the 1930s, keeping pace with increasing national authority and with the greater variety of class forces benefiting from national action. Increasing business hostility, matched by growing congressional-executive conflict over presidential authority, exacerbated the U.S. governing crisis. The resulting New Deal political stalemate set the stage for the battles over World War II mobilization.

The first stab at building national economic governance occurred during the Progressive Era. The statebuilding imperative gripped U.S. national officials as economic and social crises overwhelmed subnational governments and exposed the weaknesses of the traditional governing mechanisms of "courts and parties." Attempts to forge an independent regulatory and administrative base for assertive national authority proceeded haltingly, precisely because of threats to established intragovernmental and state-society relations. Expanding government power threatened to increase national authority over the states, strengthen the presidency over Congress and the courts, and disrupt or even displace the private prerogatives of powerful class forces in American society. Given the stakes involved, building national governance raised tensions between capitalist development and democratic accountability, igniting struggles within and over the state system. In attempting to resolve these tensions, Jeffrey Lustig concludes, the period witnessed "burgeoning government activity and diminishing public authority," since national officials did not use expanding responsibilities to challenge growing corporate power. Instead, the Progressive complacency about the distribution of economic power in U.S. society diminished the potential for democratically accountable public authority. In this way, Progressives helped to construct a consensus among corporate liberals that subordinated national policy to dominant corporate interests.[1]

Rhetorically, of course, Teddy Roosevelt's "New Nationalism" and Woodrow Wilson's "New Freedom" both sought to recast the emerging corporate order in terms of democratic norms and increasing public accountability. In this sense both projects responded to the rising public clamor for positive state action against the harsh exigencies of corporate capitalism. But fears that a broadly accountable interventionist national state would erode the nation's economic strength led national officials to limit regulatory initiatives. Wilson, for example, expressed reservations about concentrations of economic power that interfered with opportunity and prosperity. But his main reform efforts—the Federal Reserve Act of 1913 and the Clayton and Federal Trade Commission Acts of 1914—were not designed to challenge the new corporate economy but rather to liberalize trade and spur economic expansion.[2]

Progressives justified the actual subservience of national regulation to the national corporate economy in terms of progress, efficiency, scientific management, and corporate social responsibility. It was not corporate power per se that threatened the public interest and body politic, they argued, but rather the abuses of the aberrant bad "trust" and the economic and social maladjustments of inevitable corporate-capitalist development. The Progressive construction of state power thus focused on "adjusting law and government policy to the new economic order" and managing the aberrant side effects of otherwise laudable corporate concentration. Weakened parties and the vigorous resistance of Congress and the courts continued to hamper coherent national administration. Still, Progressive success can be measured by the containment of democratic agitation for a publicly accountable and assertive national authority.[3]

World War I and the War Industries Board

Although much wartime experimentation proved makeshift and patch-work, the hothouse environment of war nonetheless produced crucial new legacies well suited for the exclusionary dynamics of 1920s politics—the most important being government-sponsored, industrial self-government embodied in the War Industries Board. Because national administrative coherence and strength were impaired by ambiguous legislation, pressure by powerful regulated interests, regulatory agency divisiveness, and an often hostile Congress and judiciary, national officials leaned heavily upon voluntary corporate action in managing the war crisis. Of course, reliance on corporate management capacities reflected preference as well. National officials for the most part proved ideologically and sociologically predisposed to rely upon private, corporate personnel; they respected corporate leaders and had close ties to them. In turn, the new ideology of corporate liberalism reinforced the structural division of labor between state and economy. National officials, including President Wilson, did not want to trespass on corporate prerogatives; instead they wanted to protect the corporate economy from any uncontrolled expansion of the state's coercive and bureaucratic authority.[4]

Wanting to put a business-friendly face on his administration and to be seen at the forefront of preparedness as war intensified in Europe, Wilson supported efforts to bring private-sector business advisors, including financier Bernard Baruch, into his administration. The 1916 Army Appropriations Act created a Council of National Defense (CND) staffed by key Cabinet members, who would in turn appoint and oversee a National Defense Advisory Commission (NDAC) staffed with these private-sector experts. At first the business advisors enjoyed no clear authority or mandate and so occupied an ambiguous position in relation to both the national state and the corporate economy. Creatures of the private economy, they sought the prestige that affiliation with the national administration would bring, but they were also driven by a strong desire to protect the private economy and their corporate brethren from expanding the control of the national state. To minimize statist precedents they sought to carve out a place for themselves within the national administration, although given their lack of formal authority and uncertain political standing they had to focus on developing an informal and voluntary system. They set about developing voluntary industry-wide agreements on prices and production and organizing informal business-government administrative mechanisms to coordinate the economy. Although they hoped to showcase for peacetime uses the successful wartime synchronization of corporate and state power, their immediate goal was to draw other industry leaders into their orbit and build a voluntary public-private partnership to forestall the need for a full-blown, state-led mobilization effort.

Bernard Baruch, a well-known Wall Street financier and an original NDAC appointee, became a central figure in industrial mobilization because his pragmatic methods tended to work. Baruch's "elitist conception of mobilization" was simple; as raw materials coordinator he built an informal network of the acknowledged leaders of the industries he oversaw. Knowing that large producers had the most experience with price controls, industry cooperation, and planning—not to mention their effective domination of various industrial sectors—Baruch sought their cooperation first. Baruch also brought prominent industry personnel into the NDAC on a "dollar-a-year" basis to facilitate agreements within their industries. Baruch showed that effective national economic management, even if organized by industry advisors, required cultivation of a direct relationship between state and corporate officials. Relying upon the personnel and networks of private industry, he helped secure industry cooperation in the absence of statutory authority. And Baruch's particular talent in building relations with President Wilson, key industrialists, and knowledgeable industry personnel propelled him to the forefront of mobilization efforts.[5]

Baruch's ad hoc system of industry leaders formed into "cooperative committees of industry" depended for its success on centralized control within an industry and on voluntary cooperation of prominent industrialists. Yet, although highly competitive industries had a difficult time reaching stabilizing agreements, even more oligopolized or monopolized industries faced problems as well. Reliance on voluntary industry agreements left participants vulnerable to cheaters or to legal challenge due to charges of collusion and price fixing. For all its general effectiveness, Baruch's voluntaristic system exposed the need for centralized, formal authority to protect participants from antitrust prosecution and to guarantee industry-wide cooperation.[6]

Such difficulties in organizing effective agreements between businessmen corresponded to, and were exacerbated by, efforts to overcome the anachronisms and divisions of the U.S. national state. Most acute and omnipresent were divisions within the military services. Although the army and navy competed for goods and services, the most daunting hurdle became the competitive autonomy of army supply bureaus (at first five and later eight). When war was declared in April 1917, the army began a fivefold expansion. Individual army bureaus, subject to no outside coordination, quickly overwhelmed the production capability of the nation's industries as they scrambled to fill their own individual orders. To make matters worse, Secretary of War Newton Baker supported the army supply bureaus in their tenacious resistance to any external control or coordination.[7]

Decentralized and uncontrolled army procurement itself threatened to bring down the entire economy. Not only did business advisors have to organize each industry, but they had to somehow link up the industry with the relevant military bureaus. Even then, overall coordination was stymied by profligate military contracting. Without centralized authority to prioritize demands, prices shot up and disorder reigned. Ironically, the business advisors discovered that weak and disorganized government proved a greater threat to business freedom and economic stability than a strong and effective one. They were careful, however, to demand that increased state power be well insulated from politicians and the general public and constituted to facilitate "private rather than public supervision."[8]

In this search for a friendly form of national economic governance, Baruch enjoyed the support of President Wilson, who did not wish to disrupt or supplant basic corporate prerogatives by developing an intrusive and burdensome state bureaucracy. Still, because of the War Department's "paranoia" toward businessmen, it was extremely difficult to establish external coordination of military procurement. Army leaders had been fighting for decades to rein in its bureaus and now faced the threat of having to surrender control to business advisors. Wilson, resistant to expansive governmental authority over business and protective of traditional governmental functions, proved reluctant to countenance broad executive power such as that required by the creation of a munitions ministry. And so, as a temporary fix, Wilson accepted Secretary of War Baker's plan for a War Industries Board (WIB) in January 1917. Wilson saw the idea as a welcome compromise; its creation would meet the growing public and congressional clamor for change while providing cover for continuing private cooperative arrangements. Wilson found a central place within the WIB for the business advisors, but the board answered to Baker and the CND.[9]

Despite Wilson's hopes for this new setup, Baruch's industry committees invited scandal as dollar-a-year businessmen acted both as government contracting agents and as their firm's contractors. It certainly did not help that Baruch's ad hoc mechanisms did little to resolve the overall coordination problem; the deteriorating economic situation reinforced a crescendo of public and congressional condemnation of the informal collusive system. Baruch's cooperative committees of industry, at the center of the profiteering scandal, were forced to disband as section 3 of the 1917 Lever Act prevented business officials from influencing the awarding of contracts to their firms and industries.[10]

To get around the new restrictions, the WIB enlisted the U.S. Chamber of Commerce to establish new industry bodies capable of formal and open cooperation with the WIB. Theoretically, the chamber, a private organization, would shoulder responsibility for organizing new industry associations called "war service committees." And these, in turn, would negotiate with public sector WIB businessmen and industry dollar-a-year men. The more formalized relationship between distinct public and private officials proved palatable to Congress and the American public, despite the fact that the new system often simply masked Baruch's old system of gentlemen's agreements. One major advantage of the new system, of course, was broader protection from antitrust prosecution, because the Wilson administration found itself encouraging, if not demanding, the collective organization of most industries. For the business advisors, the organization of trade associations was crucial to legitimating their industry-centered management of mobilization. Certainly, the war saw a great expansion in the number and importance of trade associations, a development crucial to business-government relations in the interwar period.[11]

Of course, rationalizing industry participation through war service committees could not rectify the WIB's lack of authority or overcome chaotic army procurement. In fact, the economic situation deteriorated by the winter of 1917–1918 as uncontrolled procurement led to chronic shortages, recurring bottlenecks, and spiraling inflation. Congressional investigations resulted in calls for ending independent bureau procurement and creating a civilian ministry of munitions. These threats finally forced Baker to reorganize army machinery, shake up bureau leadership, and establish greater central oversight over bureau purchasing. Improvements came too late, however, to save the existing system. Facing increased business and congressional pressure, Baker finally made concessions designed to strengthen centralized authority.[12]

Wilson reorganized the WIB and installed Baruch as chairman, granting him executive authority. Congress, in turn, passed the Overman Act, giving the president expansive power to rearrange governmental bureaus and wartime administration. Wilson subsequently placed the WIB under his own authority, independent of the obstructive force of the CND and Baker. The WIB received power to clear all government purchases, to prioritize production, to fix prices, and to conserve materials and industrial plants by eliminating wasteful production. Still, the WIB never gained control of military procurement, partly because of military stubbornness and partly because Wilson, the Congress, and the U.S. public doubted the disinterestedness of the businessmen in control. As historian Robert Cuff affirms, Wilson did not wish to upset the balance of power between the state and society (that is, between government and business) by authorizing a new national munitions bureaucracy. But, by the same token, he hesitated to grant the WIB more authority because every gain for the WIB "signified a gain for business power."[13]

Under the new system, a semblance of order was enforced by industry dollar-a-year advisors within the WIB commodity sections working in concert with industry war service committees. War service committees, guided by an industry's leading producers, faced sympathetic counterparts in the WIB commodity sections. Industries were encouraged to collectively devise policies relating to pricing and labor costs in the name of organizational efficiency and production effectiveness. In the process, antitrust enforcement obviously fell by the wayside, and profits skyrocketed. This easy departure from antitrust law heralded political developments in the 1920s and during the early New Deal.[14]

Predictably, the war's end brought the dismantling of most emergency agencies, including the WIB. Still, the WIB experience left a powerful legacy for future U.S. political development. First, it was now part of the national memory that emergency expansions of governmental authority could be fashioned through corporate administrative and personnel capacities. Second, during the 1920s and early 1930s many corporate executives began to espouse the development of the government's capacity to support private-sector stabilization efforts. Third, Congress passed the National Defense Act of 1920 in the war's aftermath to address both the serious deficiencies in the military's mobilization capabilities and the deep tensions between the military services and corporate personnel World War I had exposed.

In contrast to the unalloyed benefits to U.S. business, organized labor experienced both gains and losses in World War I, with its losses clearly predominating despite the beneficial conditions of wartime full production: labor benefited from a political coalition with the Democratic Party, from war imperatives that necessitated cooperative management-labor relations, and from a severely tightened labor market. The national state remained for the greater portion of the war hopelessly divided over issues of labor organization. While American Federation of Labor (AFL) President Samuel Gompers became an official member of the NDAC alongside the likes of Bernard Baruch, business advisors infiltrated the state in greater numbers and their staunch anti–closed shop stance found great support throughout the national administration and judiciary. Conservative business and political forces gained an important advantage by linking labor's aggressiveness to the avowedly radical Industrial Workers of the World (IWW, or "Wobblies"). Success in tarring the IWW as obstructive and even seditious exposed all of labor to the state's coercive and judicial authority. With even the AFL supporting attacks on its IWW competitor, the Justice Department carried out raids and gained indictments against IWW leaders. Troops were sent to western states, where the IWW's strength was greatest, to crush their unions. Once on the scene, the army set up company unions and suppressed all strikes and attempts to organize, whether led by the AFL or the IWW.[15]

Wilson appointed a special mediation committee under Felix Frankfurter late in 1917 to investigate wartime labor troubles, but there remained no centralized labor policy by the winter crisis of 1918. In response to an epidemic of strikes Wilson finally appointed a National War Labor Board (NWLB) in April 1918. Under the forceful and sympathetic leadership of Frank Walsh, the NWLB brought gains for labor including, in various industries, the eight-hour day, wage gains, equal pay for women, and protection from employer backlash against union activities. Prospects definitely brightened for labor as unions also scored huge gains in membership during the war (a 70 percent gain of two million new members from 1917 to 1920).[16]

Nonetheless, the exigencies of wartime had only temporarily boosted labor's bargaining position. With the war's end, employers acted to expunge labor's wartime gains and prepared for what George Soule called "a war of extermination against organized labor." Employers were aided by the Wilson administration's quick retreat on wartime controls, by the state-guided Red Scare campaign against alleged leftists (including those in the labor movement), and by the employer-centered "American Plan" that portrayed closed-shop unionism as anti-American. Labor's hopes and employers' fears coalesced in a mammoth strike wave in 1919. Coming on the heels of the sweeping Republican congressional victories of 1918 and the fear-inspiring Bolshevik revolution, labor's attempts to capitalize on its wartime successes were smashed—as exemplified in labor's resounding defeat in the monumental steel strike of 1919 and, later, in the 1922 strikes by coal and railway workers. As Mike Davis concludes, "It would be difficult to exaggerate the magnitude of American labor's defeat in [this] period." Squeezed by both the state and business throughout the 1920s, labor retreated to the limited rationality of economic and organizational survival, however costly the concessions.[17]

In summary, then, the WIB demonstrated to influential corporate officials that increased government authority could be channeled in ways hospitable to corporate power, especially if corporate personnel gained positions of state authority. In addition, nothing in their previous experience could have provided more dramatic evidence of the great potential of state expenditures than spending for World War I. Needless to say, corporate officials remained wary of or ambivalent toward expanding government authority, fearing that autonomous state power could be utilized to trespass upon managerial prerogatives. Yet, although the state's expansion of the rights of labor offered more evidence of the potential contradictions of increasing governmental authority, corporate officials were reassured as national officials in the 1920s used their authority to smash labor organization. Here, indeed, was more dramatic evidence that an alliance with national officials needed to be cultivated and nurtured.

1920s Associationalism and the Road to the Great Depression

Thanks to political animosities roused by the postwar economic collapse, the effort to sustain the industrial self-government of the WIB did not succeed. Yet, despite the quick demobilization of the WIB, attempts were made immediately after the war and throughout the 1920s to recapture the benefits of business cooperation and business access to state power.

Agitation for a friendlier government attitude toward business self-regulation (albeit with government assistance) encompassed the decade of the 1920s and involved the Justice Department, the Federal Trade Commission, and the Commerce Department under Herbert Hoover.[18]

Despite—or, just as accurately, because of—the apparent prosperity of the 1920s, the U.S. economy remained plagued by growing weaknesses as advances in mass production and scientific management techniques increased the productivity of an ever more disorganized labor force. Besides prosperity, the results of such productivity gains included overcapacity, overproduction, cutthroat competition, and a corresponding relentless attack on labor costs. Although offered the ostensible carrot of company unions and "welfare capitalism," organized labor suffered through the 1920s under the stick of the state's judicial and police power, wielded alongside industrial espionage and private-sector coercion. Ironically, the very success of such attacks on labor's bargaining position led to stagnant wages, underemployment, and a reduction of the mass consumption required to stabilize profits. The national and subnational states picked up some of the slack through investments in construction of roads and buildings, but the coalition between Republicans and business that dominated Washington greatly limited the scope of U.S. politics and the likelihood that national reform efforts designed to strengthen economic stability would succeed.[19]

Firms and industries sought stability instead through mergers and acquisitions (giving the twenties the label the "era of consolidation") and through collective, associational strategies. The latter appeared especially promising because of their seeming wartime success and the growing competitive pressures plaguing many firms and industries. However, the political climate turned increasingly hostile to any postwar revision of the antitrust laws because of leftover Democratic personnel in the Justice Department and Federal Trade Commission and because a postwar depression deepened public and congressional suspicions of associational activities.[20]

At the same time, the influential secretary of commerce, Herbert Hoover, sought to bend the law to encourage certain types of associational practices. Hoover recognized that a reorganized and strengthened Commerce Department could empower those trade-association practices designed to stabilize the economy. Yet Hoover's goals for his invigorated Commerce Department took Baruch's fear of strengthened governmental powers over industry into account as well. As Hoover himself remarked, "The sole function of government is to bring about a condition of affairs favorable to the beneficial development of private enterprise." Hoover feared governmental intervention in business activities as an all-or-nothing affair—the slightest formal state interference with market activities would be like a peek into Pandora's box.[21]

Still, Hoover's thinking transcended simpleminded laissez-faire; like Baruch, he pursued the creation of a particular type of positive governance that subordinated the authority of the national state to the requirements of capitalist stability. "Paradoxically," Ellis Hawley finds, Hoover "saw himself both as an anti-statist and as an ardent champion of one form of positive government and national planning." Accordingly, Hoover initiated and utilized new types of governmental authority but made sure the goal remained assisting cooperative and voluntary associational activities. In the end, despite antitrust pressure Hoover helped to launch hundreds of industry agreements, thereby anticipating many aspects of early New Deal's National Industrial Recovery Act.[22]

As the economy recovered from its postwar collapse, and as Harding and Coolidge personnel assumed positions within the Federal Trade Commission (FTC) and the Justice Department, the political climate again favored associational activities, which gained legitimacy in turn from Justice Department and FTC encouragement of associational endeavors.[23] Hoover nonetheless kept his Commerce Department a safe distance from the more radical practices of the Justice Department and the FTC. Although Hoover would subordinate the state to capitalism, he feared capitalist oligarchy as much as bureaucratic tyranny, fascism, and socialism. Hovering between free and controlled competition on the one hand and industry- and state-guided regulation of competition on the other, Hoover encouraged associational practices that skirted the law in cases of destructive competition. But he resisted Commerce Department involvement in associational practices that might taint his reputation and opposed any formalization of increased governmental powers over industry. Fearing that an increasingly extensive reliance on associational practices would quickly usher in statist bureaucratic controls, Hoover, similar to Baruch, wanted to reap the benefits of associationalism while assiduously avoiding any formal government regulation. His ideals would be greatly tested by the Great Depression.[24]

Despite the growth of associational practices during the 1920s, few concrete gains were possible given the inability of associations to coerce cooperation. Industries remained bedeviled by the dilemmas of capitalist collective action throughout the interwar period. And the contradictions of flourishing mass production and withering mass consumption combined with the era's freewheeling financial markets to create a system that "accentuated maldistribution, encouraged speculation, piled up excessive savings, destroyed its own markets, and plunged the nation into . . . depression."[25]

Hoover, the brilliant technocrat, became president on the cusp of the catastrophic free fall of 1920s prosperity. Because Hoover feared disrupting the balance of power between government and business, he proved unwilling to truly test the national government's capacity to meet the economic crisis. No coherent governance project emerged to bind state and corporate officials. Instead, Hoover relied upon exhortation and voluntarism until very late in his administration and utilized national power primarily to sponsor conferences of private associations and state and city governments to focus on what could be done through existing public and private instrumentalities. Legendary are his exhortations that prosperity was right around the corner if only businesses and local governments would maintain wages, hire workers, and undertake new construction. Yet private associations of business leaders and the cities and states proved incapable of doing much to meet the crisis. In the face of the enormous economic crisis, the failure of voluntary cooperation became complete.[26]

As the deepening economic crisis took its toll on the nation's banks, Hoover finally sacrificed some of his ideals and intervened using national authority. The highlight of his new activism was the Reconstruction Finance Corporation (RFC). Convinced that the continuing depression was being fed by tight money markets, but unable to rouse the private banking community to action, Hoover agreed to an RFC modeled on the wartime War Finance Corporation. The RFC would unsuccessfully attempt to restart the economy by furnishing credit to tottering large banking institutions and railroads. Hoover eventually relented on unemployment relief as well, signing a bill broadening the RFC's lending powers to include money for state-level relief and work relief. But relatively few funds found their way to the unemployed because of strict eligibility tests. The hard irony of Hoover bending his ideals for established bankers but not for the impoverished was impossible to miss.[27]

Despite Hoover's reticence, the RFC represented a dramatic shift in the use of peacetime state power and marked the end of an era when it was assumed that the economy was self-regulating. The fact that Hoover's hand was forced displayed the bankruptcy of business voluntarism; since corporate leaders could not save their own system, national intervention became the sine qua non for national economic stability. Corporate leaders, incapable of coherent voluntary action in the best of times, remained for the most part fearful and befuddled by the continuing depression. The best they could do at the time was to turn to World War I and to 1920s associationalism as models for utilizing national authority on behalf of capitalist stability. Thus, the most coherent business plans for recovery, developed by Gerard Swope of General Electric and Henry Harriman of the U.S. Chamber of Commerce, emphasized the suspension of the antitrust laws and government-supervised, industry-wide planning through trade associations. Their plans, historian William Leuchtenburg reports, "drew on the experience of the [WIB] because it offered an analogue which provided a maximum of government direction with a minimum of challenge to the institutions of a profit economy." Still, business plans lacked imagination, since corporate leaders were driven more by fear than by consistency or coherency; they feared the devastation wrought by the depression and feared congressional proposals for granting the peacetime state unprecedented regulatory authority. As historian Robert Himmelberg recognizes, U.S. businessmen were driven by the "fundamental attitude . . . that economic power and the determination of economic policy were as much as possible to be reserved to the business community; responsibility and accountability to political agencies to be avoided at all cost." The New Deal shift in governance threatened this corporate longing for autonomy, however, and set the stage for a monumental struggle over the direction of U.S. statebuilding.[28]

"The Revolution of 1932" and the Vagaries of New Deal Statebuilding

E. E. Schattschneider, an uncommonly astute political observer, calls the 1932 election a "revolution" because it heralded nationally competitive elections (outside the South), forged a closer relationship between national parties (especially the Democratic Party) and popular majorities, and dramatically shifted the content of U.S. public policy. Previously, 1920s Republican hegemony and the national state's close alliance with business had insulated the government from the influence of more popular class forces (workers, small farmers, the elderly, and the unemployed). But now economic depression initiated a political process that would dramatically alter the strategic relation between the state system and class forces. The depression undermined the legitimacy of the prevailing accommodation between class forces and the state, reduced the leverage and prestige of businessmen over and within the state system, increased the authority of national officials and especially the president within the U.S. state system, and awakened popular class forces to the potential of political action.[29]

Businessmen of all stripes sought political intervention because of their utter failure to discover and implement their own voluntary collective solutions. And yet, while believing they could contain and control governmental initiatives, executives were troubled by two aspects of the new political shift. First, Roosevelt's election initiated an expansionary political dynamic, an expanding scope of national interventionism that, over time, displaced many class conflicts from the economic to the political sphere. Rising popular expectations, increasing popular political agitation, and the expanding relations between the Democratic Party and a growing urban electorate threatened to erode the preexisting business hegemony within the state system. Second, U.S. businessmen seem conditioned to worry that increasing national authority might be a harbinger for a statist attack on private economic prerogatives. Because New Deal national intervention exceeded all previous parameters for national action, only the most prescient and politically astute of businessmen were not frightened into some form of opposition.

Most businessmen are generally threatened by any political shift that leads to either more autonomous or more democratic governance, and many New Deal programs raised the specter of both these threats. National authority greatly increased during the 1930s and in the process national officials imposed a greater degree of public accountability upon most corporations. And increased national intervention made the state system a more overt arena for class conflict. Growing pressure from popular class forces increased, yet also channeled, the options available to national officials—that is to say, popular pressure and agitation increased the space for state action independent of business forces, but at the same time popular forces prodded national officials to respond to their escalating demands. The New Deal should not therefore be conceptualized as simply a case of increasing political autonomy. Indeed, as Schattschneider observes, "The Democratic Party in the 1930s became the reluctant instrument of a revolution it did not plan and did not produce." Those national officials so disposed could, of course, harness the rising social agitation as a resource for imposing greater accountability and responsibility upon the U.S. business community. Yet it is difficult to envision the dramatic policy shifts of the 1930s in the absence of the popular agitation and burgeoning radical threats to the existing order. What makes the 1930s so compelling, then, is that alternatives ripened within that decade that had never before seemed possible: C. Wright Mills proclaims that "for the first time in United States history, social legislation and lower-class issues became important features of the reform movement." In these respects, the Great Depression and the resulting social upheaval increased the consequence of politics, and national officials became more directly responsible for mediating class conflicts and stabilizing the system as a whole.[30]

The 1932 election provoked deep concern among the U.S. corporate community over the landslide electoral victory of Roosevelt, a relative unknown with ominous rhetorical appeals to the "forgotten man at the bottom of the economic pyramid." Roosevelt's first moves as president, however, seemed designed to convince financial and industry leaders of his orthodox deflationist intentions. By signing a conservative bankers' bill (the Emergency Banking Act) designed to arrest the sudden and alarming collapse of the banking system, and by committing himself to cuts in federal wages and veterans' benefits, Roosevelt calmed business fears. But his next moves forcefully broke with the past. Roosevelt quickly overrode Hoover's reluctance to preempt local responsibility and initiate a national program for the unemployed. Creation of the Civilian Conservation Corps was soon followed by the Federal Emergency Relief Act, which provided, through state and local administration, direct relief payments to the unemployed. As Frances Piven and Richard

Cloward stress, the precedent of asserting national responsibility for unemployment relief "had taken protest and the ensuing fiscal and electoral disturbances . . . and it took continued protest to get the legislation implemented."[31]

Industrial recovery presented a more problematic task. As was his wont, Roosevelt waited until prevailing sentiment of important economic and political interests coalesced around a particular scheme for promoting industrial recovery before taking action. Ultimately, however, although the U.S. business community remained divided, his hand was forced, as every account recognizes, by the passage of Senator Hugo Black's thirty-hour-workweek bill. Only then, confronted by legislation that roused significant industry opposition and that he feared would worsen economic conditions, Roosevelt began actively to synthesize existing proposals into a viable industrial recovery alternative.[32]

As business antagonism buried Secretary of Labor Frances Perkins's amendments to the Black bill, Roosevelt separately encouraged Raymond Moley of his brain trust and Senator Robert Wagner to develop an alternative. Moley signed up former General Hugh Johnson, a close associate of Bernard Baruch's who had served as the army's representative to the War Industries Board. Johnson, in turn, drafted a proposal meshing the corporatist experience of the WIB with the trade-association plans championed by businessmen Swope and Harriman. Meanwhile, and by contrast, Wagner developed a close liaison with an eclectic group, including on the one hand planning and spending proponents such as Rexford Tugwell and labor leader Sidney Hillman and, on the other, Assistant Secretary of Commerce John Dickenson, an advocate of industry self-government through trade associations who also shared the belief in boosting mass purchasing power. Both groups were either inspired by, or lobbied heavily to lean on, the experience of the WIB and the trade-association developments of the 1920s. Wagner's group also promoted labor's collective bargaining rights and championed a public works program to help boost mass consumption. At this early stage of the New Deal, with few alternative organizational or policy legacies and surprisingly few dents in the armor of business hegemony, Roosevelt was obliged to rely heavily upon the legacy of the WIB.[33]

After drafting their respective proposals, key members of both groups were exhorted by Roosevelt to forge a compromise bill. An amalgam of divergent and contradictory remedies, the National Industrial Recovery Act (NIRA) suspended antitrust enforcement and empowered trade associations to formulate "codes of fair competition." Under the loose direction of a National Recovery Administration (NRA), each industry would design codes regulating prices and limiting production. The aim, of course, was to stabilize and even increase profits. So, the NRA, like the WIB, was dominated by trade associations and their officials, and the codes themselves reflected the preeminent position of the largest producers in every industry. Hawley and others have shown that industry representatives played a large role in defining industry codes. Many NRA officials came from industry, thus reproducing the industry-men-in-government oversight of industry actions from the WIB. Also, trade associations remained the only organizational means readily available for implementing industry codes. Reliance on them led to similar patterns of industrial self-government as displayed during World War I, although under the NRA businessmen made a sport of evading code regulations. Himmelberg sums up most scholarship by concluding that the NRA "established cartelist patterns which survived the demise of the agency itself" and also displayed "a disturbing tendency on the part of businessmen to seize state power and use it to defend their position and improve their wealth."[34]

The NRA was not, however, simply a replay of the WIB experience. First, this was not a wartime emergency where business-government collusion could be easily concealed. By introducing the notion of citizens' economic rights and national responsibility for alleviating the depression, Roosevelt had raised expectations and focused public attention on the politics of industrial recovery. Second, because of the depression, the balance of political forces was less favorable to a revival of business-friendly corporatism. For example, the NIRA was notable for legitimizing the rights of organized labor. Section 7a of the act, which outlawed "yellow-dog" contracts and declared labor's right to organize and to bargain collectively, was thought to be a bone thrown to labor to solidify support for the bill and to increase the potential for mass consumption. Yet its existence also testified to the increasing electoral significance of labor, the rising agitation of the employed and unemployed, and the growing congressional support for labor concerns, especially among urban liberals like Senator Wagner from New York. In fact, Wagner threatened to hold up the industrial recovery bill if 7a was not included with the original language intact: as he put it, "No 7a, no bill." Labor's actual participation in the fashioning of NRA codes was minimal, owing to business dominance within the NRA; yet inclusion of section 7a alongside the introduction of large-scale national unemployment relief indicated a substantive break with the business-government relations of the recent past. Given the eventual demise of the NRA and subsequent passage of the Wagner Labor Relations Act, section 7a can be counted as the most permanent governmental legacy of the NIRA.[35]

Thus, even as the NRA ratified a form of government-sponsored industrial self-government, it also led to expanding governmental authority over business for two interrelated reasons. First, government regulatory capacities grew to compel adherence to and oversee compliance with NRA codes. Second, discomfort with big business dominance of the codes resulted in pressure for greater independent government oversight of code authorities. Initially, though NRA administrator Hugh Johnson often resorted to threats and exhortation, he relied primarily upon the discretionary and informal code-making process that evolved under trade-association dominance. But popular patience with codes fashioned by industry leaders eroded quickly as prices rose while wages fell and competition atrophied. As consumers and many small businesses paid the price for stabilizing profits in monopoly-sector firms and industries, their complaints about Johnson and his informal system flooded Congress, inevitably weakening the NRA. Likewise, workers increasingly protested the failure to deliver on the promise of section 7a. In the end, the NRA was thus undermined by intraclass and interclass conflicts.[36]

To be sure, the more volatile political circumstances of the 1930s also made revival of a WIB-style departure from antitrust law problematic. Pressured by Senate progressives Gerald Nye and William Borah, Roosevelt appointed a National Recovery Review Board under Clarence Darrow. In turn, Johnson—before he was eased out—was forced to gradually share power with representatives of labor and consumer interests. Likewise, the NRA moved, albeit slowly, to increase independent governmental oversight of the business forces dominating the NRA and its codes. Accordingly, business regarded the NRA with increasing suspicion and hostility. Already many firms distrusted the NRA because of growing governmental intrusion and the willingness to sacrifice marginal producers that had resulted in greater economic concentration. Once forced to share power within the NRA, and faced with growing governmental authority, many monopoly-sector firms had reason to turn against the NRA as well. As historian Robert Collins reports, by the summer of 1934 "a generalized fear that the New Deal threatened business autonomy developed among businessmen of all sorts" because of increasing governmental authority and the state-labor accommodation manifested in section 7a.[37]

In another unintended consequence of the NRA, section 7a revived moribund labor unions and spurred labor struggles as labor gained the legitimacy of national law and an apparent presidential endorsement. Although neither Roosevelt nor the authors of section 7a intended or envisioned the social disruption that ensued, Roosevelt's election, his activist initiatives, and his on-again, off-again populist rhetoric combined with 7a to spur rising labor agitation. Labor militancy in the face of employer resistance to the closed shop quickly burst the bounds of the traditionally conservative American Federation of Labor's craft unions, proceeding to threaten major mass-production industries and, consequently, economic and political stability. Unlike government leaders in the 1920s, however, Roosevelt and many Democrats, reliant upon working-class electoral support, declined to turn the state's coercive power against labor. Instead, to placate labor and resolve the growing number of industrial disputes, Roosevelt created in August 1933 a National Labor Board (NLB) with Senator Wagner as its first head. Although the NLB scored some quick victories in settling disputes, its rulings against company unions caused increasing opposition from powerful industries and firms and from Hugh Johnson. Accordingly, without enforcement powers and reliant upon quickly dissipating presidential support and industry cooperation, the NLB (and its successor, the National Labor Relations Board) atrophied.[38]

Many firms, blaming section 7a for the sudden escalation of labor disruption and seeing labor influence increase within the national state, increased their opposition to unionization by relying upon well-worn techniques of violence and intimidation and by expanding the use of company unions. Increasing numbers of businessmen also moved to oppose Roosevelt and the New Deal. Roosevelt, in turn, hedged on pursuing further reform, because of a fear of 1934 midterm congressional losses and because he still wanted to placate most interests, including most importantly the U.S. business community. Thus, he preempted Wagner's labor legislation by pressing for a joint congressional resolution allowing him to create a National Labor Relations Board, and he deferred action on public works, old-age pensions, and unemployment insurance.

Although a business offensive proved generally successful in resisting unionization after labor's initial surge in 1933, mounting labor militancy became a bellwether for the popular surge to Democrats in the 1934 midterm elections—described by the *New York Times* as "the most overwhelming victory in the history of American politics." Up to this point, Roosevelt had remained especially attuned to the hopes and fears of major U.S. firms and industries, considering their demands central to recovery. However, plagued by competitive disorganization and a confused search for profits, business forces increasingly strayed into formal opposition to Roosevelt and the New Deal even as the labor insurgency, the general expansion of popular radicalism and unrest, and the overwhelming progressive makeup of Congress all tilted the political balance toward activist reform initiatives.[39]

Although the 1934 election forced Roosevelt to recognize this shift in the balance of class and political forces, his conversion to an activist and reformist agenda was neither simple nor quick. Yet, refusing to lead, Roosevelt was prodded by an increasingly activist popular base and especially by the building momentum for a labor rights act. Orchestrated and tirelessly promoted by Wagner, the National Labor Relations Act threatened to become law without Roosevelt's blessing. As continued labor strife threatened economic and political stability and as conservatives and businessmen continued to turn against the New Deal, Roosevelt slowly drifted from ambivalence to tepid support of a labor measure. Only when the Supreme Court struck down the NIRA in the 1935 *Schechter* decision did Roosevelt—confronting a "regime crisis"—finally turn to complete support of the Wagner bill. Roosevelt's conversion was certainly helpful, but it was less decisive than Wagner's persistent efforts. Even Wagner's endeavors, however, paid off more because of popular insurgency, especially from workers, than because of Wagner's work in and of itself.[40]

Roosevelt's belated progressive shift seemed to boost his confidence in the face of business opposition and the 1935 *Schechter* decision. Passage of the Wagner Act rescued and strengthened the part of the NRA concerned with collective bargaining, and it represented an important step toward asserting an independent governance project based on Keynesian principles. It also augured the beginning of a series of legislative enactments often cited as the Second Hundred Days. A seeming decisive break but also a pragmatic recognition of great human suffering, overwhelming public and congressional sentiment, and disruptive social movements, the reform initiatives of the so-called "second New Deal" nonetheless found Roosevelt continuing to hedge in his support for reform. Reflecting Roosevelt's practical irresolution and the continuing divisions within his administration, many of these measures embodied the ambivalence that characterized much of the New Deal; even as they intensified the national government's responsibilities to greater numbers of persons, they incarnated and represented a conservative compromise. For example, the Social Security Act of 1935, notwithstanding its essentially regressive (in terms of taxation) and conservative (in terms of who it excluded) elements, redistributed income and extended national responsibility to ordinary citizens. Leuchtenburg thus deems this legislation "inept and conservative," but recognizes that "it reversed historic assumptions about the nature of social responsibility, and it established the proposition that the individual has clear-cut social rights." Accordingly, many businessmen perceived a clear antibusiness threat in these enactments and in the disturbing emergence of the avowedly militant Congress of Industrial Organizations (CIO). As David Vogel concludes, "It is not surprising that the reforms of the second Roosevelt met with far more extensive hostility from business than those of the first. The former were less under their control and thus resulted in a relative strengthening of the authority of government."[41]

The "New" New Dealers and the Attempt to Fashion a Coherent Governance Project[42]

Roosevelt's convincing reelection landslide in 1936 seemed to verify that tilting toward reform could pay massive electoral dividends. Permanent additions like those of the Social Security and Wagner Labor Relations Acts combined with temporary and less legitimate jobs and relief programs to cement the loyalty of a majority coalition to Roosevelt and to the newly invigorated national administration. And yet, driven it seems by overconfidence, Roosevelt chose to expend his newly gained political capital in the pursuit of two seemingly disastrous policy goals over the first year of his new term. First, he sought the authority to "pack" a hostile Supreme Court with friendly justices. Second, he retrenched national expenditures to make good on budget-balancing promises made in 1932. The first campaign turned into a political rout, the second, an economic debacle. Yet neither can be considered an unalloyed setback in the effort to establish a coherent, popularly oriented New Deal governance project.

Roosevelt considered it imperative to confront the Court because of the challenge it posed to any national regulatory project. When, beginning with a Washington state minimum-wage case and again in upholding the Wagner Act, Justice Owen Roberts joined the Supreme Court's liberal bloc, an intractable roadblock to the development of the national regulatory state seemed to have been removed. But the price was high. The Court plan dominated the 1937 congressional session to the exclusion of other business and brought failure and derision upon Roosevelt and confidence to the conservative coalition that coalesced in opposition to the plan. Tommy Corcoran, one of Roosevelt's top advisors, even argued that the Court fight was less about the actual merits of Roosevelt's plan than a convenient opportunity for Congress to rein in Roosevelt's powers now that he was considered a lame duck. Likewise, historian James Patterson reports that many conservative southern Democrats, frightened by rising expectations among southern blacks and an increasingly urban constituency, and especially galled by an alliance between Roosevelt and the CIO, had already turned against Roosevelt's newfound reform efforts before the Court fight.[43]

Alongside the Court fight, Roosevelt, overconfident about the ability of the economy to stand on its own and pressed by conservatives, brought more derision upon himself by instigating the 1937–1938 recession-within-a-depression through cutbacks in work relief and public works programs. The so-called "Roosevelt depression" dramatically weakened the CIO and the "left wing of the New Deal" and emboldened conservatives in Congress and elsewhere who had been made quiescent by Roosevelt's tremendous reelection victory. Still, Roosevelt's increasing estrangement from conservatives in his own party did not spell an end to the search for a New Deal governance project. Given the shifting strategic relation of Roosevelt to Congress (especially after the 1938 election issued a blow to progressive New Dealers—Republicans gained 81 seats in the House and 8 in the Senate, with all of the Democratic losses coming from outside the solid South), Roosevelt moved from a legislative to an administrative strategy, and from extension of the New Deal to consolidation. Thus, the shrinking number of senators and representatives who counted themselves New Dealers in the late 1930s was offset by a growing number of New Dealers ensconced in many regular departments and New Deal agencies. As New Dealer Tommy Corcoran proudly noted at the time, "These people scattered all through the government amount to an espionage system, as well as a technical and administrative force. Particularly in the agencies where the official powers are conservative, they watch policy, and if policy takes a wrong direction, they mobilize the whole Kitchen Cabinet group [including Corcoran, Ben Cohen, and Harry Hopkins at the top] to bring pressure on the wrongdoers." Thus, while congressional conservatism checked many new legislative initiatives, Roosevelt operated from a hefty statutory base of existing New Deal measures and an organizational base of new agencies and personnel, which together wired the U.S. state system up for national, and specifically presidential, supervision and management of economic stability.[44]

Although popular support for Roosevelt softened in the wake of the 1937 recession, a major reorientation of public attitudes had nonetheless been achieved. The American public looked to the president for leadership and generally rallied around broad national interventionism; and, certainly, the persisting economic crisis and high unemployment meant that most emergency New Deal stabilization programs were secure as well. Accordingly, Congress canceled few programs until the crisis of war revived the economy and ended the crisis in unemployment. Roosevelt could therefore bypass his party to a degree in substantiating a new governance regime in the United States; in fact, he operated from a large base of potential authority. As Barry Karl reports, "The creation of new administrative agencies, whose responsibilities for distributing and managing the nation's resources were so complex that Congress could no longer directly oversee them, gave the administrative branch of the government its greatest infusion of potential power in peacetime history."[45]

Roosevelt had begun his first term by requesting emergency power: "I shall ask the Congress for the one remaining instrument to meet the crisis—broad Executive power to wage a war against the emergency, as great as the power that would be given me if we were in fact invaded by a foreign foe." And he expanded and enhanced presidential authority throughout the years of the economic emergency. Since he did not trust the holdover personnel inhabiting existing departments, Roosevelt utilized the emergency authority during the early period of his first term to create temporary agencies staffed by his personal appointees. As Stephen Hess reports, "When the President felt most strongly that a job was important . . . he often simply ignored the departments and created a new agency."[46] This experimentation led him early in his presidency to augment his cabinet with an ever-shifting cadre of personal staff that he used as personal assistants and as intermediaries to the permanent departments. Once reelected in 1936, he sought to remake the national executive and so enshrine presidential governance by institutionalizing this experimentation. Roosevelt's

Court-packing plan, however, tainted and doomed the plan for executive reorganization. Congress rejected his reorganization bill and only passed a stripped-down version as the war emergency loomed.[47]

Needless to say, the national state remained throughout the late 1930s intensely divided, and executive-congressional conflict forced New Dealers on the defensive on many fronts. But they remained on the offensive in some important areas as well. Throughout the closing years of the decade a group of statist economists and lawyers operating within the Roosevelt administration developed the intellectual and policy framework for a coherent governance project aimed at expanding and managing mass consumption. As the renewed economic downturn of the late 1930s discredited the balanced budget approach of Treasury Secretary Henry Morgenthau Jr., this group, in alliance with a new generation of labor leaders and progressive corporate liberals, initiated a broad debate over alternative positive measures, including deficit spending.[48] This debate gave these "new" New Dealers an opportunity to clarify and formulate a coherent national governance project, one that had been slowly percolating throughout the years of depression. The recession of 1937–1938 was a turning point since it convinced many of Roosevelt's key advisors that the depression was not just another business downturn but rather a permanent condition reflecting the "secular stagnation" of a "mature economy" and the dominance of monopoly-sector firms capable of imposing "administered prices."[49] Since recovery could not therefore be expected simply as a result of various encouragements designed to boost business confidence, more permanent and formalized governmental involvement would be necessary. Accordingly, although New Dealers up to this point had primarily pursued adaptation to corporate power, these "new" New Dealers sought to strengthen national authority over the corporate economy in order to strengthen popular class forces and weaken the hold of major corporations over the national economy.[50]

Although public planning, the state's most aggressive option, had been discredited (ironically, by the failure of the NRA), there remained plenty of activist national policy alternatives. The proposed shift to a fiscal project of deficit spending hinged on a debate over what a program of public investment would actually entail—more specifically, whether the fiscal remedy could stand alone or be complemented by strengthened governmental oversight of those firms and industries that exhibited monopolistic or oligarchical market power. Marriner Eccles, head of the Federal Reserve and leader of the so-called "spenders," thought of deficit spending as an alternative to increased governmental regulation and planning. As he put it, "I would like to see as little regimentation—as little direct regulation . . . as possible. I would like to see the Government's function to be that of the compensating factor." By contrast, Leon Henderson, another key New Dealer and Eccles's ally, promoted a new antitrust effort and some measure of government involvement in decisions concerning production and prices in key industries.[51]

Still, for Henderson, as for most New Dealers, spending and greater governmental authority over corporate firms and industries went together. Most New Dealers distinguished between earlier attempts at temporary "pump priming" and the now-accepted need for a permanent public investment program. A national spending program would necessarily be more interventionist than the monetary and security regulation implemented earlier in the New Deal.[52] A national investment program would necessitate a mix of the executive administrative capability to plan and implement public investment strategies, the capacity to regulate destructive monopolistic or competitive tendencies, and the ability to redistribute income. Such a program in turn would represent a shift from "extensive" investment into the domestic frontier (now closed) and international markets to "intensive" investment in public infrastructure and natural resources requiring government planning and even some government ownership to spur economic development and achieve full employment. Thus, a wide range of alternatives for national interventionism remained on the table in the late 1930s.[53]

Both strands of the new thinking—Eccles's more passive "fiscalist" alternative and Henderson's more statist "administrative" approach— were promoted and developed separately and as two parts of a single strategy, until war arrived. The fiscalist alternative was immediately implemented in 1938 as Roosevelt easily convinced a Congress anxious over midterm elections to authorize new spending for public works and work relief. Though Eccles and others thought the program too tame, Robert Lekachman reports that, owing to deficit spending of $2.9 billion, "a grateful economy responded appropriately: GNP in 1939 returned to its 1937 level." Meanwhile, the administrative alternative was embodied most actively in Thurman Arnold's antitrust offensive, which began with his appointment in 1938 and finally ran out of steam by 1942 when the wartime emergency encouraged the very industry collusion Arnold fought against. Until then, Arnold not only tried to reinvent antitrust enforcement (prosecuting "bad" firms who controlled prices and hampered consumption rather than "big" firms per se) but also tried to develop and legitimize a permanent state administrative ability to regulate monopoly power. Likewise, alongside Arnold's ongoing endeavors, other New Dealers led by Leon Henderson orchestrated a massive joint congressional-executive investigation into the workings and structure of the U.S. economy. Henderson and others intended that the Temporary National Economic Committee (TNEC) investigations would serve to guide and inform the national interventions that would complement a public investment program. As Henderson, and his New Dealer soul mate Isador Lubin, stated in their personal statement attached to the final TNEC report:

> The [TNEC] was charged with the fundamental problem of devising ways
> and means of utilizing fully our men, our machines and our materials so
> that the economic paralysis of the early 1930's could not occur again. . . .
> The testimony . . . has demonstrated clearly that private enterprise does not
> adjust itself quickly to violent economic disruptions, that in any major crisis
> of peace-time or war-time, Government leadership and Government partici-
> pation are required to help get the job done and avoid great social and eco-
> nomic hardship. . . . Surely it should be possible, with this great wealth of
> evidence, first, to formulate more clearly our national economic objectives
> and second, to offer a concrete program geared to the needs of our times.[54]

This appeal for "a concrete program," however, went nowhere. Still, despite internal divisions (Lekachman counts "five rival theories" contend-
ing for presidential favor) and the quickening drumbeats of war, the new
New Dealer vanguard struggled mightily, as historian Alan Brinkley concludes, "to establish the ideological and institutional foundations for a
strengthened national state" in the time they had. Falling short of such a
program, they hoped (and feared) that the war would provide the context
for establishing the guidelines for positive governance in the United States.
To that end, once war appeared likely, they poured their energies into the
burgeoning administrative controversies over wartime mobilization. And
many corporate executives, fearful that a war emergency would herald
new threats to corporate prerogatives and profits as aggressive New Dealers
expanded public control over the national economy, prepared to resist
New Dealer control of mobilization and gain authority for themselves.[55]

▼ ▼ ▼

What do we make of the momentous changes of the New Deal period, especially in terms of the struggle to define a stable governance
project? As the Great Depression forced the development of national interventionist capabilities, New Deal programs fundamentally transformed the distribution of power within the U.S. state system as well as
redefined the national state's relationship to the private economy and
corporate firms. A key economic issue throughout the 1930s remained
the extent to which the national state would gain the capability to
guide the economy and shape economic relations. The related political
dilemma concerned the practical difficulties of constructing a stable
framework for national governance capable of unifying the state system
and a class-divided society. It seems clear that, by 1940, these difficulties
had not been successfully negotiated or resolved; New Dealers, that is,
had not managed to establish a stable governance project acceptable to
a broad enough coalition of state and class forces.

Roosevelt's reelection in 1936, alongside the emergence of the new
mass industrial unionism and the retreat of most organized business or-

ganizations into what Robert Collins calls "negativistic opposition" seemed to have turned the tide in favor of progressive statebuilding. Yet successful opposition to the Court-packing plan empowered conservative forces in Congress and their business and sectional allies. The 1937–1938 "Roosevelt depression" further emboldened conservative forces. It encouraged, for example, the conservative American Federation of Labor to awake from its somnambulation and launch a destructive civil war against the CIO over organizing heavy industry and over national policy. The AFL relentlessly and successfully attacked the NLRB for its CIO bias and lobbied against the New Dealer–sponsored Federal Labor Standards Act, and AFL leaders testified in Congress repeatedly about the ostensible communist domination of the CIO.[56]

Still, the continuing depression meant that the political initiative remained with New Dealers, especially since conservatives, whether in Congress or elsewhere, developed no clear alternative to the New Deal. In the wake of Roosevelt's decision to opt for more aggressive national interventionism, New Dealers successfully regrouped and developed a coherent national response to the continuing depression. Though what may have occurred had war not erupted is anyone's guess, certainly the New Dealers were not defeated; yet neither they nor the conservative forces arrayed against them proved capable of a strategic victory.

Although state officials define the specific resolutions to crises like the Great Depression, any broad success is ultimately contingent upon social bases of support and resistance. So it was with the "new" New Deal, whose chances of success were circumscribed by the resistance of powerful sectional and business forces. Intragovernmental competitions generated by the U.S. constitutional system were compounded by the tensions caused by class pressures focused overtly upon and within the national state. Thus, both the successes and failures of the New Deal are observed in the ability, or inability, to link new programs and agencies to class forces. Overall, we can say that the New Deal as a reform movement largely owed such success as it enjoyed to the pressure and support of a mobilized mass base that was both consequence and cause of the startling expansions of national authority during the depression. The New Deal failed when it did, however, because it aroused profound antagonisms among powerful class forces (including representatives of major corporations and the southern caste system) and among significant sectors of the existing state system. The result was that, although on one level the New Deal certainly succeeded, given the expanded statutory and administrative base of the national government and the transformation of citizen expectations, from a more general perspective the 1930s ended in a grand political stalemate.

Thus, as the United States stood on the brink of war it also stood poised at a fork of statebuilding paths. Accordingly, to New Dealers and conservatives alike, it seemed certain that the war would provide the opportunity to resolve the political dilemmas raised by the Great Depression. And indeed the war did break the impasse; by the immediate postwar years, the stalemate was resolved by the creation of a national security state. This resolution was in turn prepared for by wartime controversies involving New Dealers, the military services, and corporate officials, which closed off progressive New Deal statebuilding and laid the framework for a very different kind of governance project. Given the openings created by Great Depression and the resulting social upheaval, this fate was not a certainty in 1940.

From Depression to War

• The move toward war in the late 1930s very quickly overturned the New Deal political stalemate. Mobilization for war precipitated important changes within the national state, between the national state and industry, and within the national economy itself. As the official history of war mobilization later proclaimed, "Industrial mobilization involved not only the unprecedented production of ships, planes, tanks, guns, and ammunition; it required sweeping transformations in the entire economic structure and fundamental changes in the Government itself." Many of these transformations were actually initiated before the United States entered the hostilities, during the prewar "defense" period of mobilization, which lasted more than two years—from the Nazi invasion of Poland in September 1939 to the Japanese attack on Pearl Harbor in December 1941. Because the turn to war during this period was so interminably slow, the struggle for control of mobilization policy was protracted and complicated, involving both the procedural and substantive issues of mobilization: what type of mobilization organization would prevail, who would staff and guide it, and the extent of its responsibilities and authority. This struggle pitted New Dealer and other civilian-state forces against the military-state forces that made such a striking entrance into U.S. politics as war drew near. But this governmental struggle was greatly modified as corporations intervened to tip the balance in favor of the military services. The long transition from depression to war altered the political leverage of interested state and class forces and recast statebuilding struggles. Changing political contingencies and the shifting national balance of power shaped the defense period administrative developments discussed in the next chapter.[1]

The most obvious changes triggered by the turn to war involved increased corporate leverage over the national state and the emergence of military-state officials as central political figures. Depression conditions had reduced corporate political leverage and thereby granted civilian-state officials greater freedom of action. Yet the depression-era relationship between assertive national officials and vulnerable business forces began to turn as the onset of the war in Europe revived the U.S. economy and as the need to produce war materiel increased governmental dependence on the nation's dominant firms and industries. Henceforth, concerns about profits, market share, and expanding New Dealer authority spurred corporate executives to bring their increased leverage to bear on the mobilization process. Preparation for war also refashioned national political struggles by introducing assertive military officials as a new political force and by weakening the political influence of organized labor. All these changes in the national balance of power diminished the likelihood that New Dealers and like-minded civilian personnel would gain stewardship of mobilization responsibilities and thereby continue to influence U.S. statebuilding. Of course, throughout prewar and wartime mobilization, the deficiencies of military and business control of mobilization provided civilian-state authorities with plenty of opportunities to extend and expand their reach. And military and corporate officials continued to fear the expansion of civilian-state authority throughout the war.

Alternative Paths to Mobilization

The Nazi blitz of Poland in September 1939 prompted Roosevelt to proclaim a "limited" national emergency and begin considering options for mobilizing the nation's economy for war. At this junction between depression and war it was unclear how full mobilization, if necessary, would be organized. There were, however, two alternative and competing legacies for implementing mobilization in the event of war. World War I and the early New Deal provided one possible precedent: extensive delegation of governmental authority to corporate executives, individual firms, and trade associations. But the later New Deal provided a second influential legacy as well, one based upon independent governmental oversight of the national corporate economy. Riding their predominance within Roosevelt's administration and propelled by the belief that public authority should hold sway over private corporate interests, many New Dealers promoted a mobilization process based on expanded civilian-state authority over the nation's economy. New Dealers questioned military planning and military readiness with regard to economic mobilization, but they also believed that the military services remained far too reliant upon and solicitous of powerful corporate firms and their representatives for mobilization to proceed in a timely manner.

For many of those who fought over mobilization authority, what was at stake was not simply how best to prepare the nation for war but also the future shape of U.S. national governance and the national political economy. This was probably most true for U.S. business interests, who believed they had suffered through their worst fears during the New Deal. Trepidation that war mobilization would expand New Dealer authority and legitimate a form of national economic planning capable of impinging on corporate profits and prerogatives translated into unbending business hostility to any wartime expansions of civilian-state authority and a correspondingly strong alliance with the military services. Corporate executives supported domestic military authority because military planning in turn relied upon the World War I model of business-dominated corporatism and the 1920s ideal of business self-governance. According to that model, temporary government agencies led by corporate advisors would organize industries in cooperation with industry trade associations. This route entailed extensive delegation of governmental authority to the most influential corporate executives and the most powerful corporate firms.

Of course, New Dealers were by this time already engaged in an ongoing confrontation with conservative business forces over the social inequities and concentrations of economic power they believed were the root causes of the Great Depression. Distrusting corporate motives, New Dealers challenged military stewardship of mobilization, citing accumulating evidence that the military's reliance upon corporate voluntarism would leave the nation unprepared for war. Alert to both increasing international threats and the need for greater preparations for wartime contingencies, they maneuvered as best they could to hurry along mobilization and gain mobilization authority for themselves. And, in the late 1930s and early 1940s, because they were well positioned within Roosevelt's administration and enjoyed substantial support within a divided Congress, New Dealers proved a match for the military services. Thus, despite their expectations, military-state officials alone could not readily dominate mobilization.

New Dealers at first expressed concern that the mobilization strategy proposed by business and military leaders would enhance the economic and political power of monopoly-sector corporations while scuttling hard-won regulatory and reform victories. But they also became convinced that neither business executives nor military representatives were willing or able to make the tough calls on speeding U.S. preparation for war if such decisions threatened an industry's stability or interfered with corporate profits or managerial autonomy. Accordingly, many New Dealers sought a central role within mobilization to quicken the transition to war production and to ensure that the war emergency would not simply be an excuse to roll back the progressive gains of recent years. They sought conversion to military production and an early curtailment of excessive civilian manufacturing. They also pushed for expanded raw material production and advocated a wider distribution of military contracts to fully exploit existing industrial capacity and to break the military's reliance on the largest firms. They promoted centralized political control of raw materials distribution and insisted that military contractors adhere to recently enacted social and labor legislation. In other words, New Dealers trespassed in areas that military and business officials had considered theirs alone.

Preparation for war thus became a new arena for New Deal–era disagreements about the disposition of national authority, one in which the military services themselves entered the statebuilding struggle. Guided at this point by prominent financial leaders and by a "passion for autonomy," the services promoted their own agenda for mobilizing the nation's economy. Their interwar mobilization planning engendered close relations between themselves and corporate leaders while enhancing their institutional flexibility and boosting their desire to direct mobilization themselves, free from civilian interference. Such planning ensured that the services would, at the very least, have a strong say in any and all mobilization issues.[2]

The Military's Interwar Mobilization Planning

In response to the problems associated with uncontrolled army procurement during the First World War, Congress had designed the National Defense Act of 1920 to allow for better civilian oversight of army procurement. The act empowered the assistant secretary of war—presumed to be a civilian and preferably an industrialist—to oversee bureau procurement, to integrate industrial know-how with military planning, and to establish closer relations between U.S. industry and the military services, so as to avoid the economic disruptions of World War I.[3]

Only after an initial scuffle over jurisdictional issues between the War Department's general staff and the first assistant secretary was an Office of the Assistant Secretary of War (OASW) established and a Planning Branch created within that office to focus on planning future mobilizations. The OASW also sponsored creation of an Army-Navy Munitions Board (ANMB) to coordinate army and navy purchases in the event of war and an Army Industrial College to develop a cadre of trained procurement and mobilization officers. These mechanisms of army planning were gradually given operational shape during the 1920s, although the ANMB did not become functional until the 1930s.[4]

Bernard Baruch—previous head of the War Industries Board—had a hand in the creation of the Army Industrial College, and he and others from finance and industry formed an advisory board to ensure that the lessons of World War I, especially the central role of voluntary business participation, would be remembered. Baruch also promoted the drafting and continual updating of an Industrial Mobilization Plan (IMP) to guide mobilization in another war. As business leaders from the nation's core industries came to have a central role in army planning, this preparation came to reflect evolving business sensibilities concerning the value of industry associations, which World War I had greatly encouraged and Hoover and others had continued to promote throughout the 1920s and early 1930s. Interwar military planning found a natural point of departure in the development of trade associations; the army came to rely upon them for the voluntary participation of industry it sought.[5]

Army planning in the 1920s proved significant as it encouraged a growing relationship between army personnel, industry experts, and trade associations. Yet mobilization planning did not itself gain momentum until after 1929, when the Planning Branch drafted the first of four Industrial Mobilization Plans. Thereafter, congressional investigations of mobilization planning gave impetus to successive IMP revisions throughout the 1930s, culminating with a final version of the plan in 1939. The most thorough congressional investigation, undertaken in 1934 by Senator Gerald P. Nye's Special Senate Committee Investigating the Munitions Industry, proved critical of the cooperative relations between the military and large industrialists. Hearings focused attention on the profiteering by so-called "merchants of death" during the First World War and examined how military planning would affect organized labor. The Nye Committee concluded its investigations by vainly recommending legislation to curb excess profits and to provide the president with powers to draft industry in time of war.[6]

The Planning Branch ostensibly took into account the Nye Committee's discomfort about the growing business-military relationship when, in the wake of the 1934 hearings, it next revised the IMP. Yet, surprisingly, the 1936 version gave an even more prominent place to military cooperation with industrialists and other business advisors. The new IMP called for a War Resources Administration, staffed by military officers and business advisors, to organize industrial mobilization in concert with trade associations organized into War Service Committees. In essence, the plan sought to replicate the experience of World War I, as Under Secretary of War Robert Patterson explained to a House investigative committee in 1942:

> The industrial mobilization plan, of course, represented a study that had been made by the War Department and the Navy Department out of the 1918 experiences. It followed the general lines of the organization that had finally evolved in 1918. It advocated a system much like that under the planning agency headed by Mr. Baruch in 1918.[7]

Like the final 1939 version, however, the 1936 plan envisioned that in a future war-mobilization crisis the ANMB could serve as an interim agency preparing the way for the business-dominated War Resources Administration that would eventually take over the reins of mobilization. The military services, gaining confidence in their abilities, were obviously positioning themselves for a central role in the next mobilization. An assertive role for the ANMB, however, raised objections. Baruch, for instance, remembering the trials of World War I, strenuously resisted any kind of military stewardship over the national economy: "No Army man should be entrusted with the direction of civilian activities." As a result, the 1939 revision of the IMP specifically called for "patriotic business leaders of the Nation," and not military officials, to be entrusted with final authority over mobilization, preparing the way for the allegiance of corporate executives to military planning.[8]

Military plans are not noteworthy because they provided a solid institutional and planning base upon which the apparatus of World War II provision could be built. The opposite is true. Despite Secretary of War Henry Stimson's and Under Secretary of War Patterson's hymns of praise to interwar military planning in testimony to Senator Harry Truman's prominent investigative committee (which catapulted Truman to national attention), the plans were deficient on a number of counts. In 1945, Robert Nathan, a civilian-state planner for the War Production Board (WPB), not only declared that "the plans were not adequate" but also reported that "actually many people in the Army and Navy did not take the studies . . . very seriously." Likewise, in the same year, James Fesler, official observer of wartime battles, reported, "The realization that the [IMP] had become inadequate from a strategic viewpoint was eventually joined by the realization that the Plan was never technically adequate insofar as its calculations of military requirements were concerned."[9]

Interwar planning nonetheless proved significant. It allowed the military services, especially the army, to counter calls for New Dealer civilian-state mobilization authority by claiming that such authority would only disrupt existing plans and ongoing activities. Interwar preparations also helped allay the mutual suspicion that had marked business-military relations during World War I. Henceforth, the military's organizational reliance upon corporate advisors and contractual reliance on the largest firms meant that its plans would easily gain credibility with powerful business constituencies, who, it so happened, were hostile to the military's primary competitor, the New Dealers. In the run-up to World War II, the resultant legacy of already-constituted military plans and agencies, along with the military's burgeoning relationship to business interests, presented a serious barrier to New Dealer influence over mobilization and provided the glue for a successful military-corporate alliance.[10]

Preparation for War and the Military-Corporate Alliance

War is often considered a great spur to statebuilding; but the point here is that, insofar as World War II enhanced military-state authority while eroding civilian-state authority, it favored a particular type of statebuilding over other types. War might naturally tend to strengthen the military at the expense of civilian-state forces, but not necessarily so—especially not in the United States in the late 1930s and early 1940s, when New Dealers were so active and aggressive. Rather, explaining military preeminence within prewar mobilization means examining the alliance of military and business that resulted from corporate intervention in mobilization controversies.

Corporate personnel intervened in mobilization controversies and made common cause with military-state officials because they perceived civilian-state authority, especially as articulated through the New Deal, as a threat. In November 1941 *Fortune* magazine cited "a pervasive fear of and antipathy for the New Deal" among top corporate leaders; more than 75 percent of the corporate executives responding agreed with the statement: "Whenever possible the Administration is using the national emergency as a pretext for pushing still further the more radical social and economic aims of the New Deal." The military services, however, remained insulated from most popular pressures and aloof from the New Deal coalition. As historian Albert Blum has noted, "Army and Navy planners . . . inevitably lined up with the opponents of the New Deal," especially as the tenuous military-business relationship of the First World War strengthened and solidified itself through the interwar mobilization planning process.[11]

There was little about military planning for mobilization that threatened corporate autonomy, since the military services planned for a powerful civilian agency dominated by corporate leaders themselves. Likewise, military plans called for deferential reliance on the production and management expertise of America's largest firms. In addition, the services remained wedded until 1941 to their prewar estimates of a short war requiring limited disruption of the civilian economy: even the 1939 IMP contemplated only a two-year war effort. Based on military plans, officials from the steel and aluminum industries, for example, could confidently report (wrongly, as it turned out) that current raw material processing capacity was sufficient to meet all possible contingencies. And low military requirements meant that officials from core manufacturing firms, including most importantly the automotive industry, could argue (wrongly again) that their now-booming civilian production did not interfere with military production. The happy alliance of military and corporate forces was therefore underpinned and bolstered by the substance of military planning. As mobilization for the new war still more directly wedded industrial and military capabilities, this relationship flourished.[12]

The close relationship between military and business was further symbolized and cemented in the prewar defense period by the recruitment of Wall Street luminaries James Forrestal and Ferdinand Eberstadt and their close associate, Robert Patterson, as civilian leaders of army and navy procurement. These men remained for the most part implacably hostile to the reform dimension of the New Deal and regarded the sacrifice of social reforms a necessity dictated by the exigencies of war. Patterson, as under secretary of war, testified to Congress in 1941 that "preparation for defense is the worst possible vehicle for relieving economic and social conditions." Patterson, Eberstadt, and Forrestal—known as "all-outers" for their unequivocal desire to speed along war preparation—believed that New Dealer "all-outers" were simply using the defense emergency to extend and expand their push for social reform. Military and corporate "all-outers" thus refused to cooperate with their New Dealer counterparts, because they distrusted and feared the civilian agenda for mobilization. Historian Jeffrey Dorwart has analyzed the intensity with which Eberstadt and Forrestal opposed New Dealer influence over mobilization; in general, he finds, "corporate experts [including Eberstadt and Forrestal] thought that New Dealers encouraged wasteful spending and civilian production instead of assisting in the conversion to military production. The frantic New Deal rush to socialism, the newcomers [to mobilization] suggested, forecast a collapse of democratic capitalism and the rise of dictatorship." Fearing expansions of New Dealer authority, Eberstadt and Forrestal promoted a mobilization program built upon corporatist cooperation between the business community and military mobilization agencies.[13]

As military and corporate officials alike saw it, the more aggressively New Dealers and their allies challenged military and corporate control of mobilization, the more the military services and corporate sector had to cooperate with each other in response. An October 1941 diary entry of Eberstadt, then head of the Army-Navy Munitions Board, provides vivid evidence of the changing way that business and military personnel viewed each other. Eberstadt writes that his military aide "mentioned the fact that the civilian organization had been created at the time of the last war and this time because of the general belief that the civilians wanted to deal with civilians and not the [military] brass hats. He agreed with me, however, that there was a considerable change in point of view which had come over U.S. businessmen and that possibly the brass hats were now more acceptable to the business people than some other groups." Shared interests, including the perception of a common domestic foe, strengthened corporate-military relations, and mobilization provided the setting within which military and corporate officials nurtured their newfound friendship into a full-scale administrative partnership.[14]

Economic mobilization cannot then be understood as simply a case of corporate domination. The development of military capabilities was critically important to preclude New Dealer control of mobilization. Moreover, military officials had separate concerns that could not be fulfilled simply by reinforcing corporate power. The military services, especially the army, had suffered through the interwar years with lean budgets and damaged prestige; they were determined that the humbling demobilization of the First World War would be reversed.[15]

Before World War II the military services were among the more autonomous state institutions in the sense of their social and institutional isolation. Except for the Army Corps of Engineers, the military services did not enjoy the close relations to powerful social forces that they do today. With World War I, this isolation began to give way to a military-business cooperation that increased in the subsequent interwar period. In World War II, the former isolation of the military services from social forces gave way to extensive military-corporate cooperation. Comprehending that their isolation translated into bureaucratic weakness, the military services learned to nurture their relations with the monopoly-sector corporations they relied upon for war materiel. This proved an important step, since the military services remained reliant on business allies to win domestic battles and retain control over home front mobilization. We cannot understand the military's successful wartime ascendancy in isolation from the corporate support that made it possible.

Military and corporate personnel certainly had separate and unique reasons for cooperating as they did—the military services sought to protect and expand their bureaucratic authority by controlling mobilization, and the representatives of major firms sought to minimize governmental regulation in order to protect their prerogatives and maximize their profits and potential market position. But military and corporate personnel alike realized that together they could pursue their interests without trampling on each other's prerogatives. So, although both military and corporate forces calculated their interests independent of each other, both found it in their interest to cultivate their relationship in order to more effectively oppose New Deal mobilization initiatives. The resulting military-corporate alliance held a tremendous reservoir of power. Major firms could easily fall back on their ownership and managerial rights during the prewar period to thwart what they portrayed as dictatorial extensions of public authority into the production process. And the military services could rely upon their prewar plans and their established mobilization agencies to claim a complete and completely legitimate control over the slowly emerging mobilization process.

Still, despite the growing odds against New Dealer management of mobilization, it was never inevitable that a military-corporate alliance would dominate mobilization administration, and, during the prewar period, military-corporate success was never a certainty. On the contrary, New Deal expansion of civilian-state authority meant New Dealers and other civilian-state personnel could provide a stiff challenge to the military-corporate agenda for mobilization and influence many prewar administrative developments. As historian David Brody, among others, has argued, the "war possessed immense potential as an agent for social reform."[16]

Organizing Economic Mobilization
Political Conditions and Economic Constraints

The main issues of prewar bureaucratic infighting—conversion of civilian industries, expansion of raw material processing capability, distribution of raw materials, and military procurement—struck at what both military officials and corporate executives saw as their exclusive domains. Thus, New Dealer efforts to manage these mobilization issues would have met dogged resistance by military and corporate representatives in any case. But, within the political environment immediately before the war, corporate power and prestige increased in ways that enabled military-corporate resistance to New Dealers' efforts to be stiffer and more successful still.

Lodged between the emergencies of depression and war, the prewar defense period was characterized by a number of interacting political contingencies affecting the leverage of competing actors. In one such interaction, continued grievances over America's participation in World War I combined with the enormous unsolved domestic problems to nourish isolationist sentiment. With 1940 an election year these sentiments took on great importance for Roosevelt, especially as he positioned himself for an unprecedented third term. Accordingly, Roosevelt proceeded cautiously on all issues relating to possible involvement in the European war, waiting for public support to build before committing to any course of action.[17]

Roosevelt's managerial predilection reinforced his caution. Reluctant to delegate broad powers such as those relating to mobilization, Roosevelt preferred to retain as much personal authority as possible. Consequently, he often split responsibilities between advisors recommending contradictory policy directions, forcing them to do the spadework for new policies while he remained above the fray, in a position from which he could choose the side and policy with the most support and claim credit for its success.[18] This tendency, combined with the growing pressures of isolationism and a general muttering hostility to his bid for a third term, explains Roosevelt's halting drift into mobilization. Of course, Roosevelt's irresolution was only enhanced by the length of the prewar period itself.[19]

The point remains, however, that political contingencies increased Roosevelt's dependence on business forces. Roosevelt's inability or unwillingness to provide clear leadership limited the space for independent political action and provided anti–New Deal business forces with additional room to maneuver. The long prologue to America's entrance into the war reinforced Roosevelt's dependence on corporate officials and heightened American industry's ability to resist any mobilization process they saw as threatening to their management and ownership prerogatives. Thus, without a clear emergency (until the attack on Pearl Harbor) from which to rally his administration's flagging independence, Roosevelt succumbed to the pressure for a rapprochement with corporate leaders, whose political support he needed in the face of congressional conservatism and isolationism. Historian Paul Koistinen reports that "business in general did not seem to hold strong isolationist views [and] it tended more towards intervention than anything. However, if the industrialists became convinced that mobilization was to serve as an instrument of social reform, in self-defense [they] might be forced to support the isolationists." Likewise, in order to jump-start mobilization without causing concern to isolationists, Roosevelt needed the support and cooperation of key industry leaders. So he began to defer to their expertise and intransigence on critical mobilization questions.[20]

Under these conditions, business prestige and political influence experienced a pronounced resurgence. Previously the depression had put the business community on the defensive. Although there was little that major firms could do, on their own, to relieve the economic crisis, they were frequently painted as villains responsible for the crisis itself. But with the turn to war, business's built-in structural advantages—their managerial and ownership prerogatives—came suddenly back into play. The lengthy prewar period provided major corporations with the opportunity to resist New Deal intrusions in many cases merely by stalling preparation for war. Widespread public and congressional isolationism served to reinforce these structural corporate advantages insofar as it discouraged Roosevelt from attempting to rouse the public support needed to proceed aggressively in the face of corporate resistance. Instead, Roosevelt opted for a rapprochement with corporate leaders, and this became a key factor shaping the administrative design for mobilization.

As it was, increasing corporate leverage combined with growing congressional conservatism to dampen any enthusiasm Roosevelt might have retained for building New Deal civilian-state authority during war mobilization. Indeed, just as later presidents would prefer the world stage to bruising domestic battles, Roosevelt came to relish his transformation from "Dr. New Deal" to "Dr. Win-the-War." Thus, leftover issues relating to the New Deal governance project came to be measured against the more pressing imperatives of mobilization and foreign policy; even national security imperatives themselves often played second fiddle to the profit-making imperatives of monopoly-sector firms, in a political environment made vastly more hospitable to corporate power.

Since apparently the United States could mobilize at its leisure—it was not under direct attack or engaged in hostilities until December 1941—Roosevelt could follow a meandering route to mobilization, knowing that any attempts to expand government supervision would be met by corporate resistance. Certainly, Roosevelt could have hastened the development of authoritative civilian-state agencies if war were more imminent, since then Congress and the public would have supported more assertive civilian-state measures. But, since the political environment proved hostile to institutional innovations or to further development of New Deal institutional capacities, and because Roosevelt's political style was to roll with the punches instead of meeting them head on, war mobilization followed by default the pattern of previous governmental mobilizations, the War Industries Board and the National Recovery Administration. Mobilization thus depended upon the tools of persuasion and informal contacts within each industry. For example, civilian agencies such as the Office of Production Management relied on the prestige of their corporate dollar-a-year representatives, informal mechanisms such as industry advisory committees, and existing industry trade associations.[21]

Corporate executives pressed their advantage throughout this period, as their rebounding legitimacy buttressed their ability to shape prewar mobilization. During early defense preparations, Secretary of War Stimson summoned this legitimacy when he recorded in his diary, "If you are going to try to go to war, or to prepare for war, in a capitalist country, you have got to let business make money out of the process or business won't work." And R. Elberton Smith, analyzing army economic mobilization, noted, "Realism suggested that the best way to obtain the widespread [industrial] expansion needed in all sectors of the economy was to enlist the initiative and know-how of private enterprise. This could be done with a minimum of government supervision by harnessing the profit motive within the general framework of the existing economic and industrial system."[22]

Smith also affirms that "many individuals and groups felt that the Roosevelt administration was bent on 'socializing' the nation's economy and that it would use the defense program to further this objective." Given this sentiment, "private enterprise showed considerable reluctance to begin the [defense] task." Such reluctance is exemplified by the November 1941 *Fortune* poll of corporate executives, which revealed that "businessmen do not like the New Deal [and] Today that attitude has become a serious concern because it is affecting the management attitude toward the war." I. F. Stone reviewed in 1940 how the profit-making logic of U.S. capitalists predominated over the political logic of national security; he cited opinion makers' indignation that any motivation other than profit should move industrialists to participate in mobilization. The financial editor of the *New York Sun,* for instance, reacted to the British 100 percent excess-profits tax (a version of which was being considered in the United States) by remarking that it is "difficult for many Americans to understand how Britain can expect anyone to make the tremendous extra productive effort required by war without some stimulus other than the vague one that it is necessary to save the country."[23]

Thus, while Roosevelt worked to establish and extend his personal authority over the war effort, he was hardly likely to risk any of it to press for the extension of civilian authority over industry. For example, the invasion of Poland in September 1939 prompted Roosevelt to declare a "limited" national emergency, which he expanded to an "unlimited" national emergency in May 1941 as Nazi and Japanese military expansions continued unchecked. These declarations provided an environment that privileged executive action and Roosevelt's personal authority. Likewise, Roosevelt took advantage of the growing international crisis to issue on 5 July 1939 a "Military Order"—"a presidential power rarely invoked"—which transferred the army and navy chiefs of staff and the Army-Navy Munitions Board from the authority of the War and Navy Departments to his own direct supervision as commander in chief. Together with the soon-to-be-passed Executive Reorganization Act, this order cemented Roosevelt's wartime authority. Executive reorganization, made possible in part by the threat of war, gave Roosevelt "the essential power he wanted," including, most importantly, the authority "to coordinate military and civilian functions in the White House." Thus, by the spring of 1941, Roosevelt had clear authority to deal with a declared national emergency and sharpened tools for executive direction of the national administration through the recently implemented Executive Reorganization Act. Yet, when it came to a civilian-state mobilization effort, Roosevelt demurred. He chose not to use enhanced executive authority to command the necessary actions from industry. Instead, he made concessions to elicit industry participation.[24]

Concessions were of two related types. The first protected monopoly-sector corporate profits and market shares, and the second protected corporate managerial prerogatives. Because the monopoly-sector firms that dominated wartime prime contracting naturally wanted to maximize their booming profits during the prewar period, they would brook no interference with their civilian production and would not tolerate any disruption of civilian markets. Military production, therefore, would be housed in separately constructed plants paid for by public funds or through accelerated five-year amortization of private investment. As Secretary of the Interior Harold Ickes complained, "This is abandoning advanced New Deal ground with a vengeance." Responding to Roosevelt's "capitulat[ion] to the big interests, not only on the taxes to be levied but particularly on the amortization of plants and equipment," the secretary of the Interior reported vainly recommending that "the Government ought to build its own plants and conscript the necessary managers to run them." In addition to governmental financing for monopoly-sector plant and tool expansions, there would be no rigid profit limitations, contractors could safely ignore New Deal social and labor legislation, and "cost-plus" contracts were reintroduced. Koistinen caustically reports "it was called patriotism plus 8 per cent—or 20 per cent, or 50 per cent, or 100 per cent if business could get it." Profit limitations on shipbuilding and aircraft manufacture legislated by the Vinson-Trammel Act were repealed through the Second Revenue Act of 8 October 1940 (the same act that contained the five-year tax amortization plan). This legislation "made it decidedly profitable for contractors to convert to war production and removed much of the sting of high wartime tax rates." Under the plan, a corporation's tax bill became an asset, as it invested these funds internally instead of surrendering them to the U.S. Treasury.[25]

During the four months it took Congress to pass the Second Revenue Act, aircraft manufacturers delayed action on government orders, awaiting a favorable legislative outcome before proceeding with production. This was the celebrated "sitdown strike of capital" in which the aviation industry—"acting as a front for big business," according to I. F. Stone—flexed its newfound leverage and deferred action on U.S. military orders until favorable amortization and excess-profits legislation had been secured. Organized labor found it ironic, to say the least, to be publicly denounced as treasonous for its increasing militancy during 1940 in the face of eroding labor laws while self-serving corporate delays in the production of critical war goods escaped critical attention or harsh punishment.[26]

Besides protecting their profits and market shares, corporate executives also wanted their management prerogatives protected from New Dealer and labor interference. So they pressed for an administrative process that maximized their discretionary authority and thereby minimized independent civilian-state oversight of the national economy. As Bruce Catton, a participant in mobilization battles, has explained:

> A key point in the adroit leadership which was lining up as the ultimate foe of the Axis was the necessity to bring into the defense effort, as active co-operators, the proprietors of the nation's chief physical assets. The job couldn't be done without them, but their fears and suspicions—which, where Franklin Roosevelt was concerned, were deep and beyond number— had to be allayed. For the duration of the prewar defense period, therefore, the game had to be played their way; whatever preparations the nation made had to be made within the bounds of territory that was familiar to these men. This meant the rules were not to be changed.

The need for a rapprochement with business led Roosevelt both to restrict the utilization of existing government agencies and to curtail the development of substantive new civilian administration. Instead, as described in chapter 4, he relied upon temporary agencies heavily staffed with business advisors.[27]

Organized Labor and the Turn to War

Given the substantial gains for organized labor during the New Deal, and the overt alliance between organized labor and the New Deal administration, it seems odd that labor proved unable to hold its own politically or to help New Dealers more in their struggles with corporate and military officials. As in World War I, preparation for war brought both trouble and opportunity for labor. By the late 1930s organized labor occupied a much stronger position than it had at the beginning of World War I. Labor was expanding its ranks (having grown threefold since the beginning of World War I) and winning important battles for recognition within major industries; the Supreme Court had recently upheld the Wagner Act; and expanding war-related production had rescued labor from the doldrums and setbacks of 1937–1938. In addition, the president of the CIO, Philip Murray, presented a visionary outline for labor-management councils designed to increase military production and cope with the expected demands of wartime production while holding forth the promise of an equal partnership with corporate management. Walter Reuther of the United Automobile Workers and Ben Riskin of the International Union of Mine, Mill, and Smelter Workers in turn developed specific plans for cooperative arrangements between labor and management in their respective industries designed to speed conversion from civilian to military production and to increase the production of military requirements. Likewise, through the appointment of Sidney Hillman, president of the Amalgamated Clothing Workers of America and a member of the executive board of the CIO, to the first set of mobilization agencies, labor gained a voice in the central directorate of early mobilization. Conditions thus seemed ripe for a dramatically enhanced role for labor, both alongside corporate management and in the affairs of state.[28]

Yet such opportunities for labor were matched by equally large disadvantages. Fratricidal conflict grew within labor's ranks as the two labor federations, the AFL and the CIO, fought each other over new members, each "raiding" territory claimed by the other. The more conservative AFL remained the larger federation of the two, and the CIO had not yet achieved organizational stability even over its own natural base, the mass production industries, where support wavered depending on the success of union intervention over particular grievances. And the two federations disagreed over the relationship between the state and the union movement. The AFL clung to its voluntarist tradition, preferring collective bargaining between management and labor to agreements imposed by government agencies, which were perceived as biased toward the CIO.[29]

Moreover, because Hillman, chosen by Roosevelt as a compromise labor spokesman, was not wholly accepted by either labor federation, it was difficult for him to overcome the corporate and military domination of early mobilization and translate labor's strengths into mobilization policy. And, thanks to persisting unemployment from the depression, labor supply did not present nearly the obstacle to military production that dwindling supplies of raw materials and available manufacturing facilities did, so labor's problems never received the same kind of administrative attention within the evolving defense setup as did manufacturers' and processors' problems. Finally, the political mood of the nation was shifting against labor, particularly since strikes in the years leading to war posed the most visible (and widely publicized) causes of slow military production. Both the military services and industry officials exploited the new conservative milieu to isolate organized labor by misleadingly portraying strikes as the major cause of production slowdowns.[30]

Thus, plagued by organizational instability and fratricidal conflicts and burdened by an increasingly hostile political environment, organized labor became increasingly isolated from the emerging governmental apparatus presiding over mobilization. Such isolation was predictable in an emergency that provided both a pretext for industry officials to be assigned to important governmental positions and the preconditions for a corporate and congressional offensive against labor's recent gains. Organized labor, especially the CIO, relied on government agencies and the Democratic party to help maintain the political momentum for the union movement to develop and flourish. This reliance on allies within the national state only increased as congressional conservatism grew and labor militancy was blamed for mobilization problems. Although John L. Lewis turned away from Roosevelt and the Democrats during the 1940 election, the rest of the CIO remained utterly dependent on the president. The threat of national service legislation (a labor draft) or of a military seizure of strike-slowed industries seemingly left the CIO with few other options, although its leadership increasingly opted for cooperation because of the organizational security offered in return. Accordingly, first the AFL and then, after Pearl Harbor, the CIO as well agreed to a no-strike pledge and vowed to cooperate with a National War Labor Board (NWLB) in return for a "maintenance of membership" formula that channeled the flood of new wartime workers into existing union ranks and promised tripartite (business, government, and labor) mediation of labor grievances.[31]

Although these agreements resulted in a tremendous expansion of the number of unionized workers during the war (from 10.5 to 14.7 million members), the nature of union leadership changed dramatically, as did the relationship between leaders and the rank and file. Labor's agreement not to strike during the war highlighted the irony for union leadership contained in the very establishment of collective bargaining: labor leaders could only achieve legitimacy as bargaining partners by curbing the very militancy that secured bargaining privileges. In effect, the road to "responsible unionism," whose trailhead was the 1935 Wagner Act, now turned into a fully paved one-way street for labor leaders. Yet, during the war, labor leaders were increasingly challenged by their own membership. As the draft swept away many experienced trade unionists, newly hired workers engaged in ever-increasing wildcat strikes due sometimes to wage issues but more often to shop-floor grievances related to arbitrary managerial actions and the breakdown of grievance procedures. Expanding wildcat strikes increased government pressure on union leadership to discipline its own rank and file or risk retraction of membership guarantees by the NWLB or the imposition of national service legislation. Thus, the union movement was transformed as tendencies toward bureaucratization and organizational oligarchy were exacerbated by the war.[32]

Notwithstanding the conservative drift of its leadership, labor was never able to gain the substantive role within mobilization that industrialists achieved. Neither Hillman nor other labor advisors could counter the influence of corporate and military advisors, because they lacked operational or policy-making authority, because early mobilization agencies proved weak and divisive, and because organized labor itself was often riven by factional discord. Moreover, whereas monopoly-sector corporations had central access points to the mobilization leadership through which they could address their concerns and focus their clout, labor's concerns were divided administratively into separate, competing organizations concerned with labor relations and labor supply. Hillman worked aggressively within these constraints, but he failed to expand the scope of labor's involvement. Increasingly estranged from his union base and caught between feuding labor leaders, hostile military and industry officials, conservative members of Congress, and a restless rank and file, Hillman sought shelter in his top-level position and the official acceptance offered him by his colleagues in the mobilization process, New Dealer and industry men alike. Desiring to protect his position within government and prove himself to his colleagues, Hillman even spoke out against the Murray industrial council plan, which would have organized labor-management councils for deciding questions for each major industry: "In short, 130,000,000 people cannot delegate to any combination of private interests final decision on matters of basic policy." Such a statement ignores what should have been obvious to Hillman—that private corporate interests were intimately involved with mobilization policy.[33]

Hillman's isolation and weakness were most dramatically manifest when, despite marshalling all of the prestige and authority of his position, he failed to budge the military from its policy of granting contracts to labor-starved areas and to firms violating labor laws. In the face of pressure from John L. Lewis and threats of labor unrest, Roosevelt initially supported Hillman's campaign to direct work to areas of high unemployment and hold defense contractors to all labor laws, including the Walsh-Healey Act, the Fair Labor Standards Act, the National Labor Relations Act, and all state and local labor laws. Accordingly, the first mobilization agency, the National Defense Advisory Commission (NDAC), promulgated two policy directives in September 1940 that tied the distribution of defense contracts to reducing unemployment and to complying with labor laws. Attorney General Robert Jackson followed up by ruling that labor laws would be enforced for those receiving military contracts. And civilian leaders for the army and navy directed their respective supply bureaus to honor the directives.

Although the army and navy formally agreed to follow the NDAC's directives, there was really no way to enforce the policy in the face of industry resistance; many army and navy contracting personnel simply ignored the directives, allowing big contractors like Ford and Bethlehem Steel to flout applicable labor laws. And, when Hillman announced the new policy to the press, industry officials, with no hint of irony, denounced it as a form of "blacklisting," and William Knudsen of General Motors, ostensibly Hillman's friend and partner within the first set of mobilization agencies, openly showed his management bias and fear of civilian-state meddling in industry affairs by declaring "We don't want any part of the Russian system over here." In turn, the same army and navy representatives who had previously agreed to the policy, joined by Attorney General Jackson, assured outraged conservative members of Congress that Hillman had it wrong. Congressman Howard W. Smith's hostile investigation forced the retractions, and even Hillman was forced to back down. As Koistinen reports, "Hillman's surrender . . . was ordered from the White House." This type of reception awaited labor throughout the war as a combination of corporate executives and military officials supported by congressional conservatives continually overwhelmed labor initiatives.[34]

Labor's hopes throughout the war remained pinned to a vision of a tripartite relationship between itself, business, and government. The stakes were extremely high. The government had politicized industrial relations through the Wagner Act, and the CIO tried to exploit this opening by gaining a voice in the management of the nation's industrial assets. CIO president Philip Murray announced in December 1940 a visionary plan for labor-management councils to plan the conversion of major industries to defense production. Such corporatist arrangements would exploit both the growing authority of the national state and labor's friendly relationship with government officials to labor's benefit. And, thanks to corporate management's manifest lack of action to mobilize their industries for war, the Murray plan and, even more so, the Reuther plan for converting the automobile industry to wartime production found a receptive audience among those civilian-state "all-outers" promoting speedier mobilization. Even though labor geared its initiatives to relieve "priority" unemployment (unemployment due to the growing scarcity of certain raw materials) and dislocation of workers, their initiatives dovetailed with plans of "all-outers" for immediate conversion of civilian industries and for maximum utilization of existing industrial capacity. As I. F. Stone concluded at the time, *the worker's interest coincided with those of the defense program, the manufacturer's clashed with it.*[35]

In the face of industry's stalling and resistance to industrial conversion and expansion, organized labor's willingness to take the initiative upped the ante in its ongoing contest with industrial capital. Labor was moving to a qualitative new position, from earlier efforts to gain recognition for purposes of collective bargaining to an insistence that they share in sacrosanct management decisions. Historian Nelson Lichtenstein hails this agenda as "the CIO's corporatist vision," which sought to project the voice of organized labor into "production goals, investment decisions, and employment patterns of the nation's core industries." By pressing for such a vision, labor was not only "trespassing" on the traditional prerogatives of management but was also linking up with those national officials wanting tighter control over the nation's core industries. Corporate management therefore saw a multiple threat to their immediate profits and to their future managerial prerogatives from increased government regulation and from expanding union influence. Fortunately for major corporations, their representatives occupied key positions within mobilization from which they could thwart any labor or civilian-state intrusion into their business. The NDAC, and its successor, the Office of Production Management (OPM), spoke with their voice, and as Eliot Janeway noted, "OPM regarded the problem [of conversion to war production] as one for industry to decide."[36]

Walter Reuther's plan to convert the auto industry (Reuther was vice president of the CIO's United Auto Workers) received the greatest attention, not least because it was the most detailed and workable of the CIO's proposals and involved the nation's largest and most critical industry. Reuther's "500 planes a day" plan excited Roosevelt and New Dealers in the OPM's competitor, the Office of Price Administration and Civilian Supply (OPACS), because of its promise to dramatically increase defense production. Reuther's plan also fit labor's immediate goal to employ the large number of experienced assembly-line and tool-and-die workers laid off during the auto industry's yearly six-month retooling period. Reuther recommended that all Detroit-area production facilities be surveyed to determine existing capacity and to plan conversion of currently unused plant and equipment. In addition, he proposed to delay retooling the industry for new auto models, thereby making available fifteen thousand skilled machinists for retooling factories for the mass production of fighter planes. In this way, the seasonally un-employed and the smaller tool-and-die shops could be absorbed into the defense effort.

Though it called for only partial conversion of the auto industry, Reuther's plan conflicted substantially with the industry's desire to cen-tralize military contracts and new military production facilities in the hands of the largest manufacturers. Auto firms also feared what the plan implied for industrial relations and for mobilization in general. As *Fortune* reported, "The heart of the Reuther Plan was not only the sugges-tion that existing Detroit facilities could be immediately converted to the making of planes; it was, more importantly, the suggestion that the entire plane program could be managed by a committee consisting of representatives of management, labor, and government." Production men, especially former head of General Motors and then director gen-eral of the OPM, William Knudsen, sought to discredit the plan by pick-ing at minor details. For example, Knudsen and the auto industry ar-gued that existing plants could not produce aircraft because of the very small tolerances required, particularly for aircraft engines. Besides, deci-sions about such matters were management's territory, and Reuther was not management. Of course, the industry's positions conveniently fit within their ongoing resistance to converting the industry to war pro-duction; they preferred to reap enormous profits from their now-booming civilian operations while the government financed an entire new industrial empire for military production alongside them.[37]

For his trouble, I. F. Stone reported, Reuther was "assailed . . . as a Communist" and his "plan was never given a hearing."[38] Yet, as the Tru-man Committee later discovered, the auto industry had misrepresented the facts to serve its own needs. When Truman's committee had argued in the summer of 1941 for immediate conversion of the auto industry to war production, Under Secretary of War Patterson testified that, accord-ing to the auto companies, the tolerances of existing machine tools were too large to be of any use. (The military services, of course, displayed their usual willingness to rely on industry information without ques-tion.) Subsequently, however, when Japan's attack on Pearl Harbor forced an end to civilian auto production, the industry suddenly an-nounced that, indeed, it could utilize existing plants and equipment for war contracts. The Truman Committee therefore concluded, "It is quite evident that the information furnished to the Under Secretary of War by the automobile companies and the OPM was quite inaccurate. We could have and should have made use of automobile plants and tools." "In the end," as Eliot Janeway put it, "it was not reason which converted the auto plants, but Pearl Harbor."[39]

The notion that labor's traditionally silent and submissive role should be transformed into a more active and expanded partnership with management was rebuffed not only in industry but also in the mobilization agencies. There, though labor officials had expected to have more leverage, labor advisory committees never gained the stature of industry advisory committees; more generally, labor officials never achieved the kinds of input that corporate representatives did. For example, when the uniform industry advisory system was established under the OPM, industry was granted the formal and central place in the administrative process that labor was denied. Hillman was quick to act on this neglect, and the OPM established a labor advisory system that, at least on paper, offered labor the same advisory status as industry advisory committees. But these labor advisory committees received their lease on life fourteen months after mobilization had begun, by which time labor became an unwanted intruder in an already functioning administrative process in which industry committees had long since been deeply rooted and fully involved. Henceforth, in effect, the OPM's industry officials permitted labor committees to sign off on plans already formulated in order to secure the appearance of labor input and head off potential labor problems in advance. Of course, this attempt at co-optation was transparent to labor advisors. As George Brooks, an aide to Hillman, reported in 1945:

> The labor advisory committees were "hopeless affairs." The members of the committees, labor men long accustomed to having decisions reached after a conference, were baffled and bewildered when, after they had come to Washington, and presented their views and recommendations . . . , they were merely thanked for attending the meeting, and so far as they knew, nothing was ever done to implement their recommendations.

Labor advisors struggled for more substantive input, especially regarding labor dislocations and regional unemployment. For Knudsen, however, labor representatives had no right to share in management's privileged access; he put off those seeking to expand labor's input in the administrative process, saying, "I believe the meeting [as now constituted] would then become too large to be workable." In other words, industrialists, having helped construct an administrative process that secured their predominance within mobilization, would brook no interference by labor with these arrangements. As Steve Fraser concludes in a recent study, labor committees "were held in contempt by government and corporate functionaries alike. Once America became an active combatant, all social and political pretensions about their role were unceremoniously dropped."[40]

Labor's marginalization was built into the administrative circuitry of the defense agencies themselves: labor committees had their input channeled through the Labor Division of the OPM, and industry committees had direct access to the OPM's industry branches, where effective policy-making power came to be lodged. In turn, industry branch chiefs, many of whom came from management's ranks, shared Knudsen's goal of insulating mobilization administration from labor's input. Official observer Edythe First found at the time that "some branch chiefs were frankly unsympathetic to organized labor"; no matter how sympathetic the OPM official, "he was not likely to free himself so completely from years of industrial indoctrination as to share labor's enthusiasm for equality of management and labor in the defense production program." Nor did it help that Hillman divided his OPM Labor Division into two branches—Labor Supply and Labor Relations—filled, respectively, with labor economists and union men who, despite their desire to counter industry influence, embodied rather distinct interests and often found themselves mired in disagreement. In the end, labor could do little more than express frustration with their meager role in mobilization. James Carey, secretary of the CIO, complained to Congressman John Tolan's investigative committee that labor's advisory committees presented only the appearance of labor input "which did not go down to the operating level."[41]

Carey articulated labor's basic problem: through Hillman, it seemed to have a voice in the formulation of mobilization policies, but the facade of Hillman's top-level participation masked negligible labor input everywhere else. Labor was granted the semblance of power while the administrative mechanisms of mobilization operated either to co-opt labor leaders or to tantalize them with visions of substantial participation that would always prove chimerical in the end. Because labor had required the support of national officials to secure its gains throughout the 1930s, labor officials inferred that a state-led mobilization effort would offer a prime opportunity to advance their interests. But corporate infiltration of defense agencies now meant that labor became dependent on those who would absorb and weaken their influence. And, more generally, because labor supply never posed serious problems during this period of preparation for war, given the reserves of unemployed workers, administrative mechanisms dealing with labor's problems were allowed to languish, with labor representatives relegated to second-class status.

Yet the government could not completely ignore industrial relations, if only because strikes were increasingly—and inaccurately—touted as the chief cause of slow defense production.[42] Accordingly, in the spring of 1941, Roosevelt established the National War Mediation Board (NWMB) to placate a growing chorus of antilabor sentiment in Congress and to deal with a wave of strikes. Despite hysterical reports promoted in Congress and by the services about "fifth column activity," these strikes resulted from the failure of wages to keep up with rising profits and prices triggered by expanded defense production. Anxious about production slowdowns and impatient with the administrative complexities for dealing with strikes, the military pressed Roosevelt for the authority to intervene forcibly to end strikes and for some type of national service or labor draft legislation. The NWMB fell short of embodying such authority; yet, until its collapse in November 1941, when CIO representatives resigned after the board refused to rule in favor of the closed shop for miners, it provided an effective mechanism for mediating strikes, especially as employers recognized the value of unions and collective bargaining as labor markets tightened.[43]

The attack on Pearl Harbor prompted replacement of the NWMB. Roosevelt called together labor and management representatives to work out a no-strike, no-lockout agreement and to agree on an acceptable mediation mechanism. After twisting a few arms to obtain an agreement to form a National War Labor Board (NWLB), Roosevelt left the new organization to sort out disputes over the closed shop by itself—and also went beyond the scope of the initial agreement by assigning the NWLB compulsory arbitration power.

Finally, at least in the realm of labor relations, organized labor obtained the tripartite mechanism they had been arguing for all along. Labor also received a "maintenance of membership" agreement through the NWLB (with a 15-day "escape clause" that made it palatable to management) that channeled all new war workers into existing unions, and laborers gained a limited wage hike through the "Little Steel" formula (allowing a maximum 15 percent wage hike). But the price for these concessions was high: the security guarantee for unions ultimately gave management a large degree of leverage since it forced union leadership to discipline their own rank and file, and kept wages, relative to inflation and profits, very low. As Lichtenstein argues, the NWLB was "as important as the Wagner Act in shaping an American system . . . of routine and bureaucratic industrial relations."[44]

In the end, the labor movement remained on the defensive throughout the war, thrown against the ropes by a combination of fratricidal conflict, the loss of experienced trade unionists to the armed forces, and, probably most important, by the combined hostility of business and the military services and by Congressional conservatives who harried labor throughout the war with threats of a labor draft.

▼ ▼ ▼

Labor's increasing weakness and the concomitant increase in corporate leverage shaped the trajectory of wartime statebuilding. The changing political contingencies of this defense period enhanced the structural leverage corporate executives enjoyed by virtue of their ownership and managerial prerogatives. Such strengthened corporate leverage ensured that Roosevelt would be heavily reliant upon corporate willingness to participate in mobilization and, in turn, that corporate leaders' willingness to cooperate depended upon Roosevelt's willingness to allow them a decisive influence over the shape and speed of mobilization.

Corporate officials thereby managed to parlay their control of the nation's industrial resources into a central role for themselves in mobilization. Many mobilization decisions resulted from their calculated inactivity—for example, delays in converting their industries to war production in order to reap increasing profits from expanding markets. But dollar-a-year corporate advisors and their cohorts on industry advisory committees, critically positioned within budding civilian agencies, also actively resisted the expansion of interventionist government policies, preferring to rely on voluntaristic and noncoercive mechanisms to mobilize the war economy.

THREE

Building the Wartime State

• Changing political contingencies and the shifting national balance of power greatly influenced prewar administrative developments. The evolving administration of mobilization during the period leading to war, especially the growing power of military-state agencies, led to a domestic military ascendancy that was partly an outgrowth of the expanding political influence of prominent corporate executives. Corporate personnel used their growing influence and prominent governmental positions within mobilization to shape the national state's response to war. They agitated for a voluntarist mobilization process to limit expansions of civilian-state authority over industry, and to the extent they accepted the need for centralized national authority they promoted military-state stewardship. Thus, as corporate representatives gained central positions within civilian agencies—both at the apex and within the operating levels of mobilization administration—they helped military-state agencies gain control of industrial mobilization.

New Dealers often found themselves overwhelmed by the new political conditions that reduced their power relative to their military and corporate competitors. As the national focus shifted to war mobilization, both military and corporate officials could claim greater legitimacy within the councils of national governance. In addition, New Dealers working to mobilize the nation had to fight both internal and external battles to expand civilian-state authority. More adept at bureaucratic infighting than at exercising authority responsibly, the military services jockeyed with civilian agencies for control of expanding mobilization responsibilities. And, while military agencies were strengthened by the corporate personnel within their ranks, civilian mobilization agencies were weakened by the inevitable conflicts between corporate dollar-a-year advisors and New Dealers. At the same time, New Dealers within these divided civilian agencies had to confront the intransigence of corporate firms, who resisted surrendering any of their managerial prerogatives to a civilian-state mobilization effort.

War Resources Board

The experience of the War Resources Board (WRB), Roosevelt's first stab at mobilization administration, is instructive. As a token of his changing stance toward corporate executives, Roosevelt on 9 August 1939 assigned the corporate-dominated board—headed by Edward Stettinius Jr., chairman of U.S. Steel—to study and recommend a course for mobilization based on the military's interwar planning. Although mostly discounted as a failed exercise because its select corporate personnel caused a storm of complaints among New Dealers, the WRB's administrative recommendations were prescient. Operating from the assumption that Roosevelt would veto the military's plan to concentrate authority in a superagency controlled by corporate and military leaders, WRB businessmen, in a report orchestrated by Bernard Baruch, recommended instead a decentralized and voluntaristic administrative framework that would nonetheless maximize business discretionary input. In their 12 October 1939 report to Roosevelt, the WRB firmly stated:

> Adequate powers must be given to experienced executives having the confidence of industry. . . .
>
> American businessmen, like all Americans, are accustomed to democratic procedures. More effectiveness can be obtained through voluntary cooperation than through force.
>
> We recommend that wartime powers be vested in specially-created wartime agencies which will be automatically demobilized when war is over. Should wartime powers be granted to existing executive or quasi-judicial agencies of the government, it will be next to impossible at the end of the war to separate the wartime from the peacetime functions of the government.[1]

Like their War Industries Board predecessors, the businessmen of the WRB feared potentially permanent expansions of independent government authority. They preferred the use of "emergency" agencies, which were more easily dismantled at the end of the war and more easily dominated by corporate executives. Their recommendations, of course, assumed military willingness to place authority with business leaders. Thus, in effect, the WRB report both illustrated the allegiance of corporate executives to the military model for mobilization and outlined the way in which they would henceforth seek to gain strategic positions for themselves within the wartime state. As historian Paul Koistinen has concluded, "What was intended as a board to study mobilization, the War Department attempted to use as a means for instituting its plans. And since the plans appealed to them, the representatives of the business community took advantage of the situation, just as they had done under the National Industrial Recovery Act."[2]

Although Roosevelt subsequently dismissed the board and buried the report, he remained heavily dependent upon corporate cooperation. As a result, mobilization did indeed follow the informal course laid out by the WRB. Edythe First, one of the first to analyze the development of mobilization administration, observed: "Though the President had discarded the War Resources Board and established a new industrial mobilization agency, he forged a strong link between the two by entrusting Edward R. Stettinius Jr., former chairman of the War Resources Board, with one of the most far-reaching phases of [its successor's] work." For Roosevelt, hemmed in by isolationist sentiment and considered a lame duck, his obvious choice for surreptitiously moving mobilization forward without causing concern to isolationists and without pushing business to oppose the administration at a delicate moment lay in simple reliance on the existing networks of large, established corporations. The government would in any event have to rely on the industrial capacity of monopoly-sector firms to prepare for war. The issue remained, however, whether these firms would have to submit to external political control. As I. F. Stone remarked in 1940, businessmen "have a place in the defense structure and it is no small one, for one of the resources of our country lies in the ability of its businessmen; but this does not mean that they are qualified to make fundamental economic decisions of the defense program, nor that the predominance of a few great monopolists is the way to tap the business genius of America."[3]

Roosevelt's political calculus meshed with the self-serving agenda of corporate executives and resulted in a strategy of slow and limited mobilization guided by industry voluntarism, a route that granted industries maximum discretion over how mobilization would proceed. In addition, because the civilian-state mobilization effort that Roosevelt patched together possessed only limited and fragmented authority, the military services acquired greater authority by default. Corporate executives buttressed military claims by adhering to the military's mobilization plan, which allowed them to protect their profits on the one hand and their prerogatives on the other.

There were two immediate consequences of the reliance on business voluntarism: fledgling civilian agencies became top-heavy with dollar-a-year corporate advisors, and industry advisory committees began to shoulder important responsibilities. Although formal civilian-state authority would eliminate the need for the voluntarism through which major corporations first gained such intimate access to policy implementation, it would prove extremely difficult to undo these relationships under the emergency conditions of wartime.[4]

National Defense Advisory Commission

The volatile mix of dollar-a-year corporate advisors and New Dealers created a split within the first defense agency, the National Defense Advisory Commission (NDAC), which hampered the development of civilian-state authority and made it difficult for the agency to proceed authoritatively. James Fesler, in an internal War Production Board analysis, reported:

> The Advisory Commission suffered further in its fight for power because of an internal split among the members of the Commission. One group, spearheaded by Knudsen [of General Motors] and Stettinius [of U.S. Steel] . . . tended . . . to look to big, well-established companies as the logical producers of defense items, and to oppose consideration of labor standards and other "New Dealish" policies as factors relevant to the award of defense contracts. These were attitudes with which the Services were generally sympathetic. The other group in the Commission . . . sought power over the Services in order to press for distribution of contracts to smaller companies, the location of munition plants in the less industrialized areas, and insistence that defense contractors observe labor standards established by the Government.[5]

The NDAC perfectly fit Roosevelt's needs. Still authorized under a World War I statute, "legally powerless," and with no provision for a single administrative head, the organization was revived in May 1940 in response to renewed Nazi offensives in western Europe and the British withdrawal from Dunkirk. Housed in the recently activated Office for Emergency Management of the Executive Office of the President, the NDAC was staffed by a heterogeneous group of seven individuals with no provision made for any kind of centralized coordination between them. This setup ensured that Roosevelt would have the final word, which was as he wanted it; he had no intention of abdicating final authority over mobilization to anyone at this early date.[6]

Notable among the NDAC commissioners were William Knudsen, president of General Motors, in charge of industrial production; Sidney Hillman, president of the Amalgamated Clothing Workers of America, in charge of labor; and Edward Stettinius Jr., who had earlier headed the WRB, responsible for industrial materials, and who, as the official history of mobilization reports, "represented, through his own affiliation with the United States Steel Corporation, and family connections with E. I. Dupont Nemours, Inc., and J. P. Morgan & Co., the 'big business' of the Nation."[7] Harold Ickes, secretary of the Interior, grumbled about the choices in his "secret" diary:

> I regard the Knudsen appointment as particularly bad. General Motors has a very heavy investment in Germany, which might conceivably be a hostage to fortune so far as the president of General Motors is concerned. Moreover, General Motors is a du-Pont-controlled corporation and the du Ponts have vast interests in all parts of the world, including munitions. I don't believe anyone ought to be on this commission or in a position of authority with the Government, in connection with the whole rearmament campaign, who has financial interests in Germany.[8]

Also notable was the appointment of Leon Henderson to take charge of price stabilization. Henderson, a staunch New Dealer, had played a key role in the Temporary National Economic Committee's investigations of monopoly economic power. Other members assumed responsibility for transportation, agriculture, and consumer issues. And Donald Nelson, an executive vice president of Sears, Roebuck & Company who had been on loan from Sears to the Treasury Department as a purchasing expert, joined the NDAC shortly after it was formed as the coordinator of national defense purchases to help streamline military procurement. Nelson, who later figured prominently in mobilization as head of the War Production Board, had experienced government service before as resident director of the National Recovery Administration's Industrial Advisory Board; he was also a well-known corporate liberal and a key member of the Business Advisory Council, "big business's" advisory voice in the Roosevelt administration's Commerce Department.[9]

Although the NDAC remained advisory to the army and navy (and to the president) and operated without an administrative head, the vacuum in civilian-state authority and expanding military contracting pressed the seven commissioners to act in some key areas.[10] Of course, Roosevelt, recalling the chaotic bidding wars between government agencies during World War I, did transfer authority to the commission for reviewing and clearing large defense contracts (those exceeding $500,000). The commission also prepared the way for industrial expansions by organizing a program of tax amortization to speed construction of defense-related facilities and by pressing the military services to expand their requirements. As the official history of mobilization reports, "The major contribution of the Commission was that it persisted, often over service protests, in getting industrial production expanded. It was the industrial expansion planned in 1940 and laid down in 1941 that made possible the huge production of 1942-43."[11]

In trying to gain civilian-state oversight of the military's issuance of priorities, however, the NDAC clashed head-on with the Army-Navy Munitions Board (ANMB), the agency headed by the under secretaries of war and the navy to coordinate and manage procurement and priorities among the military branches. Priorities stipulated the precedence of goods to be produced by guaranteeing specific contractors access to scarce raw materials and components. Bernard Baruch called this power "the synchronizing force" behind governmental direction of resource allocation during wartime. Interwar planning and the military's Industrial Mobilization Plan had recognized that civilians should manage and oversee the determination of priorities in order to weigh military needs against other claimants and to maintain the principle of civilian control of the military, and Nelson and Henderson aggressively fought for civilian-state oversight of priorities. The military services, however, through the ANMB, battled for sole stewardship of priorities. In this fight, Nelson and Henderson battled not only the ANMB but also an internal foe in Knudsen, who believed the NDAC civilians should concern themselves only with priorities relating to civilian production instead of worrying about overall supervision. In the end, although Roosevelt empowered an NDAC Priorities Board headed by Nelson to help manage priorities, the services retained the ability to assign most priorities outside of Nelson's purview. This episode was indicative of what was to come: the military services fiercely resisted any and all attempts by civilians to gain supervisory control over military operations, and their defiance proved successful. After all, the military controlled procurement, and priorities by necessity followed contracts; they had an operating national staff in place, giving them de facto control by virtue of the vacuum in civilian-state capacity; and they could always argue that civilian-state control interfered with military strategy.[12]

Even as some NDAC commissioners struggled to project greater authority over the military, military officials were busy entrenching their control over procurement and priority orders. Military assertiveness proved all the more effective, of course, thanks to divisions between New Dealers and corporate executives within the NDAC. A powerful group of industrialists within the NDAC, including Knudsen, typically sided with the military on important controversies while gaining military support in return. In fact, the military's hostility to their civilian-state counterparts contrasted sharply with its receptiveness to corporate executives. As Ferdinand Eberstadt, head of the ANMB and later top-level member of the War Production Board, recalled, "These fellows [military personnel] are terribly impressed by business success [and the] other side is terribly impressed by general's uniforms." Military historian Walter Millis elaborates:

> NDAC attained no great popularity with the War and Navy Departments. The civilian heads [of those departments] were accustomed to men like

Stettinius and Knudsen, but Henderson, [Agricultural Commissioner] Davis and Hillman were outside their ken as working partners. The reactions of uniformed officers tended to be even more emphatic. Some of them stood in unreserved awe of executives of companies like U.S. Steel and General Motors; but there was far less community, on both sides, between the military and the representatives of other segments of the economy that were included in NDAC.[13]

Roosevelt, ever conscious of isolationist sentiment and concerned to protect his own authority, did little to expand NDAC authority over the military. Yet, although the NDAC represented a halting start to projecting civilian-state authority over mobilization, it laid down the tracks on which future mobilization efforts would travel: limited civilian-state stewardship based primarily on the prestige of businessmen, combined with unsupervised military-state control of procurement.

The onset of the European war increased the pressure for more action on the mobilization front. But the changes Roosevelt made in the mobilization setup were a response not only to war in Europe but to the exigencies of the 1940 election as well. Of course, mobilization and the politics of war dictated that Roosevelt make his peace with business and with the political opposition alike to smooth the way for his reelection bid. Toward this end, in the immediate wake of France's fall to the Nazis in June 1940 he appointed two prominent Republicans, Henry Stimson and Frank Knox, both members of the internationalist and interventionist wing of the GOP, as secretaries of the army and navy. Stimson and Knox in turn hired new under secretaries. These positions held the real power over mobilization, and Stimson choose Robert Patterson, a federal judge and past and future member of a top New York legal firm, and Knox settled on James Forrestal, a conservative Democrat and partner in the New York investment-banking firm Dillon, Read. These appointments, along with those of the businessmen already serving, created the "national unity" front with which Roosevelt would simultaneously undergird his third-term campaign and prepare the nation for war.[14]

Only with the 1940 election out of the way did Roosevelt turn his full attention to the mounting international crisis and to the administrative arrangements for mobilization. Problems of home front mobilization increased dramatically when Roosevelt promoted a British aid program on top of $11 billion in prime contracts awarded by the military services from June through December 1940. Increasing orders from Britain combined with expanding military contracting to burden the national economy and to expose the weaknesses of the NDAC as a coordinating institution. And, once again, members of a restive Congress began to propose their own plans for centralizing civilian-state authority, thereby placing that much more pressure on Roosevelt to speedily reform mobilization.

Office of Production Management

Following the 1940 election, Roosevelt thus sought to remedy the administrative weaknesses of mobilization by replacing the NDAC with the Office of Production Management (OPM) on 7 January 1941. In the OPM, however, Roosevelt replicated the NDAC's division of power by assigning two codirectors, Knudsen the industrialist and Hillman the labor leader, naming Knudsen the spokesman for the agency. These two, along with the secretaries of the army and navy, made up an OPM Policy Council (the "Big Four"), responsible for overall policy. As Nelson reports, the president "informed us that he was going to run the new show just as he had run the headless NDAC. He was not going to cede or delegate any powers to an 'economic czar.'"[15]

Although Roosevelt delegated official powers to the OPM ostensibly to help it increase defense-related production, the existing problems of divided authority and reliance on corporate voluntarism continued to hamper effective civilian-state stewardship. Besides the separation of authority between Knudsen and Hillman, the OPM operated through three independent divisions: a Division of Production under John Biggers (president of Libby-Owen-Ford Glass Company), a Division of Purchases under Donald Nelson, and a Priorities Division under Edward Stettinius. Up to June 1941 all three divisions established separate relations with military procurement agencies and with each industry, causing undue confusion owing to the replication of functions and inadequate coordination between the Divisions.

The OPM's ability to provide effective stewardship and coordination suffered from this unnecessary replication of agency functions and responsibilities. But it also came to be hindered by a competitor agency that shared its administrative bailiwick. Roosevelt, observing the disruptions to the civilian economy and concerned about the corporate domination of the OPM, assigned responsibility for controlling prices and stabilizing the civilian economy to a separate organization, the Office of Price Administration and Civilian Supply, created on 11 April 1941, headed by New Dealer Leon Henderson, and staffed by New Dealer and other civilian-state personnel.[16]

These responsibilities with regard to mobilization and its impact on the national economy were far weightier and more explicit than the NDAC's had been. Its charge was to measure military requirements and industrial capacity, coordinate government procurement, regulate production, plan the conversion of civilian industries to war production, expand production capacity, and establish priorities for the delivery of raw materials and finished goods. To help fulfill their responsibilities, Roosevelt eventually delegated to the OPM his priorities power and his power to place compulsory manufacturing orders.[17] Yet, although its grant of authority and stated mission seemed broad, OPM statutory power was not much greater than that of the NDAC. As Roosevelt's executive order stated, the OPM "does not negotiate, award, or execute contracts. Nor does it finance, build, or operate plants. All this work is done by the War and Navy Departments and other operating defense agencies." Knudsen, ostensible head of the new organization, noted to Senator Truman's investigative committee, the Special Committee Investigating the National Defense Program, the OPM's built-in subordination to the military:

> We took over priorities and purchases so that we are set up as what you might call an expediting agency. We make no contracts with anybody; we can't sign a contract. The contracting is purely under law invested in the Secretary of War and the Secretary of the Navy.

Philip Reed, a dollar-a-year advisor on leave from his position as chairman of the board for General Electric and with the OPM's Materials Division, explained the office's subordination to industry: "OPM has no authority over industry; it has nothing it can do to industry to command them to do this or to do that." As Donald Nelson wryly concluded:

> I have said that OPM, with its lack of any police power, inherited all the troubles of NDAC. In some instances we were like a judge who, after listening to elaborate testimony, orders an injunction which is blithely ignored by the defendant. Such a judge would feel that he might have spent his time to better advantage picking beans or working crossword puzzles.[18]

For the fact that the OPM presented more bluster than muscle, Roosevelt certainly bore much of the blame. After Congress expanded the president's authority over priorities on 31 May 1941, for example, it took Roosevelt three months to pass it on to the OPM. Moreover, the office's limited authority made it vulnerable to predation by competitor agencies. Existing federal agencies understandably resisted the OPM's attempts to secure control over the home front, and Roosevelt further undermined its authority in such matters by delegating to a "czar" (in this case, Secretary of the Interior Harold Ickes) control over petroleum, thus removing a vital area of economic activity from OPM control. Even worse, as political scientist Herman Somers reports, "The armed services presented a far greater problem to OPM. The War and Navy Departments were not eager to concede much power." Military agencies retained operating authority over procurement and priorities, and they resisted any substantive intrusions into what they considered, by this point, their exclusive domain.[19]

The OPM, moreover, was dominated by dollar-a-year corporate advisors who dragged their feet when it came to implementing substantive controls over their counterparts in industry or forcing conversion from civilian production. As the Truman Committee reported, "The principal positions of the [OPM] were assigned to persons holding important positions with large companies who were willing and anxious to serve on a dollar per year, or without compensation (w.o.c.) basis." Although the percentage of corporate dollar-a-year advisors to the total administrative workforce was relatively small, official historian James McAleer reports that "the importance of this group far exceeded its numerical strength," since they made up the "large majority of top officials." Only 3 percent of top officials came from the ranks of organized labor, 4 percent from universities or foundations. As Philip Murray, president of the CIO, reported to his membership in late 1941: "A horde of representatives of the large corporations [has] descended upon Washington and [has] attempted to assume complete control of our defense effort through the dollar-a-year men within the [OPM]." As Harold Ickes put it, "Big business is certainly not overlooking any opportunity to entrench itself [in mobilization] and it is working through its dollar-a-year men in Washington."[20]

These corporate advisors proved hostile to formal governmental controls and did little to expand OPM authority over the military. In general, the Truman Committee found "numerous instances of gross inefficiency [in the defense program] and still more instances where the private interest of those concerned have hindered and delayed the defense program." Dollar-a-year advisors, the Truman Committee noted, had exhibited a natural tendency to favor the interests of their firm, their industry, and even business interests as a whole in their decisions concerning the implementation of mobilization controls. As the committee report states, "No man can honestly serve two masters." The Truman Committee worried as well about the likelihood that corporate representatives would inherently promote the interests of larger firms in general: "All important procurement contracts must be approved by these dollar-a-year and w.o.c. men, which means that contracts must conform to their theories of business. Since they represent the largest companies, this means that the defense program in all its ramifications must obtain the approval of the large companies." Dollar-a-year and w.o.c. advisors were seen to "subconsciously reflect the opinions and conclusions which they formerly reached as managers of large interests with respect to Government competition, with respect to taxation and amortization, with respect to financing of new plant expansion, and with respect to the margin of profit which should be allowed on war contracts." In fact, Senator Truman's investigative committee essentially blamed those who led the OPM (specifically, dollar-a-year advisors) for the weaknesses in civilian-state control:

> The [OPM] was properly given a very great amount of freedom to determine its own organization and the interrelations between the various departments and divisions of that organization. This freedom . . . carried

with it a corresponding duty on the part of the responsible heads of the [OPM] to see to it that an efficient, workable organization was created. If the powers given to them were not sufficient to accomplish that end, they had a plain duty not only to call attention to the lack of power but themselves to present a carefully prepared request for the Executive orders or legislation which they needed. . . .[21]

Civilian-state mobilization authority was thus stymied by the predominance of corporate dollar-a-year advisors within the civilian agencies, by the aggressiveness of the military services, and by the unwillingness of corporate advisors to challenge expanding military authority. This is especially clear in the case of William Knudsen, former chairman of General Motors (a corporation that came to dominate wartime contracts) and head of the OPM, who was regarded by the War Department "as its ally and advocate" while the OPM itself came to be regarded as "virtually the civilian auxiliary of the War and Navy Departments."[22]

Military and Industry into the Organizational Vacuum

Independent military procurement had a long tradition, but World War I had exposed the military's anachronistic and destructive practices and led to civilian-state review of military procurement. Civilian clearance was instituted to bring coherence to military procurement; civilians were to coordinate War, Navy, and Treasury Department purchases and contract placement to ensure that military needs were filled with the least disruption to the civilian economy. However, the military rejected this scenario and resisted all civilian-state attempts to regulate their procurement practices.[23]

Beginning with the NDAC, military procurement was reviewed by Knudsen and Donald Nelson, who shared the authority to clear all contracts exceeding $500,000. But the extent of their authority was never clear. Knudsen and Nelson usually were given only 48 hours to clear contracts, which were handed to them in their final form, after they had been negotiated. Their options in most instances were either to rubber-stamp a fait accompli or to risk shouldering the blame for holding up production: "To exercise a veto [over a contract] . . . would be to assume the responsibility for a protraction of the defense effort." The "bottle-neck-or-rubber-stamp" dilemma continued under the OPM, but within a context of increasingly aggressive military resistance and intra-OPM disputes over the civilian review and clearance function.[24]

Nelson, head of the OPM's Purchasing Division, was also stymied when OPM Director General Knudsen and his close associate, OPM Production Division Director John Biggers, argued that Nelson's jurisdiction should apply only to "soft goods" (commercial items or quartermaster supplies) and not to military hardware. According to their interpretation, Nelson's division would be purely advisory to the armed services, without any real, independent authority. As Koistinen notes, "The Knudsen-Biggers interpretation was precisely that held by the Army and Navy." Nelson successfully fought to gain formal authority to coordinate the placement of military contracts and review and clear all military purchasing, but in a familiar pattern the de facto reality substantially departed from Nelson's hoped-for scenario. In some cases the army and navy simply awarded contracts without clearance, but nothing stopped the services from altering or renegotiating contracts once they had been cleared, thus effectively nullifying any effect that civilian clearance may have had. Thus, as the official history of mobilization concludes, "The Armed Services, in short, remained for all practical purposes autonomous with respect to procurement."[25]

Unplanned military procurement conflicted with civilian-state plans for spreading contracts to those areas still suffering from the depression and to smaller firms who suffered as war-related work became concentrated in the largest monopoly-sector manufacturers. New Dealers and others thought that contracts could be distributed so as not to inundate certain regions and firms with defense work while others went begging. Nelson, a corporate liberal sympathetic to the New Dealer agenda for mobilization, testified to Congress: "I think one of the worst things that could happen to us, [is] if we built a tremendous, big defense program . . . [and] in doing it, we created economic deserts over the U.S. by causing an unnecessary migration of workers. . . . I think that insofar as it is humanly possible, we should plan this program, so that when it is over, we will have a better country and not a poorer country." Marriner Eccles, the proto-Keynesian head of the Federal Reserve, echoed Nelson's sentiments: "The economic dislocation should be lessened to whatever extent it is possible to do so if we are going to meet in any reasonable way all the post-defense problem. We certainly don't want to start out here thinking that defense is an end in itself. The defense program is a means to an end, and the end is the preservation of our democratic way of life, and if, in trying to secure the end, which is preserving the democratic way of life, we destroy it through the means we choose, we will have been very shortsighted."[26]

But the army and navy remained unmoved by the potential for serious economic dislocation and the failure of smaller firms when placing contracts, if only because they simply did not have the administrative capability to break their dependence on the largest and most established firms, who could relieve the services of the detail work related to the placement and completion of defense orders. The services also successfully rejected adherence to social and labor legislation as a prerequisite for corporations receiving military contracts. Primary consideration for placement of contracts was essentially quickness of delivery, with the consequence that most contracts gravitated to the largest firms and to regions already bogged down with work. As the official history of mobilization reports: "Of the more than $11 billion in prime contracts awarded by the Services during the seven months from June to December 1940, 60 percent went to 20 firms and 86.4 percent went to only 100 companies." As a result of this trend, during the very critical early period of the war, May–September 1942, 80 percent of all contracts went to areas experiencing labor shortages. Concentrating contracts in the hands of the largest firms was promoted by the OPM's Knudsen, who advised the services to contract only with those firms "big enough to handle [the job]." This stance, of course, often prevented the assimilation of smaller firms into the defense program, but it also delayed mobilization in general, since many prime contractors delayed production of military hardware until new, specially built plants were ready; they wanted no interference with their now-booming civilian production.[27]

Despite their administrative shortcomings, the military services managed to extend their authority during the defense period by claiming that they needed control of priority orders (orders ensuring access to scarce materials) to fulfill their procurement responsibilities. World War I had demonstrated the importance of the priorities power as a central device for coordinating national production, and interwar planning models intended to place this device in civilian-state hands. Despite such intentions, the services gained control of priorities during the prewar period and simply refused to give it up. With the increase in military orders (domestic and allied) of 1941, the services thereby gained enormous authority over the nation's economy, from raw materials to end products—an authority through which, by giving preference to military orders over civilian ones, they effectively deprived many smaller firms of access to raw materials. Liberals in Congress became so alarmed about the resulting disappearance of smaller businesses and the mass dislocation of workers that they opened investigations of mobilization, including most prominently Senator James Murray's Special Committee to Study and Survey the Problems of Small Business Enterprises and Congressman John Tolan's House Committee Investigating National Defense Migration. Harry Truman's Special Committee Investigating the National Defense Program could be added here as well, since much of its work proved critical of the military and corporate forces that had gained control of mobilization.

Lacking the staff and organization to rationally distribute priority orders, the military services also exercised the priorities power with brutal inefficiency, creating a chaotic situation reminiscent of World War I. They flooded the economy with priority orders (up to 25,000 a week), quickly negating any controlling effect these orders might have had. With so many priority claims outstanding, their value as a rational tool to distribute scarce materials greatly diminished. Each individual claim became little more than an invitation to scour the markets for scarce materials and then to horde whatever could be found.[28]

Of course, the military's disastrous use of priorities for the most part did not affect the nation's largest producers, although its contractual reliance on these producers exacerbated conditions for other firms. Priorities were granted first to the military's prime contractors (likely to be the largest corporations), who often used scarce materials to build new plants and factories for war work, reserving their existing plants for civilian production.[29] Expanding the capacity of a few large firms tied up tremendous amounts of critical resources to create new machine-tool capacity and new plants while great numbers of smaller plants were shuttered for lack of materials. Smaller firms were allowed to wither, and scarce raw materials were diverted into creating new plants and tools for already dominant monopoly-sector firms. As the Truman Committee reported regarding the automobile industry: "The capital expenditures for plant improvements for defense purposes will ultimately provide them with some of the newest and finest machine tools and factory buildings, practically free of charge . . . —it is clear that their [prime contractors] competitive position in the economy is being vastly improved by the war, and at the [same] time . . . tens of thousands of small businessmen are being forced to stop production." This problem was in fact recognized fairly early, by the fall of 1941, but little was done to remedy the situation. As Senator James Mead, a Democrat from New York, exclaimed to Floyd Odlum, the OPM's director of contract distribution:

> We are losing plenty of time here because we have permitted the larger manufacturer or industrialist to expand his plant so that he could do every bit of the work under his own roof [instead of subcontract to smaller firms], and in doing so we overemphasized the construction [or expansion] program. . . . Too much material has gone into construction and too little has gone into production.
>
> I believe we have overemphasized the construction program and we have permitted all these big industrialists with these large contracts to secure preferential priorities in order that they might complete a model plant which would be theirs after the war is over.

Odlum agreed that "it is bad from every standpoint to build up a lot of new plants . . . , while at the same time we are letting existing plants fall into disuse." This policy course, in turn, led to a slow death for smaller firms cut off from scarce materials because they did not have defense contracts.[30]

In sum, in the absence of substantive civilian-state authority, the military services expanded their preexisting mobilization prerogatives. Military stewardship did not emerge because of the military's proven administrative capacities, nor was it a result of interwar planning. The interwar military-corporate agenda for mobilization had called for an assertive civilian superagency run by corporate advisors; but this alternative was blocked by the presence of assertive New Dealers and other civilian-state personnel, able and willing to take the initiative themselves. Military officials had been willing to defer to a civilian agency run by corporate advisors but not to one run by New Dealers. So, together with most corporate advisors, officials in the armed services easily shifted strategy and supported military stewardship of mobilization, all the more so as corporate advisors flooded the military's mobilization ranks. In fact, in one case, auto industry representatives willingly deferred to the military services precisely because their counterparts already dominated the Army Ordnance Department: "One of the reasons for the Services taking over almost complete authority on some of the [production] programs lay in the fact that the Automotive Industries' men had gone heavily into the Ordnance Department of the Army and that the War Production Board staffed the [WPB] Automotive Division quite weakly with salesmen [from the industry]. Under the existing system, the Automotive Industry is in a sense regulating itself."[31]

The OPM's authority was stymied both because of military assertiveness and because the corporate executives dominating the OPM proved averse to the potentially precedent-setting example of expansive governmental authority over corporate firms. The resulting vacuum in authority created by the OPM's abdication was accordingly filled not only by the military but also by a great onrush of corporate volunteers and great reliance on industry voluntary action. Industry advisory committees, like their World War I predecessors, the war service committees, flourished as both the civilian NDAC and OPM and the military's ANMB utilized them to decide upon and implement policies affecting industry. Advisory committees offered readily available expertise, a business-friendly source of policies with which firms would be that much more likely to comply. The official history of mobilization explains: "Since OPM had no power to change the operating pattern of industry, reliance had to be placed on voluntary action to bring about substitution of materials, conservation, conversion, and similar changes in industrial practices, and it was anticipated that the major functions of industry committees would be to recommend such programs of voluntary action." Advisory committees thus became another mechanism for industry to infiltrate or colonize the mobilization policy-making process.[32]

In an indispensable account of industry advisory committees during the defense period, Edythe First has concluded that under the NDAC the "war service committees" concept of World War I was revived: "The weight of precedent [was] . . . wholly on the side of industrial self-regulation, achieved through hand-in-glove cooperation between the mobilization agency and industries' existing organizations." As First discerned, the emphasis on limited civilian-state authority meant that "a large measure of the progress toward defense goals that the . . . Commission achieved was powered by these industry groups." The disadvantages were numerous, however. One such disadvantage was that reliance on industry groups magnified and accelerated cartelization of industry, as past experience (in the WIB and NRA) had shown. Another was that industry committees often acted irresponsibly. In their overriding concern to prevent any displacement of their civilian markets, they often exploited the government's reliance on them and hindered mobilization. Committees tended to be dominated by the largest firms in an industry, and therefore they represented industry's political strength in two senses: They had the expertise and status necessary to mobilize their respective industries, and by virtue of their ownership and managerial prerogatives they could also effectively resist any mobilization route that might threaten their interests.[33]

Monopoly-sector prime contractors, whose representatives dominated industry advisory committees, would accept the benefits of military contracts as long as they suffered no disruptions to their civilian business. For example, raw materials industries such as aluminum, steel, rubber, zinc, and copper feared the destabilizing market effects of excessive processing capacity and the government controls that would follow upon reports of material scarcities. Industry committees therefore "fought the extension of allocations or mandatory priorities; they opposed price control; they tried to avoid the expansion of facilities; and they opposed the curtailment of nonessential [civilian] production." To reduce pressure for expansions in processing capacity and to limit the introduction of intrusive governmental controls, industry committees hedged by reporting sufficient production capacity to handle any and all contingencies. Senator Truman exposed the resulting problem of relying on corporate personnel in these committees:

> It looks very much to me as if the voting members of the [OPM Aluminum and Magnesium Priorities] committee represent dupont, General Motors, and the people who are most interested in these priorities. I can't see that this is for the welfare and benefit of the country. I don't believe that this is good public policy. The . . . fellow who is most vitally at interest in this thing makes the decision for his own welfare and benefit.

As Nelson put it, "Of course, the steel industry [eventually] did a superlative job, but there were weeks and months when it resisted any and every impulse to admit the need for priorities or for any hard-boiled schedule of allocations. To have done so would have been to admit that it had missed the target somewhat in its own handling of materials, that it had failed to anticipate munitions requirements, and had misjudged its own productive capacity."[34]

Similarly, manufacturers, with the powerful auto industry foremost among them, resisted the conversion of their industries to defense production in order to maintain relations with their civilian customers and maximize their booming profits. The war was a distraction that manufacturers would not allow to interfere with their "business as usual": "Since war seemed remote to many, it was difficult for industry to pattern its day-to-day behavior on a contingency that might not materialize, while unprecedented civilian and defense demands were creating an exhilarating boom." Industry's unwillingness to revise its behavior was implicitly supported by industrialists within the OPM. Knudsen's "sympathy with the big business point of view," reported the official history of the period, "made him reluctant to force conversion of large manufacturing plants to full scale defense production as early as would have been desirable."[35]

As noted earlier, the military and corporate agendas dovetailed in ways that strengthened the willingness of each to rely on the other in their shared battles with New Dealers. Prewar "defense" preparation illustrated the military's inability to offer a vision of war mobilization that fit the new realities of warfare and their inability to challenge industry's unwillingness to interrupt their civilian business. The services, despite the growing anxiety of the civilian leadership, failed until late 1941 to reconsider their 1939 Industrial Mobilization Plan appraisal, which contemplated a short conflict requiring little disruption of the civilian economy. Luther Gulick wrote in 1946: "Up until December 7, 1941, in spite of tremendous prodding from the White House, the military leaders could not bring themselves to envision even remotely the extent of the prospective supply needs of a total war waged all over the world. This lack of imagination was duplicated by the industrial leaders." Military calculations fit nicely with both corporations' unwillingness to expand the industrial base and the corporate preference for booming civilian profits over conversion to military production. Based on flawed, anachronistic military plans, industry advisory committees could confidently and legitimately state that their current raw material processing was sufficient to supply any emergency. Accordingly, with proposed military requirements lagging far behind adequate estimates of the growing international military threat, there was little pressure on manufacturers, particularly the auto industry, to convert from their civilian production.[36]

Yet New Dealers did enjoy some success in countering the influence of industry advisory committees, thanks to efforts by Thurmond Arnold of the Justice Department's Antitrust Division to curtail formal reliance upon agreements arrived at through industry collusion.[37] To head off Arnold and the threat of antitrust prosecution, however, industry committees often requested and received Justice Department clearance in advance of their proposed cooperative actions. The military services went even further and lobbied for suspension of the antitrust laws for the duration of the emergency. In response to these pressures, John Lord O'Brian, OPM general counsel, worked with the Justice Department to formalize rules restricting industry groups to solely advisory functions. Reflecting on the matter in 1944, O'Brian (who would go on to be general legal council for the War Production Board) reported:

> Relations with the Anti-Trust Division [of the Justice Department], particularly when Thurman Arnold was directing it, had been especially troublesome to OPM's and WPB's efforts to get industry cooperation. O'Brian . . . realized early that joint action by industry would be necessary to get the war job done. On his second day here, O'Brian spent the evening with Robert H. Jackson, the Attorney General, and they discussed candidly the need to protect businessmen who entered into joint arrangements for defense purposes which ordinarily would be violations of the Anti-Trust Act.[38]

Thus, although the new rules prevented a full-scale revival of the type of business dominance present under the War Industries Board and National Recovery Administration, they did little to mitigate the thoroughgoing reliance on industry action that marked prewar mobilization. In fact, one wartime analysis describes how the effect of O'Brian's rule changes was to secure a "broader role for the committees":

> On the industry side, its advisory committees became primarily a device for steering OPM in directions the industry considered desirable, for restraining it where industry felt action would be disadvantageous, or for tempering the quality of action that was inevitable. On OPM's side, the committees became important chiefly as a medium for securing understanding and support of its policies or practical aid in their formulation.

Thus, despite O'Brian's rules, the scope of advisory committee influence remained extensive under the OPM and continued so under the wartime War Production Board.[39]

Office of Price Administration and Civilian Supply

Booming civilian production and increasing U.S. and allied military orders increased scarcities and disruptions within the civilian economy. Because the OPM remained narrowly focused on facilitating military production, Roosevelt created yet another new agency in April 1941—the Office for Price Administration and Civilian Supply (OPACS)—to stabilize prices and protect the increasingly fragile civilian economy. That office, in turn, offered New Dealers an administrative base from which they could challenge the authority of the corporate-dominated OPM and its industry advisory committees. Disputes between the two agencies were inevitable, since the line separating military from civilian production was impossible to maintain, especially given the dependence of military production on critical civilian needs such as transportation and housing. And such jurisdictional conflicts became exacerbated insofar as the OPM and OPACS were staffed by, respectively, dollar-a-year men and New Dealers. As V. O. Key, then an administrative analyst for the War Supply Administration Section, described the situation, the OPM was "staffed in its key positions by business men, on the whole not characterized by an intense and uninhibited desire to accelerate interruptions to normal business production" while OPACS personnel were career government men and academics "animated by considerable zeal and not a little idealism" who were "quite certain not to develop congenial relations with the OPM."[40]

The OPACS staff, led by New Dealer Leon Henderson, became particularly disturbed over the continuing increase in civilian production, especially in the auto industry, while the defense program languished. New Dealers sought more substantive civilian-state authority as it became clear that neither the military nor corporate executives were pushing for adequate preparation for war. For example, OPACS personnel aggressively sought to curtail civilian production, promote conversion to military production, and secure civilian-state input over priorities. But, although New Dealers could draw attention to the sometimes glacial pace of conversion to military production, they were stymied by their own lack of authority and by the hostility of corporate advisors in the OPM and in the advisory committees.

The most outrageous example of expanding civilian production during the growing emergency was in the automobile industry. Koistinen reports that the auto assembly lines "consumed 80 per cent of the nation's rubber, 11 per cent of its tin, 23 per cent of its nickel, 14 per cent of its copper, 18 per cent of its steel, 12 per cent of its zinc, 34 per cent of its lead, and 10 per cent of its aluminum." Yet, with most of these materials scarce by 1941, "automobile production was one million cars above 1939." Accordingly, Leon Henderson, head of OPACS, battled with General Motor's William Knudsen, head of OPM, over curtailment of auto production, especially given the auto industry's huge consumption of scarce materials. In a letter to Knudsen, Henderson complained about having found out through the morning newspapers that Knudsen had scheduled a meeting with auto industry representatives on the same day that Henderson was to meet with them. Henderson recognized Knudsen's right to oversee conversion of the auto industry to military production, but he firmly reminded Knudsen of his own authority over the auto industry: "It seems to me equally clear that the use . . . made of whatever material, equipment, facilities and the like remain [after use for military production] is a civilian matter for which I have responsibility. I propose to make clear this division of responsibility . . . to the representatives of the [auto] industry with whom we propose to confer, and I trust that you will do the same with those representatives with whom you may meet."[41]

The two agencies also clashed over priorities. In May 1941 Roosevelt declared an unlimited national emergency and asked Congress for more substantive priorities power to control the distribution of raw materials. Although Congress granted this request by amending the Priorities Act, Roosevelt interminably delayed delegating the expanded power, thereby sparking a lengthy OPM-OPACS struggle and exacerbating an already troubled administrative situation. The conflict effectively scuttled any rational use of the priorities power. As one official observer reported, during much of 1941—a period in which Nazi forces continued to rack up a startling array of victories as they raced across the Soviet heartland—"the entire field of priorities procedure was one of confusion and ambiguity." And the ensuing OPM-OPACS (corporate–New Dealer) impasse, lasting throughout the summer of 1941, only undercut the efforts of those trying to establish wide civilian-state authority over mobilization and allowed the military services to further entrench themselves in mobilization. Roosevelt finally delegated the priorities power to the OPM, but this did not represent a victory for OPM corporate advisors, since Roosevelt also transferred overall decision-making power to a new coordinating agency, the Supply, Priorities, and Allocations Board (SPAB).[42]

Supply, Priorities, and Allocations Board

The board was established on 28 August 1941 as a top-level policy-making and coordinating center for the entire defense program. Civilian and military supply responsibilities—the cause of so much conflict—were merged by dissolving the OPACS and placing within the OPM a Division of Civilian Supply (DCS). One part of the OPACS was reconstituted as a price control agency, the Office of Price Administration (OPA). Donald Nelson was elevated to executive director of the SPAB and to director of priorities for the OPM. Leon Henderson too was given mixed responsibilities in the new set-up: he became DCS administrator and first director of the OPA, and by virtue of this latter position he received a seat on the SPAB as well. Many commentators have noted the confusion caused by this reorganization. SPAB members Nelson and Henderson made the decisions that the OPM was to follow. Then, as OPM members, they were to follow these directives and act under the direction of Knudsen, their equal on the SPAB. Nelson later wrote, "As Executive Director of the new board I gave orders to OPM; as Director of Priorities I received orders from OPM." The confusion was legendary.[43]

There was a certain logic to Roosevelt's actions, however. On the one hand, in joining together representatives of the major claimants on the nation's resources, he characteristically sought that elusive balance of competing interests. Besides Nelson, who Roosevelt appointed director of the SPAB, there were seven members: Knudsen, Hillman, Stimson, and Knox, the four members of the OPM Policy Council (which ceased to function), representing the military services, industry, and labor; Harry Hopkins, head of the lend-lease program; Henry Wallace, vice president and chairman of the Economic Defense Board, now appointed vice chairman of the SPAB; and Leon Henderson, head of the OPA and director of civilian supply in the OPM. Jesse Jones, commerce secretary and director of the Reconstruction Finance Corporation (RFC), would later join the SPAB as well. On the other hand, the SPAB embodied a shift of power from the conservatives of the OPM council to those seeking quicker conversion and greater governmental authority over industry; these "all-outers" (so-called because they pressed for an all-out mobilization effort), including Wallace, Hillman, Hopkins, and Henderson, represented a majority on the board. The SPAB was similarly important for Roosevelt because it constituted a majority in favor of increased aid to Britain and especially the Soviet Union—aid that the military services opposed as their own demands increased.[44]

The SPAB also brought together those who were eager to devise a coherent overall mobilization program under the terms of an executive order that empowered the SPAB to determine the total expected defense requirements of the nation and to oversee the division of scarce raw materials and finished goods between competing claimants. Military, civilian, defense aid, lend-lease, and all other claimants to the nation's goods had to go through the SPAB. Yet the board did not execute its own decisions; it was a policy-making body whose decisions were implemented by the OPM, OPA, and military services and whose staff support was supplied by OPM personnel who were often already burdened by other important responsibilities.[45]

Despite—or because of—this lack of operating authority, the SPAB's tenure marked important gains. It provided an opportunity for New Deal planners finally to gain a foothold within mobilization administration. Although they never became a central directive force within mobilization (under the War Production Board they were scattered about, although many came to reside in the WPB Planning Committee), New Deal planners would nonetheless provide a crucial counterbalance to military authority. For the first time an agency existed to sponsor some measure of central planning and to press for quicker mobilization. The SPAB did not supplant the military services' control of procurement or dislodge corporate advisors and industry advisory committees. But the board did allow New Deal planners a central venue to promote their own vision for mobilization.

The SPAB was specifically charged by Roosevelt to "determine the total requirements of materials and commodities needed respectively for defense, civilian, and all other purposes" and to plan policies for controlling the distribution of materials and components between the various claimants. The importance of this type of planning cannot be overstated. The military services had only just begun to calculate what they might need in the event of all-out war, and their initial, fumbling attempts to calculate total prospective military needs were in fact driven by the need to justify "the U.S. Army's preeminent claim upon the nation's resources" in the face of intensifying pressure to send war materiel to the Soviets.[46] At this point there still was no comprehensive idea of what the military might need for fighting a world war. The military procurement offices contracted blindly, as they would throughout the war, piling up orders for contingencies they could not foresee. Planners within the SPAB began the task of calculating the overall requirements for war and rationalizing the placement of military contracts while analyzing the capabilities of the U.S. economy and determining whether it could handle the huge demands about to be placed on it. SPAB successes included the first full estimation of the basic production requirements—military, civilian, and allied—needed to defeat the Axis powers. These assessments thereby injected the first healthy dose of rational planning into mobilization. The SPAB also forced the military services to increase their dangerously low estimates of what they required to fight the war; they began the process of converting from priorities to allocations in the distribution of scarce materials; they set out the argument for protecting the civilian economy in the event of all-out war; they restricted the use of critical and scarce raw materials; and they urged the expansion of metals production facilities. These important steps, critical to the success of any future mobilization, resulted from handing overall policy determination to civilians committed to thorough preparation for emerging contingencies and less concerned about the consequences for private corporate interests.[47]

Unfortunately, war cut the SPAB's progress short after only a few short months, long before it had the time to assert itself fully. The SPAB and OPM were replaced in January 1942 by the War Production Board, and a key opportunity for civilian-guided mobilization was lost. In the end, in fact, all reorganizations before the war provided at best only minimal opportunities for the development of a strong civilian authority. As Louis Koenig reports, "There rarely was a reorganization of the agencies in the sense that some agencies were abolished and their useful functions transferred. Agencies were multiplied; they were not consolidated. The labyrinth always became more complex." Yet, as the experience of the War Production Board would make clear, the legacy of defense period development of authority had substantial implications for the wartime to come.[48]

Creation of the War Production Board: Confirming the Prewar Legacy

The surprise attack on Pearl Harbor finally spurred Roosevelt to allow concentration of authority in one agency, operating under the direction of one man. Under the auspices of the Office of Emergency Management and under the authority granted him by the War Powers Act of 18 December 1941, Roosevelt created new agencies and reorganized old ones. To head the new War Production Board (WPB), Roosevelt chose former Sears, Roebuck executive Donald Nelson and allowed him to define the contours of his authority by writing the executive order, which, as written, assigned enormous powers to "exercise general direction over the war procurement and production program." Preexisting mobilization agencies such as the SPAB and OPM were abolished, their functions and operations going to the WPB and Nelson, who enjoyed final authority over the actions of the WPB.[49]

With Nelson in charge of a powerful WPB, central authority at last was lodged in a civilian agency, under the direction of a single administrator. Nonetheless, Nelson remained caught within the web of preexisting relations constructed and controlled by the military services and industry personnel. As James Fesler, official observer of wartime controversies, remarked in 1943:

> Although new laws and executive orders, and new needs of the war period, have served to strengthen the central [civilian] agency, the dead hand of the past has never been wholly absent. Early decisions are not lightly reversed and squatters are not always dislodged by mere fiat. Since many of the key officials of the Office for Production Management and the War Production Board "grew up" in the 1940 setting, it was naturally difficult for them to assert definitive authority over the Armed Services to which they had originally been merely advisors.[50]

Nelson's continued reliance on the armed services and on dollar-a-year corporate advisors and industry advisory committees was much criticized but largely inevitable, given the constraints and resistances set into place by the prewar accumulation of authority and, accordingly, by the expectations of monopoly-sector prime contractors and the military services. Indeed, the WPB's own official history reports that Nelson's "authority was not fully exercised . . . over production and procurement, for that would have required his shouldering aside powerful agencies and officials already well entrenched and well staffed." Since civilian-state authority remained relatively undeveloped throughout the prewar defense period, Nelson felt he had little choice but to submit to the military's de facto control.[51]

Nelson's delegations of authority found many critics. Although he has been described as a master conciliator who patiently sought ground for compromise between the disparate interests wrangling over mobilization policy, this very virtue implies that he "was not," as the official history noted, "aggressive about his jurisdiction and his powers." He often hesitated when decisive action was vital, and as a result he lost power and implicitly encouraged predatory conduct by his bureaucratic competitors. Yet, although it may be abstractly true that someone other than Nelson might have done more, Nelson was chosen precisely because of his propensity for patient compromise. As a corporate liberal and a purchasing expert from Sears, he was not an industrialist, and therefore he was equally acceptable to administration and congressional New Dealers, to organized labor, and to industrialists.[52]

As the WPB history explains, moreover, it was never expected that Nelson would exercise all mobilization authority; rather, his authority was specific to production and procurement. Yet, even in these specific areas, Nelson began to relinquish authority to separate agencies concerned with manpower, food, smaller war plants, and rubber. Nelson's reliance on agencies other than the WPB for enforcement and implementation of his decisions thus magnified his weaknesses as an administrator. Nelson's most significant delegation, however, left procurement authority with the military services. He justified this decision as necessitated by the time and legal constraints to setting up a new purchasing organization, by expected criticisms of the dollar-a-year procurement officials the WPB would need to recruit, and by a disinclination to interfere either with the military's strategy decisions or with their existing relationships with prime contractors. In essence, Nelson admitted the need to surrender to the military's prewar accumulation of authority and their de facto control.[53]

Nelson's delegation of procurement powers to the military, however necessary, made civilian-state coordination of mobilization increasingly difficult, and it increased domestic military prominence more generally. Nelson nonetheless believed he could achieve effective oversight and control of military procurement, albeit indirectly, by placing handpicked assistants in the army and navy procurement offices. But his assistants were quickly assimilated into the military agencies they were supposed to oversee. W. L. Batt, head of the WPB Requirements Committee (and previously president of SKF Industries and chairman of the Business Advisory Council), confirms that, "as soon as they got into uniform, there was no question as to where their [Nelson's deputies'] allegiance had to go." Military control of procurement also led to military intervention in other phases of mobilization. As Bruce Catton, an assistant to Nelson, put it, "The War Department, retaining the power to buy the munitions it needed, promptly translated that power into an assertion, endlessly repeated, of the right to say how the munitions should be produced and how the civilian economy should be operated."[54]

Besides surrendering control of procurement to the military services,

Nelson decided to continue the broad reliance upon corporate dollar-a-year advisors and industry advisory committees. Senator Truman's wartime investigative committee, having traced many of the problems of prewar mobilization to dollar-a-year men, would take Nelson to task for relying upon industry personnel. When, at his confirmation hearing, members of the Truman Committee expressed apprehension regarding such reliance, Nelson argued that he could not do his job without the aid of corporate advisors and that these men could not afford to sacrifice their corporate earnings because of existing financial obligations. Given the committee's long-standing insistence that authority be centralized under one man, they did not want to criticize too harshly or withdraw their support from Nelson, and they agreed to disagree with him.[55]

The dollar-a-year issue arose again in 1942, when Robert Guthrie, a WPB branch chief, resigned, alleging that dollar-a-year employees were sabotaging the program to convert major industries from civilian to military production in order to protect their civilian markets. Guthrie found a receptive audience among the senators in Truman's committee, who had reached many of the same conclusions a few months before. Since industry personnel dominated the WPB Bureau of Industry Branches, which was responsible for converting industry to military production, blame for slower-than-expected conversion justifiably fell on their corporate shoulders.[56]

One of those Guthrie criticized, Philip Reed, dollar-a-year chief of the Bureau of Industry Branches on leave from his position as chairman of the board for General Electric (and still drawing his $60,000 annual salary), testified that corporate advisors could be trusted to do what was in the public interest and, moreover, that the WPB was organized to ensure that New Dealers and labor representatives could oversee the activities of dollar-a-year advisors who dominated the industry branches. Senator Brewster responded to the first point by saying that Reed's own situation was indicative of the problem the committee was exploring: "Certainly you would agree, wouldn't you, that the average man in America can't contemplate the necessity of $60,000 a year to live on. You see the problem in a democratic world, Mr. Reed?" In response to Reed's argument that corporate executives were unable to make the financial sacrifice of stepping down to a government salary, Senator Truman retorted, "A very great many of the $21-a-month boys [in military service] have very abruptly changed their standards of living, also." As for Reed's second point, that adequate checks and safeguards existed to prevent corporate advisors from abusing their position, it was true that noncorporate civilians in the WPB Planning Committee, the Office of Civilian Supply, and the Labor and Legal Divisions could oversee, advise, and criticize. Still, they lacked operating initiative. James Knowlson, director of WPB Industry Operations and former president and chairman of the board for the Stewart-Wagner corporation, affirmed that the top men from any given industry held the real initiative: "The first step [in converting an industry] is to bring in one, two, or three absolutely top production people from that industry that know the companies."[57]

As members of the Truman Committee and some members of the WPB itself well understood, reliance upon industry personnel often resulted in stalled or slowed conversion. New Dealer economist Robert Nathan, head of the WPB Planning Committee, became aware that, even after Pearl Harbor, industry remained reluctant to disrupt its civilian businesses. He wrote Nelson in March 1942, insisting that the WPB needed to take charge: "Normal production of the durable goods industries must be ruthlessly ceased. The industries will not engage in an all-out conversion until they are absolutely closed. Where a market output is absolutely essential, then this output should be confined to the smaller plants in the industry." Later, when asked by Senator Truman whether there had been industry resistance to conversion, Nathan replied:

> Undoubtedly there was resistance by industries in certain areas against giving up the production of normal civilian goods. Conversion . . . is not an easy matter. It means giving up the production to which firms have been accustomed over years; it means giving up markets, the channels of distribution; it means giving up efficient and profitable operations for uncertainty.

By depending so heavily upon industry personnel to decide the pace of conversion, national officials in essence capitulated to industrial-sector corporations reluctant to move as fast as strategic circumstances seemed to dictate. Truman himself recognized the inherent problem of relying upon dollar-a-year advisors in his sharp retort to one industry witness: "We can't help but think if a man's whole life has been spent in the creation of an industry, . . . and that he is now receiving a tremendous salary . . . his loyalty naturally would come first to the place where his heart has been and where his bread and butter is." Yet the pattern of reliance on industry personnel, whether formally a part of the national government or not (in the case of industry advisory committees), continued throughout the war as mobilization again and again conformed to a logic and rhythm defined by industry personnel. Even during total war, civilian-state officials could not wrest control of mobilization policy from the hands of industry men.[58]

Nelson also acquiesced to continued reliance on industry advisory committees. Of course, as formal governmental powers expanded with the arrival of war, committee influence was formalized to erase any hint of scandal. Increasing government authority further replaced the ad hoc actions of industry. Reliance on industry committees continued, however; industry was still needed, but the appearance of impropriety had to be reduced, thanks to public and official sensitivity to potential abuse by the monopoly-sector firms that often dominated industry advisory committees. In fact, beginning with the OPM, formalized rules were set in place to govern committee activities, even as those committees' violations of antitrust laws came to be accepted as inevitable and justified. As the head of WPB Industry Operations, James Knowlson, instructed his staff: "Plans and programs worked out by the Industry Committees shall be submitted to the Branch Chief for approval. . . . However, possible conflict with the antitrust laws is not to be permitted to restrict the scope of planning such steps as may be necessary to the war production job."[59]

Such formalized rules (stipulating representative memberships, open meetings, written records, etc.), constructed to ensure that the largest firms did not dominate proceedings, could only be so effective, especially since the routines and relationships of industry advisory committees were already so well established by the time war arrived. In effect, the rules had changed, but the same industry personnel remained in charge. In particular, trade-association members, banned from dollar-a-year positions, stayed on in their advisory committee roles. While some such committees were expanded to represent a broader cross section of the industry involved, most remained dominated by industry leaders. In addition, as one contemporary observer reported, "Many [of the government's] presiding officers . . . leaned heavily on the judgement of their industry advisory committees and . . . interpreted their own function as protection of the industries they directed from excessive restriction or regulation."[60]

Moreover, despite the establishment of these formalized rules, an informal system flourished as committees met outside of government auspices and simply ignored the new guidelines. Informal gatherings of trade-association committees or other industry groups had already emerged as a problem in the days of the OPM, when unregulated and unsupervised meetings resulted in unauthorized industry agreements and improper industry influence over mobilization policy and administration. Because unsupervised meetings had been the modus operandi of the NDAC and OPM, many WPB Industry Branch officials empowered to oversee advisory committees continued to avoid formal procedures, especially since they viewed the formal route as slow and cumbersome. But industry representatives also resisted any extensions of formal governmental authority over industry on the presumption that government lawyers "were indulging in bureaucratic expansion of authority" and that this indulgence "justified recourse to irregular methods of obtaining industry advice." Thus, attempts to control informal gatherings of industry committees often proved unsuccessful. The evidence suggests, then, that even under the WPB an articulated system of ad hoc relations between industry and government was well entrenched—albeit one masked by a veneer of formal rules and regulated conduct. Formal rules did, in fact, curb some of the more egregious examples of industry action, yet the Truman Committee continued to point out the extent to which industry committees consistently bent the formal rules for their own gain:

> The WPB committees selected to pass on the [steel] expansion program were dominated by officials of the five largest steel companies and did not even have a representative of the small companies or of labor to voice any opposition. The public could hardly be expected to rely on the wisdom or impartiality of the committees so constituted.[61]

Rules by themselves could not negate the state's dependency on industry action, nor could the rule changes negate the ability of corporate leaders to resist policy initiatives. On the contrary, advisory committees and dollar-a-year men were key features of a strategy by which national officials legitimized the expansions of national authority over industry and into ostensibly sacrosanct managerial territory. In effect, national officials did not intrude. Rather, reliance upon corporate advisors and corporate-dominated institutions safeguarded the basic division of labor between state officials and business firms and ensured that the firms dominating the military's prime contracts would gain a large measure of the wartime expansion of state authority for themselves.

▼ ▼ ▼

Obviously, greater state authority was needed in the Second World War than in World War I, given the enormously increased scale of the mobilization task. Yet the mobilization program that emerged from the prewar struggles constituted a revival of the War Industries Board model of World War I. Expansive state authority was provided through strengthened military bureaucratic authority, which itself, for the most part, offered a front for extensive corporate discretion. New Dealer pressure resulted in a much more formalized process than in the First World War, and such formal procedures helped prevent some of the most abusive business practices while more efficiently preparing America for war. But, by and large, the development of civilian-state interventionist authority was stymied, resulting in a lack of influence that itself greatly influenced the trajectory of wartime statebuilding.

The Politics of Wartime Mobilization

• As it produced new laws, agencies, and personnel, the New Deal had gradually yet persistently increased momentum for a politics and administration independent of the machinations of powerful corporate and sectional elites; hence it also generated increasing controversy and hostility. War mobilization, however, displaced the New Deal search for a national governance project and returned U.S. politics to the familiar ground of close collaboration between political and economic elites. In wartime controversies—as had been the case earlier—expansive domestic military authority translated into extensive delegations of mobilization authority to the military's prime contractors, to corporate dollar-a-year advisors, and to industry advisory committees. These delegations and the related strengthening of the military-corporate alliance secured the allegiance of powerful class forces to a particular type of strong national state based on military-state capabilities. Thus would mobilization independently influence the trajectory of U.S. political development.

Prewar institutional disputes pitting New Dealers and their academic and labor allies against the military services and their corporate allies continued throughout the war. As noted, the predominant role of corporate executives within the War Production Board (WPB) and the mobilization authority retained by military officials largely foreclosed any true civilian-state authority over mobilization, but civilian-state personnel continued to battle over the feasibility of military requirements, the distribution of scarce raw materials, and the control of production scheduling. Investigating these battles illustrates that, despite formal civilian-state stewardship, and despite the military's administrative deficiencies, military agencies gained substantial authority over much of the mobilization program. Also, such deficient and maladroit military administration was bolstered and upgraded primarily through the delegation of authority to the military's prime contractors and the integration of corporate personnel into military ranks. Even so, recurrent crises due to military maladministration left the door open for civilian-state personnel to continue the fight for mobilization authority.

Problems with Military Procurement

The military's administrative deficiencies, combined with its effective control of procurement, led to a great concentration of contracts in a relatively small number of economically powerful firms. De facto decentralization of procurement authority to individual procurement officers reinforced the military's organizational reliance upon the largest monopoly-sector corporations. Such procurement officers were in no position to develop the innovative contractual relationships necessary to spread work to a wider spectrum of the U.S. business community, especially since any failures in procuring needed supplies and war materiel would fall heavily upon the officer himself. As Senator James Murray's investigative committee reported in early 1942:

> There was a wealth of testimony that the training and experience which Army and Navy procurement officers have had . . . has incapacitated them from forthright and effective action in wartime. They have learned that a single mistake is liable to wreck a career. . . . Consequently, they feel that the only safe thing to do is to give contracts to big companies with a reputation for performance.

Likewise, W. L. Batt, who worked for civilian mobilization agencies from the NDAC through the WPB, noted that "the deep sense of responsibility of each procurement officer for obtaining scheduled delivery of items contracted for, led the individual officers to place contracts with the large and therefore supposedly 'sure' companies."[1]

The surprise attack on Pearl Harbor and other early military setbacks only reinforced the tendency to pile contracts in the hands of a relatively few firms. And, of course, the producers themselves reinforced this trend. The Budget Bureau's history of mobilization notes that after Pearl Harbor:

> Industry was now eager to get into war work, especially as the WPB materials orders and limitations orders began to interfere with normal production of civilian items. The services were equipped with high priorities, which gave the contractors confidence that they would be able to get the materials and components they required, price arrangements were gener-

ous and elastic, and the manufacturers were not unwilling, under pressure, to sign additional contracts even when their plants were already full, hoping to expand, or find some other method of discharging their inflated obligations.

Once government controls drastically reduced civilian production, monopoly-sector firms clamored for the lifeline of government contracts and the attendant access to scarce materials and components.[2]

New Dealers did not regard this reliance on monopoly-sector firms as inevitable, nor were they happy with the results. Senator Truman's committee concluded that a wider distribution of contracts could have been achieved but for "the lack of advance [military] planning": military procurement officers "did not have sufficient knowledge of the manufacturing problems involved and of the existing facilities available through subcontracting to insist that certain parts be manufactured in the existing plants of the large manufacturers or in the plants of small manufacturers available through subcontracting." The military's reliance on the largest firms was also a concern insofar as, in the words of the official WPB history, "the Services' distribution of munitions contracts could materially reshape the national economy, particularly with regard to geographical centers of industry and with regard to concentration of economic power in large corporations." John Tolan's investigative committee also worried about concentrating "the bulk of production of military articles in large corporations [whose concerns are] not entirely confined to matters of national necessity."[3]

In addition to relying on relatively few prime contractors, the services made extensive use of corporate advisors to bolster their meager administrative capabilities. Traditionally, procurement and supply had not been prestige positions within the services and therefore did not attract quality personnel. As John Millett, official historian of army mobilization activities, reports, army supply functions suffered before the war because of the low esteem and prestige of officers assigned to Robert Patterson's Office of the Under Secretary of War, the "business side of the War Department": "The officers assigned to [Patterson's office] sometimes felt that they had reached a blind alley in their careers. Often their military rank was too low to permit effective performance of duties." This attitude, by one official account, "made it difficult to get and retain the most capable officers in [Patterson's office]." Of course, at the lower levels of army procurement, this difficulty was even more profound.[4]

Patterson compensated by recruiting civilians—most of whom were "lawyers trained at Harvard and with professional practice in the New York area"—who reportedly had an "important and often decisive influence . . . in the Under Secretary's office, as well as elsewhere in the War Department." In early 1942, when the War Department was reorganized, most of these civilians transferred to Lieutenant General Brehon

Somervell's Army Services Forces, which certainly needed the help: "On one occasion, the [army's] Chief of Statistics complained that a number of his statisticians were former cavalry officers who had been rendered useless along with their operation." And army procurement bureaus needed even more help. Millett judged these bureaus to be "mere skeleton organizations" up to 1940, and even during the defense period "they had been slow in building up their internal organizations by commissioning or hiring top-ranking civilians for key positions."[5]

Despite the manifest unpreparedness displayed by the military services, they continued to stave off civilian-state control by arguing that control of procurement was essential to strategic military planning. We have already seen how Donald Nelson acquiesced to this argument before the Truman Committee: "I consider that it is vitally essential for the services to determine themselves on a strategy basis what comes first. I don't believe it is our job to try to tell them that you should have airplanes . . . first and tanks later. I think that is a pure strategy question and it should be left to the experts to determine." Nelson need not have conceded the military's point about strategy; after all, civilians never considered dictating *what* the military could have, but rather *where, how, and in what quantities* these items could best be produced. Yet, as historian Paul Koistinen notes, "Civilians were always at a disadvantage because military personnel cloaked their contentions in terms of military strategy, of which civilians were always kept in the dark."[6]

Of course, while military representatives employed the strategy argument to cripple any opposition to their control throughout the war, for the most part the military services did not derive their procurement requests from prior strategic planning. Although army officials, seeking to quiet congressional and WPB attacks on their prerogatives, declared definitively in early 1943 that "strategical and tactical planning" guided their procurement of war materiel, the opposite had been and still was true. As the historian of army economic mobilization relates, the army waited upon rapid advances in technological and production processes before deciding grand strategy. Thus, the "sequence of . . . *planning ran from requirements to strategy.*" Rather than programming procurement on preexisting strategic plans, the army waited for the latest armaments and supplies to accumulate before developing strategy. As Major General Lucius Clay, Somervell's director of materiel, later reported, "We were building an Army in which we in supply found ourselves having to determine its size and how it was to be constituted. We were flying blind. It wasn't until late 1943 that the General Staff came up with plans for the number of armored divisions that would be required . . . and so forth."[7]

The military services stubbornly insisted on the greatest possible authority over procurement despite the fact that they contracted "blindly," with little or no conception of the nation's production capabilities, little idea of the overall requirements needed to prosecute the war, and little interest in attempts by civilian agencies to gather such information. The military attitude was clear to their contemporaries: "The Armed Services," reports the official history of mobilization, "were prone to regard the civilian economy as an inexhaustible reservoir from which materials might be drawn at will, and many military experts, in consequence, saw no reason for a high degree of accuracy in figuring requirements."[8]

Military Reorganizations

In an attempt to remedy military administrative weaknesses and disorganization, both the army and navy were reorganized in the early months of the war. These reorganizations did provide for some centralized management of army and navy procurement bureaus, although problems relating to bureau independence continued. More important, the reorganizations enabled the services to present a stronger and more unified front, which proved crucial for helping the services resist civilian-state interference.

At the time of Pearl Harbor, army command, including the organization of procurement and supply, was in disarray. The National Defense Act of 1920 had been designed to resolve the problems of command and supply that had hamstrung the army's efforts in World War I. But the dual command structure that had resulted from the act's implementation—the General Staff for central command and the Office of Under Secretary of War (OUSW) for procurement and economic mobilization activities—led to crossed and confused lines of authority that reinforced the independence of the army's separate command and procurement bureaus and exacerbated the management task facing the General Staff under George Marshall and the OUSW under Robert Patterson. The reorganization of the army in March 1942 was supposed to bring order and coherence to this system. Reorganization created three separate army commands—ground, air, and service forces (including supply, procurement, and logistics)—leaving the General Staff free for the general coordination it was created to exercise. Besides creating separate command and procurement responsibilities for the assertive army air forces, reorganization also transformed and rebuilt the organization of army procurement and economic mobilization.[9]

Prior to the 1942 reorganization, procurement and mobilization authority formally rested with Patterson's OUSW, which had grown from a staff of 181 when Patterson took over the office on 1 July 1940 to 1,200 at the end of 1941.[10] With reorganization, however, the period referred to by the historian of army economic mobilization as the "hegemony of the Under Secretary of War" was coming to an end. Somervell was placed in charge of the General Staff Supply Division, or G-4, in November 1941; with the beginning of hostilities a few weeks later he proceeded to plan the transfer of the OUSW staff and responsibilities to his own command. Somervell, who would figure prominently in wartime mobilization battles, was described by *Fortune* magazine as "every inch an Army man—but an Army man with a difference. The difference is that he has mixed in civilian affairs too." Somervell's efforts to shake up military procurement and supply acquired additional urgency in early 1942 as he discovered ongoing air corps and General Staff planning for army reorganization. As Somervell pressed to include the army's supply functions in any reorganization scheme, Patterson, the civilian under secretary of war, was deliberately left in the dark; the army's plan was shown to Patterson only immediately before it was presented to Roosevelt. Hence, Patterson "was practically faced with choice of accepting a fait accompli, or delaying the much needed reorganization." The final plan worried Patterson's staff, since under its provisions a military officer would acquire the civilian secretary's authority, thereby disregarding the lessons of World War I concerning necessary civilian oversight of military procurement practices. Patterson, however, considered only small changes to the proposed plan. Only the Bureau of the Budget objected to the transfer of civilian authority to military hands, and even then, with Secretary of War Henry Stimson's reassurances, "the President ignored the warning."[11]

Roosevelt established the new army organization by executive order on 28 February 1942, and Somervell became the commanding officer of the new Services of Supply, which, within a year, became the Army Service Forces (ASF). Somervell's new command soon absorbed most of the power and responsibilities of Patterson's office; Patterson himself retained at best an indirect advisory role conditioned on Somervell's willingness to accept advice. Although Millett, historian of the ASF, and military historian Paul Hammond both insist that civilian control was adequately maintained, "in every case," reports Hammond, "the [reorganization] pattern was to transfer functions and responsibilities out of the civilian offices to staff or command units of the military. . . . The most extensive transfer of functions went to the Army Service Forces." As Koistinen concludes, "War Department supply operations had once again reverted to military control, despite the intentions of Congress after World War I and over twenty years of effort to bring procurement under civilian control."[12]

The navy also reorganized its command operations in early 1942 to achieve unity both of naval command and of procurement and supply operations. Command was centralized by merging the post of Commander in Chief, United States Fleet (COMINCH) with the supply command of the Chief of Naval Operations (CNO). The merged post went to Admiral Ernest J. King, who proved more interested in logistics and command of the fleet than with the supply functions of the CNO. Problems with naval procurement and supply thus came to be addressed by Patterson's navy counterpart, Under Secretary of the Navy James Forrestal, a prominent Wall Street financier "with wide connections in the upper reaches of national and international business." It did not take long for Forrestal to recognize the hopeless state of planning and procurement for naval munitions and supplies; "frustrated and surprised at finding . . . archaic precepts and procedures in the navy's contracting system," he quickly created an organization specifically charged with balancing requirements, coordinating procurement for the independent bureaus, and facilitating long-term planning "to end the irrational procedures he had uncovered in his new domain." This organization, the Office of Procurement and Material (OP&M), was created on 30 January 1942 and placed under Forrestal's supervision.[13]

Although a naval officer, Rear Admiral Samuel Robinson, was named to head the OP&M, the new organization still faced a challenge from Admiral King, who distrusted civilian intrusion and regarded the office as nothing more than the navy's representative before the WPB. It seemed to Forrestal that the OP&M could best serve as an intermediary between King's CNO and the independent procurement bureaus; overall navy requirements developed by King could be transmitted to the bureaus through the OP&M, thereby giving Forrestal and his staff the opportunity to coordinate bureau procurement and reduce interbureau competition and replication. However, navy tradition and Admiral King served to block this use of the OP&M: "In practice the Office of Naval Operations presented its requirements to the bureaus and was hostile to any review of them." Likewise, the bureaus themselves continued to operate with a large degree of independence. In May 1942 King even went so far as to attempt to absorb the OP&M into his own command, leaving Forrestal in the same position as Patterson. Roosevelt, however, rejected this plan.[14]

Despite King's attempts to short-circuit civilian oversight and coordination, Forrestal—with the support of Navy Secretary Frank Knox and Roosevelt, and driven by his own stubborn and forceful personality—successfully implemented remarkable supervision of navy supply bureaus. Forrestal imposed an impressive system of coordination upon haphazard and confusing procurement procedures by recruiting a cadre of civilian professionals from the nation's top banking, manufacturing, and legal corporations to oversee contract negotiations and to press upon the bureaus sound business practices. The bureaus submitted to external control only insofar as friendly civilian oversight (through business advisors) represented centralized review of their autonomous decentralized activities. Bureau acceptance was also ensured since OP&M management shielded bureaus from WPB oversight and interference.[15]

Thus, according to one assessment, while in "the War Department, the professional military pretty much had their own way," in "the Navy, thanks to Knox and Forrestal, there was a division of tasks based more on skill and a larger degree of civilian leadership throughout." As a result, the WPB had much less trouble with the navy than with the army; but since the army had the greatest needs, spent the most money, and let the largest number of contracts, problems of military administrative deficiencies continued to haunt mobilization and provoke further military-civilian clashes.[16]

Certainly, given the WPB's broad authority to coordinate and supervise mobilization, civilian-military clashes could be expected. Nonetheless, Nelson tried to avoid overt clashes through a series of signed formal agreements with each service, which stipulated the WPB's functions and responsibilities in relation to them. But, in the words of the WPB history, "Despite Nelson's high hopes, the agreements did not solve the major jurisdictional issues of 1942." The WPB-army agreement did, however, prove useful to Somervell in direct proportion to the disappointment it caused Nelson. Somervell used the agreement to cement and extend the army's prewar accretion of authority over mobilization by repeatedly portraying Nelson's attempts to assert WPB authority over army supply as a violation of the 1942 agreement. Certainly the agreement was ambiguous, but any ambiguity worked to Somervell's advantage, since the weight of precedent favored the military services. Alongside Nelson's decision to leave procurement to the services, then, these agreements therefore provided an important ratification for existing military authority over procurement and production. Indeed, after the war Nelson reported that "the agreement with the War Department crumbled before General Somervell's refusal to recognize any degree of subordination to WPB, his insistence on a dominant say-so with respect to matters involving the civilian economy, and his incessant striving to extend the limits of his jurisdiction at the expense of WPB."[17]

In the wake of these reorganizations and agreements, the secretaries of war and the navy requested that Roosevelt strengthen the Army-Navy Munitions Board (ANMB) and even make it (and, through it, the military services) rather than the WPB the administrative successor to the OPM and SPAB. Adhering to the strong views of his budget director, however, Roosevelt declined to elevate the ANMB and instead established the WPB as its administrative superior. Although the military's interwar planning presumed the disappearance of ANMB upon the creation of a top-level civilian agency such as the WPB, Somervell acted to ensure the former's continuance by bringing it under the jurisdiction of the ASF.[18]

Already, prior to army and navy reorganizations, Patterson and Forrestal had called on Ferdinand Eberstadt, another investment banker and close friend of Forrestal's from their days together at Princeton University and the Wall Street firm of Dillon, Read, to study and recommend alternatives for reorganizing and better utilizing the ANMB. Following Patterson and Forrestal's lead, Eberstadt envisioned a role for the ANMB as the advocate for military demands before the WPB, as coordinator of army and navy material requirements, and as a link between military and business interests. Although many military officials eyed even the ANMB as a civilian interloper to their authority, Somervell also saw the value of having the ANMB represent the military's interest before the WPB. Whereas Eberstadt, Forrestal, and Patterson thus viewed the ANMB as potentially an independent force for coordinating military procurement and materials policies (hence the distrust expressed by some military officials), Somervell saw it as yet another mechanism for staving off more intensive civilian-state control. In this latter goal, moreover, Somervell found common ground with Eberstadt, who had come to Washington "to prevent the chaos of a 'New Deal war.'" Eberstadt proved his worth in other ways as well. He had maintained for years a "Good Man" list of prominent and trusted corporate associates who could be called upon in time of need. As Jeffrey Dorwart reports, "Seventy percent of those on the Good Man list went to Washington as so-called dollar-a-year men during the second world war."[19]

Roosevelt granted administrative responsibilities to the ANMB and Eberstadt on 21 February 1942, and Nelson delegated the ANMB authority to grant priorities shortly thereafter, thus following the pattern of lodging authority with the military agencies that exercised de facto control during the prewar defense period. Under Eberstadt, the ANMB gained two missions. First, the board aggressively advocated for military authority and blocked civilian-state oversight, thereby acting as a front for Somervell. Likewise, because Eberstadt distrusted New Dealers and feared permanent expansion of civilian-state interventionist authority under the cover of war, he strove to enhance military administration and spread authority as much as possible to industry advisors and industry committees. Yet, like his close friend Forrestal, Eberstadt also strove to rationalize the military's materials and priorities programs and to use the ANMB to relieve competition between the services' procurement agencies.[20]

The extensive military reorganizations strengthened the military's domestic capabilities and thereby fortified military-state resistance to civilian intrusions. Gregory Hooks, viewing the process through a state-centered lens, has suggested that the reorganizations of the early war period signaled the emergence of a strong independent military capable of directing the activities of monopoly-sector firms. But the evidence strongly suggests that the military gained extensive domestic authority despite their administrative deficiencies, not only thanks to the combined effects of their assertiveness and prior claims to important mobilization authorities but also because of corporate support. The services relied upon businessmen to staff and oversee their growing bureaucracies for procurement and supply precisely because they recognized their internal administrative weaknesses; likewise, the stabilizing presence of business personnel helped to bolster the military's domestic authority. But the military's administrative preeminence certainly does not mean that the military services supplanted, or even threatened to supplant, corporate prerogatives. It was the major firms, together with industry advisors in government, that exercised much of the discretionary authority over the mobilization program. Indeed, the services' administrative weaknesses translated into widespread deference to monopoly-sector prime contractors, who exploited the war emergency to tighten their already firm hold on many sectors of the national economy.[21]

Mobilization thus hardly offers a simple case of autonomous military dominance over civilian competitors, whether businessman or New Dealer. After all, business personnel held important positions in the WPB *and* in the military agencies. And the domestic military ascendancy is comprehensible only as a side effect of corporate hostility to expansions in civilian-state, particularly New Dealer, authority. Corporate rapport with the military services greatly enhanced the ability of the latter to gain and exercise mobilization authority. Since some sort of national controls were necessary, businessmen preferred to deal with the military services, who were organizationally dependent upon prime contractors and who did not threaten business autonomy. Military control of procurement thus led to extensive delegations of authority to prime contractors, who themselves relied upon industry men in the WPB industry divisions and on industry advisory committees. Thus, the ascendancy of the military within the state only served as a stalking-horse for corporate influence over mobilization. The World War II mobilization process presents us not simply with a case of expanding military autonomy but rather with an expanding military-corporate political alliance defined through a process of mutual reinforcement and accommodation between military and corporate officials.

The Feasibility of Military Requirements

With the attack on Pearl Harbor, the military's contracting escalated rapidly and quickly outstripped the production capabilities of the national economy. At this point, the feasibility of military requirements became a critical issue. Civilian-state planners studying the capacity of the U.S. economy found that the unplanned escalation of military requirements would do great harm, as it did in World War I, by overloading the economy and thereby creating uncontrollable bottlenecks and shortages. As Somervell himself admitted, ASF requirements represented a "projection of existing military plans of the United States and of the [allies] translated into supply objectives *without any consideration for the practical limitations of available raw material and other industrial resources.*"[22]

When the military services authorized in early 1942 an ambitious program for constructing new processing facilities and manufacturing plants, the controversy over feasibility began. The military insisted that construction of new plants continue despite the fact that this construction was consuming scarce resources and despite WPB projections demonstrating that there would be insufficient raw materials to supply the new plants. Civilian-state WPB personnel thought it unsound to divert scarce resources for new plants when the materials and equipment demands of existing plants could not be satisfied. Members of the WPB Planning Committee complained that such a policy would lead to "construction of new plants without materials to keep them operating, vast quantities of semi-fabricated items which cannot be completed, production without adequate storage facilities, idle existing plants due to lack of materials, and similar disrupting situations."[23]

The WPB Planning Committee, whose personnel had begun its planning work under the SPAB, pressured Donald Nelson, among others, to raise the feasibility issue with military officials and with the president. Before the war began, this group of planners had pressed for an increase in military requirements and in contracting to spur conversion from civilian production. Now they believed that skyrocketing military requirements would destabilize the national economy and so interfere with war production. Somervell, for one, picked up on this apparent contradiction when he wrote the head of the Planning Committee, Robert Nathan, to complain, "Only a few months ago this office was urged by your statisticians to increase the goals [i.e., the military's requirements]." Somervell could not, or would not, see the danger of overloading the economy with excessive demands. Rather, he viewed the issue in terms of civilians in the WPB coddling civilians at home.[24]

Somervell and other army officials also distrusted the reasoning of civilian-state planners. Millett reports that, for ASF officials, "the concept of 'feasibility' ran contrary to the widely accepted notion of setting high goals as incentives . . . [and was therefore] simply a high sounding theory." Military officials also thought any problems could be easily overcome through better scheduling, increased production, and further cuts into civilian and indirect military requirements. Corporate advisors serving civilian mobilization agencies also proved skeptical of civilian-state planners' asserting their knowledge of what the economy could handle: "Some of the business men in the war agencies were not receptive to the idea [of feasibility] because they were unaccustomed to the concepts of economic analysis involved and had no experience with labor and material shortages. . . . An added handicap to the acceptance of the feasibility concept was its advocacy by persons who were regarded as 'academic long hairs.'" The lack of enthusiasm by both dollar-a-year men and military officials left civilian-state planners pressing this issue on their own.[25]

Although the civilians in the Planning Committee convinced Nelson of the need to reduce military requirements, Nelson had a difficult time convincing the president and military officials of this. Somervell simply refused to heed the advice of the young civilian-state "long hairs" who dominated the WPB Planning Committee. Yet Somervell and other military procurement chiefs quickly proved they could not control the inflation of military requirements, which escalated rapidly throughout the summer of 1942 as both the services and even independent procurement bureaus within each service scrambled to secure their own requirements with little top-level oversight or coordination. As the solicitor of the WPB later related, "Military requirements as such weren't formulated by anyone. The Air Forces, the Navy, and the Army Ground Forces each did their own estimates." And, as James Fesler, WPB staff analyst, ascertained, top-level military review merely led to ever-more-inflated estimates of need:

> Claimed requirements . . . were often the result of a perverse "reverse effect" of hierarchy in the Armed Services supply agencies. In contrast to budgeting, in which higher levels tend to cut subordinates units' estimates, in military supply units a subordinate units' estimates were apt to be enlarged at each higher level. Asking for too much was prudent, a tactic freeing each officer from blame for losing the war by asking for too little.[26]

Ironically, it was precisely this bureaucratic disarray on the part of the military that stymied civilian-state attempts to plan wartime mobilization. Donald Nelson testified to Congress before he became head of the WPB that a comprehensive statement of the services' requirements "was a prerequisite for proper planning of war production," yet the services never provided civilians with an overall schedule of their requirements. Since the services proved unable to generate accurate and stable requirements, it was near impossible for the WPB to exercise its management responsibilities. Still, this did not mean that WPB civilian-state personnel were completely prevented from managing procurement. On the contrary, chronic military mismanagement meant that strategically placed civilian-state personnel would continue to influence a mobilization process they were unable to plan or control.[27]

A sudden increase in unplanned military requirements during the summer of 1942 provoked warnings from the WPB Planning Committee that immediate reductions in military procurement orders would be necessary. With military requirements exceeding the capacity of the economy, it was feared that shortages would develop in machine tools, certain local labor supplies, and raw materials (especially steel, copper, and aluminum), which in turn would severely disrupt existing production schedules. Moreover, quite aside from these potential disruptions, civilian production would have to be cut to one-third of depression levels to meet the inflated military needs. Reducing and stabilizing military requirements thus became a central goal of the Planning Committee, which sought to shift the military-civilian balance of power by formally recommending that production considerations be made a part of strategic planning and that a "supreme war council" be created for coordinating military-strategic and civilian-production planning. Creation of such a mechanism would mean a dramatic shift in the WPB's relationship to the military. An unpublished draft of the WPB history reports an "increasing awareness . . . that *the Board* [WPB] could not merely serve the military agencies as if the latter were our customers, but *would itself have to assume fundamental programming responsibilities even though the decisions made might bear significantly upon strategic decisions.*" Thus, the desire of civilian-state planners to limit military requirements became connected to their readiness to supplant military authority if necessary.[28]

This maneuver struck at the heart of military authority, and any such inroads would threaten the prominence of Somervell's supply command. Accordingly, when copies of the Planning Committee warnings and recommendations were forwarded to Somervell, he denounced them as "an inchoate mass of words" and concluded, "I am not impressed with either the character or basis of the judgements expressed . . . and recommend they be carefully hidden from the eyes of thoughtful men."[29] Nathan responded to Somervell (in a memorandum written by Simon Kuznets, author of the committee's original report, who went on to win a Nobel Memorial Prize in economics), "Your conclusions . . . that these judgements be carefully hidden from the eyes of thoughtful men is a non-sequitur."[30]

The WPB meeting on 6 October 1942—to consider the need to reduce military requirements and the planner's call for "a new organization to correlate strategy and production and bring procurement objectives in line with productive capacity"—led to a showdown between Somervell and the civilian-state planners. With support from Admiral Robinson of the OP&M and Under Secretary Patterson, Somervell led the military's attack and seemed poised to block any resolution of the issue by the WPB. Leon Henderson, however, struck hard against Somervell's obstinacy "and proceeded to make the most violent personal attack ever heard in a meeting of the War Production Board." Henderson declared, "I am goddamned tired of Somervell's coming in here and questioning the competence of the [WPB]. . . . I don't see how you can duck the economic and production problems when you are dealing with strategy, nor can you duck the strategy problems when you are dealing with production." He then mused aloud, "Maybe if we can't wage a war on 90 billions [the amount that Nathan calculated the nation was capable of producing in 1942], we ought to get rid of our present Joint Chiefs, and find some who can!" Henderson's attack succeeded in subduing Somervell and the other military representatives and led them to accept a compromise at the next meeting of the WPB. There, Somervell agreed that Nelson would fix the maximum size of military requirements, and any reductions would be the responsibility of the Joint Chiefs of Staff.[31]

Obviously, Somervell's ostensible compromise protected military autonomy. The WPB forced the military to accept feasible requirements goals, but the military stopped the WPB from proceeding with reorganization plans that would have shifted the civilian-military balance of power within mobilization and thereby allowed civilian-state personnel to trespass on the military's authority over procurement and strategy. This resolution fits a familiar pattern: though the services retained the authority to independently proceed as they saw fit, civilian-state personnel played a crucial role in correcting potentially serious problems resulting from military mismanagement. Civilian-state planners, although outnumbered and squeezed out of direct policy-making roles by corporate executives and military officials, thus continued to wield influence by indirectly supervising mobilization. Still, since it never developed its own machinery to review the accuracy of military requirements, the WPB could only check the worst abuses caused by uncoordinated and haphazard military procurement.[32]

Material Control and Production Scheduling

As it was, despite the Planning Committee's ability to force reductions, the military's production program remained excessive, with military agencies contracting beyond available supplies of raw materials, labor, and components. Thus, the initial storm over feasibility shifted to battles between civilian and military leaders over controlling scarce materials and then over scheduling production for huge and competing military programs. Although material control and production scheduling are clearly related issues in the management of production, the controversies around them occurred separately. Material control received attention first because of early shortages in critical raw materials like steel, copper, and aluminum. And then, as control of raw materials stabilized, attention shifted to better scheduling of the military's production programs.[33]

Civilian-state personnel never surrendered mobilization to de facto military-industry control; continued problems and crises allowed them to both stay in the fight for authority and exercise an oversight influence that proved crucial in stabilizing mobilization. Still, these controversies illustrate how the military agencies, especially Somervell's ASF, retained and expanded their influence over mobilization despite their administrative weaknesses. As the domestic battle shifted from feasibility to raw materials and production scheduling, the military services claimed ever-greater authority to stave off WPB oversight of its operations. Instead of behaving as just a claimant on the nation's economic production, the services increasingly tried to run the whole show. Besides weakening civilian-state control, ASF advances also abetted the devolution of substantial authority from government to monopoly-sector prime contractors and to industry advisors and industry committees inside and outside of government.

Civilian-state officials recognized the need for centralized coordination of raw material distribution and for centralized scheduling of competing military production programs as corollaries to reducing excessive military requirements. Stacy May, former assistant social science director for the Rockefeller Foundation and now head of the WPB Statistics Division, criticized the military's inefficient use of materials and drew attention to the military's reliance upon all-too-optimistic production forecasts. And Robert Nathan's Planning Committee—through its Committee on Control of the Flow of Materials—criticized military material-control policies and recommended specific reforms. Both Nathan and May complained about the increasing gap between forecasted and actual production and about "'paper' schedules . . . not based on a considered evaluation of productive resources," and they recommended that the WPB provide central review and guidance to the military procurement agencies.[34]

As in the feasibility controversy, however, military officials, especially Somervell, adamantly opposed any outside interference with their material-control and scheduling functions. Both services continued to view any expansions of WPB oversight as a violation of the agreement Nelson had signed with the army and navy early in 1942. And military officials hoped to trump expanding civilian-state coordination by continuing to stress that strategy must guide production decisions. But by the middle of 1942 Somervell himself faced numerous problems fulfilling his supply responsibilities due to competitive divisions within army command and the related lack of advance strategic planning. Millett, historian of Somervell's command, details feuds between Somervell and the Operations Plans Division (OPD), the unit that formulated strategic plans for the General Staff. Somervell wanted closer collaboration between strategy and logistics (and, by extension, production) and the centralization of all logistics authority in his office, but the OPD, itself responsible for logistics, would have none of it.[35]

Planning military requirements even during the war thus became a guessing game, one that promoted competition between procurement bureaus. Millett reports, "Military plans were too uncertain to enable it [OPD] to supply the definite information [Somervell] sought." In the place of concrete plans, the strategic planners simply demanded "maximum over-all [military] production" and "sufficient supplies of all kinds to meet any strategic change," favoring "oversupply rather than undersupply." Although Somervell tended to want more military production, not less, it infuriated him that a closer meshing of strategy and logistics could not be achieved, especially since his run-ins with civilians over the unregulated inflation of military needs increased the vulnerability of his command.[36]

The absence of a strategic plan and overall coordination within the military meant that goals throughout 1942 expanded according to the whims of individual procurement bureaus, who competed with other bureaus to set and to meet their unintegrated requirements. Just as there was no coordination of contracting, there was no plan for rationally distributing the priority orders that supposedly guaranteed prime military contractors access to scarce raw materials. The thousands of uncoordinated priority orders granted daily by individual procurement officers were rapidly becoming worthless paper, exposing the need for centralized control over the distribution of raw materials. In response to this need, civilian-state officials once again made their move. Nelson wrote Patterson, Forrestal, and Somervell in May 1942 to explain the imminent implementation of a new control device by the WPB: the Production Requirements Plan (PRP), a system that the WPB had been experimenting with for months. Predictably, within days Somervell attempted to preempt Nelson's plan by recommending that control over allocating resources instead be shifted from the WPB to the Joint Chiefs of Staff or the ANMB. Nelson retorted that since the cause of the current crisis is "loose issuance and extension of [priority orders] by the procurement officers of the Army and Navy and the failure of the Services to present accurate statements of their requirements . . . your proposal seems to me to be basically in error."[37]

Thus, as priority orders collapsed under the weight of their unrestrained use, Nelson rushed the PRP into use. According to its terms, all contractors would file their priority orders with the WPB Requirements Committee, which would, in turn, allocate available materials and components after taking into account all military and civilian needs. This was considered a "horizontal" distribution system because the WPB would bypass the services in order to directly distribute materials and components to all contractors. The need for quick action meant that the plan had to be implemented quickly, with almost no lead time to educate participants or to develop adequate administration. Unsurprisingly, then, given its complex filing requirements, poor administration, and rushed implementation, few were satisfied with the PRP.

Still, the greater obstacle with regards to the PRP was not the administrative difficulties of merging priorities with an allocation system but rather the resistance of military and industry representatives.[38] For the PRP or any such plan to have a chance, military and industry personnel would have to cooperate fully in changing a system that had guaranteed their predominance in material distribution. Wartime conditions allowed little leeway for controversial shifts in authority in any case. But the barriers to changing material-control policy proved even greater because the military and industry clung to the preexisting system. Both the dollar-a-year advisors, who dominated the material and industry branches in cooperation with industry advisory committees, and the military services staunchly resisted the PRP.[39]

Moreover, the services' inability to coordinate their own procurement ironically doomed the PRP and stymied effective WPB coordination in general. By inundating industry with orders at the very beginning of the war, the military services indirectly foreclosed in advance the possibility of civilian-state control. As one author of the PRP found, "The questions of paramount importance which should have been answered at the highest echelon in the Pentagon Building [and by extension, the WPB] were being answered every day, through accident or ignorance, by the managers or even the stockroom clerks in thousands of industrial plants all over the United States." Similarly, Congressman Tolan's investigative committee complained about unrestricted and uncoordinated military procurement because, "by default, the individual prime contractors have been left with the responsibility for planning and scheduling production." This, of course, was precisely why the WPB sought to bypass the armed services and to allocate materials directly to firms. Yet, by the time the WPB attempted to take charge of material distribution, decisions about material needs had already been scattered among thousands of contractors; monitoring and controlling these contractors would take an administrative effort beyond the capability of the WPB.[40]

For Nelson, part of the solution to the crisis in material control lay in finally ending the military's power to issue unlimited priority orders independent of WPB review; this he accomplished in September 1942. At the same time, to provide greater supervision of the flow of raw materials and of the military's production scheduling, Nelson reorganized the WPB, creating two new top-level positions within the board. Nelson first announced the creation of a Production Executive Committee (PEC), through which he hoped to reassert the WPB's authority over production scheduling. Nelson appointed Charles E. Wilson, president of General Electric, to head the PEC as production vice chairman of the WPB. Wilson, unlike Nelson, was a production man, who, it was thought, would get tough with the military services and be a forceful advocate for WPB control. Soon thereafter, Ferdinand Eberstadt moved over from the ANMB to take charge of the new material-control program; as Eberstadt reported, the WPB reorganization was at least partly geared to "enable the ANMB to fit into its [the WPB] processes as an integral part of the system." Eberstadt's appointment as program vice chairman was thought to be "a conciliatory gesture toward the Services." By the same token, Wilson was viewed as being "a counterweight to Mr. Eberstadt," since Eberstadt was closely associated with the military. Because Eberstadt and Wilson gained authority over complementary parts of the mobilization program—Eberstadt over allocation of materials and Wilson over production of end products and components—it was probably inevitable that they would clash.[41]

Since material control presented the most urgent problem, Eberstadt's star rose first as he set about to implement an alternative to the PRP. To be successful, any alternative materials program had to fit the pattern of military-industrial relations that had stymied the PRP. Indeed, the WPB Requirements Committee staff, studying possible alternatives for material control, concluded that "by far the most crucial test of any workable scheme for material control [was its ability to] enlist not only the patriotic support but also the personal self-interest of businessmen." Eberstadt's scheme, the Controlled Materials Plan (CMP), passed this test, rooted as it was not only in military plans but also in proposals advanced by the steel industry and General Motors.[42] The CMP was also generally welcomed because of its simplicity. It proposed to control only three critical materials upon which most production hinged: steel, aluminum, and copper. Administratively, the plan conformed to the de facto military and industry control of mobilization by granting implementation authority to the military services and by relying heavily upon WPB industry branches, which Eberstadt reorganized into industry divisions. The CMP's "vertical" allocation system—called this because of the allocations of materials from the WPB to the services and then on to prime contractors—also greatly pleased the military, since, as Millett writes, it "preserved intact an intimate association between a military procurement office and its prime contractor. No third party [like the WPB] with any authority to give separate instructions intervened in this relationship."[43]

Eberstadt's plan did enable the WPB to exercise an important measure of top-level control over materials distribution. As the WPB history reports, "CMP . . . became the backbone of civilian programming." Eberstadt and the WPB Requirements Committee were able to enforce an uneasy balance between demands and available materials by forcing the claimants, especially Somervell's ASF, to live within their allocations: "the Requirements Committee [under Eberstadt] and its network of divisional requirements committees had the final word on making materials available for actual production." Of course, the services remained incapable of adequately programming their demands. As a top-level member of the WPB observed: "There was no procedure to connect reduced allotments of materials under CMP to the actual placement of contracts by the Procurement Agencies. Everybody went on cheerfully allocating deficits."[44]

Moreover, despite the CMP's partial success in expanding top-level WPB coordination, its implementation nonetheless further entrenched military and industry control of mobilization. With the PRP, the WPB allocated materials "horizontally," or directly to firms. Through the CMP, the WPB Requirements Committee (now under Eberstadt) granted large blocks of the critical materials (steel, aluminum, and copper) to the services. The services then divided the materials between their major contractors, who, in turn, were responsible for dividing materials between their subcontractors. This vertical flow of materials gave the services and monopoly-sector contractors enormous potential authority. The WPB history cites a general "fear" that a CMP-type plan "would mean the final WPB abdication and the turning of the economy to the Services." In effect, however, military control resulted in an enormous delegation of authority to WPB industry divisions, dominated by industry personnel, and to the military's prime contractors. As one contemporary analysis of the CMP concluded, "In practice the procurement agencies must transfer their control over material procurement to their prime contractors . . . [which] means, in effect, that the *real control over the distribution of raw materials will rest in the hands . . . [of] the steel mills, the copper companies, and the aluminum company* [i.e., Aluminum Company of Amercia]."[45]

The point must be emphasized: enhanced military authority under the CMP did not occur because of superior military administration, nor did it mean increased military authority. Instead, the CMP yielded greater power and authority to monopoly-sector prime contractors and to industry advisors serving within the WPB. Enhanced WPB programming capability under the CMP ultimately meant increased authority for WPB industry and materials branches (now reorganized as "divisions"), heavily staffed by industry personnel who worked closely with industry advisory committees and military procurers. In implementing the CMP, Eberstadt transformed these divisions into the workhorses of the program. As the Bureau of the Budget reports: "In his daily operations, [Eberstadt] . . . leaned heavily on the materials and divisional chiefs and their divisional requirements committees to carry on the major operating functions of WPB in Washington. Thus . . . each industry division became a small WPB in its own area." The point of contact between industry and the WPB was now in the hands of committees controlled by industry men: "detailed programming was largely their responsibility." Operating authority was delegated downward to leave the Requirements Committee free of what would have been overwhelming detail work. And Eberstadt empowered industry divisions to maximize production in their area of responsibility, estimate the amount of supplies that production could support, reconcile competing demands with available supply, and then allocate materials to specific claimants under the broad allotments made by the Requirements Committee.[46]

This system was beneficial to industry in a number of ways. Government planning was effected through industry-dominated agencies, with the aid of industry advisory committees that were themselves dominated by personnel from the largest firms in an industry. Two of Eberstadt's aides recommended that the "use of Industry Advisory Committees from private industry to supplement the Industry Divisions should be expanded." And Eberstadt subsequently prepared a memorandum for industry and material divisions that stressed the need to consult with industry: "The use of frequent and well-prepared meetings of Industry Advisory Committees will afford War Production

Board Divisions the greatest amount of industry participation in the solutions of its problems." Eberstadt's dependence on industry advisory committees dominated by the largest firms proved so great that even John Lord O'Brian of the WPB's Legal Division, himself very receptive to industry cooperative action, warned that committee activities were violating antitrust regulations.[47]

Major firms also became the recipients of large blocks of critical materials, the use of which they determined. WPB Chairman Nelson explained the benefits of this system of private planning as follows:

> We used controls, yes—all kinds of them, yet even a device like the Controlled Materials Plan, which was certainly a far reaching exercise of government power, was basically nothing more than a device for enabling industry to get what it had to get in order to do the job. Industry told us *what* it had to have and *when* it had to have it. What we did was establish a set of rules under which the game could be played the way industry said it had to play it.

The way the game was played had serious implications for the structure of American industry, since it reinforced the economic dominance and political influence of monopoly-sector firms. The concentration of contracts meant that the CMP enabled a relatively few large firms to gain authority over materials distribution and so gain power over the smaller firms forced to subcontract from the giant prime contractors. Congressman Tolan's committee reported that, besides placing "the cloak of legitimacy and Government authority upon the independent actions of large prime contractors," the system allowed relatively few prime contractors to "exercise virtual life and death control over thousands of small and medium-sized businesses through their subcontracting powers." The committee concluded that smaller firms "could not engage in any war production unless they obtain raw materials from this small group." As the Smaller War Plants Corporation noted in its report, "Companies obtaining prime contracts secured thereby the instruments of economic power." Smaller firms obviously feared the economic power thus conferred on the large prime contractors; according to one observer, they "expressed great concern that the CMP procedure would put them at the mercy of the prime contractors, most of which were pre-war industrial giants. . . . They expressed the fear that power entrusted to large prime contractors might be used to secure commitments and favorable competitive positions for the post-war period." This fear, as it turned out, was justified. When military production began to wind down, prime contractors used their control of contracts and materials to increase production in their own plants, drawing work away from their subcontractors.[48]

At least one of the materials divisions, the steel division, exploited the opportunity provided by the CMP. Estimates of prospective supply of each controlled material—steel, aluminum, and copper—were prepared by the three controlled materials divisions, and allocations to users were made based on these projections. The steel division discovered that they could provide low estimates of projected steel production and then easily produce a surplus. Besides receiving praise for their seeming good work, the steel division, with strong connections to the steel industry, could then allocate surplus supplies according to their own discretion, which usually meant that they could continue to service selected civilian customers. Steel companies were thus able "to maintain contact with their normal peacetime customers, an advantage when the war ended."[49]

Finally, industry divisions gained authority at the expense of the WPB's Office of Civilian Supply (OCS), a New Dealer–oriented agency empowered to ensure a healthy civilian economy during the war. Relations between industry divisions and the OCS were strained from the beginning, because it was staffed by civilian-state personnel and academics while the divisions were dominated by industry advisors. The OCS and industry divisions struggled for the power to determine civilian requirements and to program materials for the civilian economy. Eberstadt, and later Wilson, increased the power of the divisions to the point that the OCS was removed as a competitor.[50]

Because the military thought implementation of the CMP a panacea for all remaining production difficulties, they did little to resolve the numerous problems on the scheduling end. Nelson had appointed C. E. Wilson (of General Electric) in September 1942 to resolve these problems. And Nelson established a Production Executive Committee (PEC), composed of Wilson and the military's procurement chiefs (including, among others, ASF's Somervell and OP&M's Robinson), as the instrument of WPB control. Wilson started out aggressively enough: "He called for careful review of the entire scheduling procedure of the procurement agencies" and sought authority to more closely match the production of military end products to available supplies of raw materials and components. His goal was to resolve scheduling imbalances—the result of competition between military procurement agencies—that resulted in overproduction and storage of some items while many crucial end products could not be finished for lack of other parts.[51]

Predictably, Wilson quickly ran afoul of the military services. Somervell and Robinson reasonably interpreted Wilson's authority within the PEC as a WPB maneuver to supplant military control of production scheduling. This represented, they argued, a reversal of the authority vested in them through the CMP and an attempt by the civilians to dictate what type of armaments the military could have. Their vigorous resistance won them a delay of two months in the implementation of Wilson's authority and a few important concessions. An agreement was finally reached, under presidential pressure, that limited Wilson's oversight to three production programs: radar, aircraft, and escort vessels.

He also gained extensive authority for general direction of other production programs, but his authority could only be implemented through the procurement bureaus themselves. As with the resolution of the feasibility dispute, the services lost none of their power to set production schedules as long as these schedules were judged feasible by Wilson. This compromise proved satisfactory to the military.[52]

As Wilson's authority became operative, however, he necessarily began to intrude upon Eberstadt's domain, and tensions between the two grew accordingly. At first, Eberstadt controlled the industry and material divisions and, with them, most of the operating authority of the WPB. When Wilson asked for control over at least those divisions relating to his new responsibilities of overseeing aircraft and radar production, Eberstadt readily acquiesced to their transfer. Wilson, however, remained convinced that to fulfill his responsibilities he needed to control all the most important industry and material divisions, including those still held by Eberstadt. Pressured by Wilson's repeated protestations to the president, Nelson reluctantly agreed, and on 4 February 1943 a number of divisions, including one of the controlled materials divisions, were transferred to Wilson's control.[53]

Obviously, Eberstadt's star was beginning to fall. Nelson would fire him within a matter of weeks, once he got wind of his own imminent dismissal, which stemmed from military and presidential dissatisfaction with an increasingly disruptive Eberstadt-Wilson feud. Bernard Baruch was slated to replace him (Roosevelt had even signed the order removing Nelson and appointing Baruch), with Eberstadt pegged as his main assistant and de facto WPB director. But Nelson prevented his expected firing by an uncharacteristic display of forcefulness: he asked for Eberstadt's resignation and appointed Wilson to the newly created post of executive vice chairman, a position that combined both Eberstadt's and Wilson's responsibilities. Nelson's sudden decisive action and his broad support made it awkward for Roosevelt to replace him as director, even though as a result of that action Wilson assumed effective operating control of the WPB.[54]

Immediately, Wilson had to deal with the military hostility caused by Eberstadt's dismissal. As a token of his good will, Wilson downgraded the status of the WPB Planning Committee, which had, along with its chairman, Robert Nathan, been a thorn in the side of military officials. Accordingly, Nathan and his staff resigned, and, in Nathan's words, "The planning function disintegrated and lost stature."[55] Another reason Wilson began to warm to the services was alluded to by his colleagues. Milton Katz, solicitor of the WPB, reported, "Wilson expressed his concern . . . regarding the threat of the Services to cancel General Electric contracts if Wilson didn't get off the Services' neck." It seemed certain to observers that members of the services also convinced two of Wilson's influential colleagues at General Electric, Gerard Swope and

Owen Young, that Wilson was headed for trouble, with the distinct possibility that his reputation could be ruined. These pressures "may partly explain Wilson's policy of knuckling under to the Services." Regardless of how Wilson's change of heart is explained, he began to ally himself with the military services, and the PEC increasingly spoke with their voice.[56]

The failure to achieve WPB stewardship over economic mobilization has been interpreted as evidence of the military's own administrative capabilities and of military independence from corporate executives. The PEC did, after all, become the operating center of the WPB, and the committee itself was made up of military procurement chiefs. Yet it is also true that the PEC brought these top procurement officers together to schedule their production programs under the direction of Wilson and his staff. Moreover, it was Nelson's initiative that brought this mechanism into being, and the services had fiercely resisted it, fearful of losing any authority. Agreements between top procurement officers that had been impossible under military command were arranged under the auspices of the WPB. And there remained the constant threat that, if the military procurers did not cooperate, civilian-state officials might gain greater authority as a result. Not only were agreements achieved through a civilian agency, but any decisions would be implemented by industry personnel whether in the WPB divisions or in the industries themselves. Likewise, it was nonindustry civilians in the WPB, not military personnel, who continued to counter the influence of corporate executives. Official observer James Fesler recounts, "The [WPB] organization was quite remarkably designed to assure review by academics and civil servants of businessmen-officials' proposed decisions affecting the economy and individual industries. And the same nonbusiness-types, plus lawyers, were in strategic advisory roles to businessmen-executives."[57]

In summary, as the procurement officers' own organizations proved incapable of the coordination the war effort required, those outside of them, whether the civilian under secretaries, the ANMB, or the WPB, provided the necessary coordination. The limitations of the military services were overcome through the delegation of authority to prime contractors and by the oversight activities of civilian-state economists, lawyers, and planners within the WPB. The services may have been able to infiltrate some of these oversight efforts, as they did with the PEC. Nevertheless, the result was more coordination than existed beforehand—and certainly more than the services themselves were able or willing to provide.

▼ ▼ ▼

The working arrangements of wartime mobilization administration heavily influenced the disposition of national governance: Civilian interventionist capacities related to the New Deal were neglected or actively destroyed while the military services gained a vastly expanded role in the national state. Wartime statebuilding, influenced as it was by the actions (and inactions) of corporate firms, privileged the development of military bureaucracies, which owed their bureaucratic successes within the state during the war years to the external influence of corporate class forces they in turn legitimized and defended. And, as in World War I, corporate officials gained first-hand experience with the benefits of increasing government responsibilities over the economy. The space for corporate involvement grew as corporate officials participated in the processes of war mobilization and as the war halted what many businessmen saw as the dangerous statist experiments of the New Deal. Mobilization for World War II thus convinced many influential corporate representatives that national intervention need not be an unmitigated threat to corporate prerogatives, especially if such intervention could be shaped according to the dictates of powerful sectors of the economy.

Nelson and others affiliated with the WPB engaged in a running battle with military officials and their industry allies. Civilian-state personnel within the WPB often lost, but even in defeat they managed to salvage gains measurable by the enhanced coherence of the mobilization program. New Dealers and allied civilian-state personnel held in check the worst abuses of the military and industrial representatives who dominated mobilization. Yet liberal New Dealers and their allies could only somewhat constrain military and industrial forces; they could neither hold back the tide of military ascendancy within the U.S. national state nor prohibit the continued concentration and centralization of economic power during the war.

Reconversion Politics

• By 1943 it was clear that wartime mobilization had marginalized civilian-state personnel, blocked later New Deal developments, and resulted in a domestic military ascendancy undergirded by a military-corporate partnership. Reconversion from the wartime economy, however, reenergized New Dealers and their allies and brought to a boil the simmering tensions over the postwar organization of power in the national state.

All forms of reconversion planning revolved around two related considerations: the immediate problem of economic disruptions during the transition from military to civilian production and the broader challenge of long-term economic stabilization. Both concerns stemmed from fears that, without the stimulus of military contracts and burdened by millions of returning soldiers hungry for work, the United States would either repeat the post–World War I economic collapse or, worse, revert to the economic traumas of the Great Depression. Reconversion thus took shape as yet another wartime controversy that pitted civilian-state forces and their allies against a military-corporate alliance. Yet whether and to what extent New Dealers and their allies could shape reconversion would be a test of the extent to which wartime mobilization and wartime politics had altered the U.S. political terrain. Corporate executives, inside and outside of government, continued to fear that New Dealers could exploit the war emergency and the concerns about postwar economic instability to expand their authority over corporate firms. They knew well that civilian-state personnel within the War Production Board (WPB) had already authored various plans and sketches of state-guided reconversions to come, just as New Dealers in Congress were already promoting a full employment bill, which would extend later New Deal developments and institutionalize broad national authority over the economy.

It took the combined efforts of corporate and military officials to bury such reconversion planning. Corporate resistance to civilian-state initiatives of this kind occurred on both fronts of the struggle over reconversion—one involving the WPB and mobilization politics and the other involving congressional and presidential politics. Industry executives within the mobilization effort actively resisted WPB reconversion planning, and corporate liberal activists outside of mobilization organized an alternative, business-centered reconversion plan that precluded the need for expansive legislative initiatives and extensive national interventionism. Likewise, the military services resisted any and all forms of reconversion planning, stubbornly maintaining that any curtailment of their prerogatives would endanger ongoing military operations.

The Office of War Mobilization and the Fight over Reconversion Planning

The formation of a Production Executive Committee (PEC) within the WPB in late 1942 shifted operating responsibilities from WPB Chairman Donald Nelson (of Sears, Roebuck) to Executive Vice Chairman Charles Wilson (of General Electric). Identified with those seeking civilian-state control of the home front, Nelson had run afoul of the military services and lost all legitimacy in their eyes. Nelson therefore relied upon Wilson to wrest control of production scheduling from the military services. But instead, heavily staffed with military procurement chiefs as it became, Wilson's PEC allowed the military to infiltrate WPB policy making, and Wilson subsequently became identified as the military's ally.[1]

Liberal congressional observers of mobilization grew concerned about the decline in civilian-state influence over mobilization and about the increasing power of the military within the PEC and over the civilian economy. In early 1943 the Senate passed legislation (S. 2871, sponsored by Senators Harley Kilgore and Claude Pepper) to reassert civilian-state control of mobilization through the establishment of a top-level government ministry. President Roosevelt, unhappy with this effort, headed it off by establishing yet another agency, the Office of War Mobilization (OWM), to provide general supervision over the mobilization effort.[2]

James Byrnes, head of the wartime Office of Economic Stabilization, was tapped by Roosevelt to head up the OWM, and Byrnes operated the OWM out of the White House, his proximity to Roosevelt underpinning his authority.[3] The WPB retained primary operating authority, but Byrnes gained a mandate to resolve disputes between the WPB and other home front agencies, including the numerous civilian-military disputes relating to reconversion. And Byrnes, a conservative, southern former senator and Supreme Court justice with close ties to Bernard Baruch, "was on the best of terms with representatives of the armed forces" and would prove receptive to the military's arguments against civilian-state meddling in reconversion matters.[4]

Meanwhile, making the most of his waning influence, Nelson concentrated on developing policies to cope with the expected traumas of reconversion. Early in 1943, he assigned Ernest Kanzler, a former WPB official, the task of studying reconversion alternatives. Kanzler responded in mid-1943 with a recommendation that reconversion responsibilities be clearly defined and delegated to a civilian agency, preferably the WPB, to avoid de facto military control of the reconversion process. Wartime controls should be used, Kanzler said, to schedule an orderly resumption of civilian production and distribution of scarce materials as military orders are cut back: "programming and scheduling of the reconversion process will be necessary . . . to make demobilization orderly and to permit maximum utilization of our resources." In late 1943, Nelson instructed the WPB's Program Bureau under Julius "Cap" Krug to prepare for the task laid out by Kanzler. Having served previously with the Tennessee Valley Authority, Krug was one of the few men in the WPB not from industry or finance; his Program Bureau, like the WPB Planning Committee, became a haven for New Dealers and academicians.[5]

Unsurprisingly, however, since Nelson at this point controlled only one faction within the WPB, those within the organization opposed to any postwar extension of wartime controls developed an alternative to the programming option. Operations Vice Chairman L. R. Boulware (of General Electric), for example, specifically advised maintaining wartime controls for military purposes only. With the end of the war, all controls would be quickly eliminated to leave the initiative for reconversion firmly with private industry. The official history of the WPB described these two reconversion alternatives as follows:

> One subscribed to the principle that an orderly transition should be effected through the established programming procedures of the WPB which, of course, meant retention of a number of controls over industrial production and the flow of resources. The other urged the discontinuance of all controls, save for a necessary minimum . . . for war and essential civilian needs during the one-front war period.[6]

Growing congressional pressure for visible progress on reconversion spurred action on behalf of both alternatives. Roosevelt assigned Byrnes of the OWM to take charge of demobilization of wartime controls in October 1943. Byrnes in turn relied on Bernard Baruch, no friend of intrusive governmental controls, to investigate reconversion alternatives. Though largely based on the WPB's own thorough considerations of the problems posed by reconversion, Baruch's report nonetheless diverged substantially from Nelson's proposal to use wartime controls during reconversion to ensure full employment and full utilization of small business. Characteristically, Baruch instead urged quick removal of wartime controls and advocated other similar policies designed to give large corporations the primary role in pulling the nation through the reconversion period. As Max Lerner maintained at the time, Baruch's report represented "an attempt to solve a crisis situation by the formula of surrender . . . to the big corporations and the petty congressional reactionaries."[7]

Nelson sought to trump Baruch's report by announcing guidelines of his more aggresive reconversion policy at the 30 November 1943 meeting of the WPB. According to his plan, as raw materials, manufacturing facilities, and labor were freed from military production, the WPB would authorize their use for increased civilian production, provided that such production would not interfere with the war program.[8] Civilian production would thus increase in roughly the same measure by which military production would decline, thereby smoothing the transition to a peacetime economy. Nelson had by this time become convinced that the full-scale programming and scheduling route previously outlined by Kanzler was unrealistic, believing that postwar governmental production planning would be unwarranted and involve too many complications. Still, Nelson and others did envision a transition period in which wartime controls—especially wage, price, and distribution controls—could and should be used to ensure a smooth reconversion. And an orderly resumption of civilian production would likewise be achieved via a progressive firm-by-firm and region-by-region relaxation of wartime controls. Nelson reasoned that civilian-state planning, besides helping to regear the nation's peacetime economy, could stabilize military production by reassuring war workers and subcontractors that the government was taking proactive steps to ensure work for all. Yet even this mildly intrusive course of action proved controversial, since it still entailed centralized decisions about *who* could first begin peacetime civilian production and allowed civilian-state personnel to use public goals such as full employment and full utilization of smaller firms as guides for policy making. Most immediately objectionable to influential industry personnel was the notion that firms without military contracts—primarily smaller firms—would be allowed to restart their civilian operations first. Although many from industry certainly supported an increase in civilian production, they opposed giving smaller producers first crack at civilian markets while the military's monopoly-sector prime contractors would be required to fulfill their military contracts before returning to civilian production. On a deeper and more general level, however, many corporate executives feared that civilian-state reconversion planning would herald a postwar return to the New Deal interventionism they hoped to have escaped.[9]

Accordingly, when military officials quickly mobilized against Nelson's plan—and thereafter vehemently protested any suggested increase in civilian production—influential WPB dollar-a-year advisors and industry advisory committees withheld support from Nelson, leaving him and his plan vulnerable to attacks by military officials, who in turn wasted little time in pressing their advantage. On the heels of Nelson's November 1943 WPB announcement regarding reconversion, General Somervell's top aide, Major General Lucius Clay (director of materiel, Army Service Forces) campaigned to place reconversion policies under the authority of the PEC, undoubtedly because of military predominance on that committee. Wilson, the WPB's executive vice chairman and head of the PEC, welcomed the army's plan. But Nelson, still titular head of the WPB, strongly opposed a dominant role for the PEC, and so he instructed his assistant Bernard Gladieux to develop alternative plans. Gladieux in turn argued that the PEC would be capable of reviewing and supervising termination of military contracts only if civilian-state representation within the PEC was increased. To handle expansion of nonmilitary production, however, Gladieux recommended establishing a separate Production Adjustment Committee "heavily weighted with representatives of nonmilitary interests."[10]

Nelson went so far as to submit a proposed administrative order based on Gladieux's recommendations, which included making Krug's WPB Program Bureau the center of reconversion planning efforts. The proposal met with immediate objections from the army and from Wilson, who protested the threat to the power of his PEC.[11] At this point, in early 1944, military cutbacks had not yet begun to affect the national economy; so, wishing to avoid a showdown with the military services and with Wilson, who was expected to resign shortly and rejoin General Electric, Nelson postponed implementing Gladieux's alternative. Wilson, however, interminably delayed his departure, even as Krug—frustrated by Wilson's refusal to countenance Program Bureau authority over reconversion—resigned to accept a commission in the navy. Although later in 1944 Krug would return to the WPB to replace Nelson as chairman, his resignation at this point closed off the alternative of Program Bureau stewardship of reconversion, since Krug's "functions, authorities, and power" as program vice chairman were transferred to Wilson himself.[12]

In early 1944 Nelson and the military also argued over whether expanding cutbacks in military contracting made it possible to increase production of essential civilian goods. Nelson—and Wilson, for that matter—believed the time was ripe for such increases, which Nelson assured the armed services would come only after all military needs were met. But Forrestal and Patterson (the under secretaries of the navy and army) effectively dismissed Nelson's assurances and ignored his desire to limit production increases to only the most critical of civilian needs.

Military opposition was premised on the specter of crippling labor shortages; military officials feared that any increase in civilian production would threaten military production, since workers would flee war work for more secure jobs producing civilian goods. Citing such fears, the military services called on the authority of the War Manpower Commission (WMC), headed by Paul McNutt, in effect exploiting McNutt's legitimate concerns about labor shortages as yet another weapon in the campaign to block increases in civilian production.[13]

With military officials successfully opposing any increase in civilian production, Nelson agreed informally to delay any concrete reconversion activities until after the invasion of Normandy, planned for sometime in June. Yet, when in May 1944 the navy announced the cancellation of fighter-plane production at the Long Island plants of the Brewster Corporation, resulting in the loss of up to 13,000 jobs, the issue of reconversion gained new life. Even the official history of mobilization characterized the navy's handling of the cancellation as "inept." Having complained about labor shortages, the navy failed either to provide alternative orders for the plants or to transfer workers to other jobs. The fired workers occupied their plants and refused to leave until one or the other of these alternatives was proffered, sparking public sympathy and demands that cutbacks be planned to minimize employment disruptions.[14]

In effect the navy's action demonstrated the validity of civilian-state fears about unplanned cutbacks in military contracts. But, given his reluctance to openly organize and promote his plan as a viable alternative during the preceding months, Nelson was now ill positioned to exploit the opening that had fallen into his lap. He was forced to sanction PEC stewardship of contract cancellations and reconversion, despite his continued hostility to PEC control. As Nelson's assistant, Bernard Gladieux, remembered: "At that [WPB] meeting, Nelson said that this order giving to PEC . . . authority over cut-backs and reconversion is wrong, that PEC was not set up to handle such policy matters as the expansion of non-military production but 'if you all want it, then go ahead with it.'" As Gladieux also notes, the "top positions in the Board [WPB] had [by that time] been filled by Wilson men," reinforcing that Nelson's surrender to PEC control had been a fait accompli. The PEC's authority was then recognized by Byrnes, who formally bypassed Nelson to grant the PEC and Wilson explicit authority to establish policies guiding the cancellation of war contracts.[15]

For Byrnes, himself antagonistic to civilian planning and friendly to the military services, such decisions came easily. Although Congress would in October 1944 expand Byrnes's authority and mission with the Office of War Mobilization and Reconversion Act—an act that "probably represents the broadest delegation of authority ever granted by Congress to an executive agency"—he remained antagonistic to planning and to planners. Accordingly, the OWMR under Byrnes never exercised the type of broad and extensive control over reconversion for which many thought it had been created. Certainly, Byrnes's mandate to arbitrate differences of opinion and practice about reconversion matters diminished the chances of expanding or implementing civilian-state planning. "Byrnes," Herman Somers reports, "with his distrust of all staffs, was particularly averse to a regular planning staff. Overall and centralized planning . . . did not appeal to him." Indeed, Byrnes prepared to testify against expansive powers for the OWMR:

> Considerable money may be saved by not establishing the new agency with the powers proposed to be conferred by this Bill. The duty of over-all planning and the duty of assisting other executive agencies in planning, would necessitate a larger staff and involve a larger expenditure. If we organize a large staff of Planners, on their own motion, they may devote a lot of time to planning to make the organization permanent.[16]

Thus, while Byrnes paid lip service to reconversion planning—"It is essential that contract termination be coordinated with a positive program of reconversion in order to avoid, as far as may be reasonably possible, unemployment"—his actions spoke differently. He granted Wilson and the PEC authority for reconversion planning after the Brewster incident forced his hand. But the PEC, heavily staffed with military officials, divided the reconversion task between two groups, one to consider the release of facilities from military production, the other to plan the use of the released materials and plants. The planning group became, not surprisingly, a casualty, because the PEC committed little time and energy to its concerns. In any case, the services quickly learned that they could squelch most reconversion talk simply by limiting cutbacks and loading the economy with massive orders until the very end of the war. PEC oversight was therefore often reduced to recording how military cutbacks in certain areas would be offset by expanding military needs in others. It was difficult to plan for cutbacks and think about increasing nonmilitary production if there were no real cutbacks to consider.[17]

With his original plans for reconversion thwarted and no one in charge of expanding nonmilitary production, Nelson doggedly prepared to implement a less ambitious, yet still substantive, reconversion policy. While the PEC primarily concerned itself with the narrower issue of reviewing contract cutbacks, Nelson proposed a revised version of his earlier plan in mid-June, shortly after the Normandy beachhead had been secured. In these new recommendations, Nelson sought increased civilian production by selectively easing wartime production restrictions.[18]

Nelson's four-step program was developed by New Dealers positioned in the Smaller War Plants Corporation (SWPC), the WPB Planning Division, and the WPB Office of Civilian Requirements.[19] Its most controversial element—"spot authorization"—would allow regional WPB offices to authorize civilian production by smaller firms as military contracts were canceled. Throughout the war, many small and medium-sized firms had managed to remain in business by subcontracting from prime contractors. Now, as military production cutbacks increased, prime contractors withdrew work from subcontractors to maintain full production in their own plants. The SWPC's Maury Maverick, a former Texas congressman and a committed New Dealer, particularly feared that monopoly-sector firms dominating prime military contracts would exploit the scarcities accompanying reconversion to monopolize materials and effectively starve smaller firms out of business. This scenario would replicate the experience of conversion (1940–1942), when, through the use of priority orders assigned by the military, monopoly-sector firms cornered critical materials for themselves.[20]

Allowing smaller firms first crack at civilian markets, however, irritated the large producers who would have to wait until they fulfilled the terms of their military contracts. These prime wartime contractors, in turn, staunchly resisted Nelson's plan. One representative industry advisory committee, asked for its views on reconversion, argued, "No new manufacturer should be permitted to produce as long as any prewar producer is unable to resume production because of war contracts or lack of necessary facilities, materials, or labor." Fairness, it seems, dictated that smaller producers not gain any advantages over the industrial giants who dominated prime contracts—and who, in contrast, suffered no moral or political qualms over the oligopolization of the economy occasioned by the war.[21]

Besides fearing for profits and market share, industry representatives worried over civilian-state planners' exercising authority over their firms and industries. The perception that nonindustry planners were negotiating a return to peacetime production by allowing smaller concerns to beat large manufacturers to civilian markets was enough to cement a hostile alliance of corporate executives, inside and outside the WPB, and military officials. Executives within the WPB had countenanced planning throughout the war, albeit through mechanisms—dollar-a-year advisors and industry advisory committees—they dominated, because it served their interest. Planning for reconversion certainly would have been acceptable if WPB industry advisors were to retain most of the discretionary authority they had enjoyed under the wartime material-control program. As one observer noted, "Programming itself was not so bad if subject to the sole control of the industry divisions." But now, as Nelson demanded that the goal of a stable postwar economy must come before the prewar market shares of dominant firms, the WPB's industry divisions (staffed mostly with industry personnel) warned against handing over reconversion to "professors and planners." For industrialists who dominated prime contracting, applying government controls to reconversion could only mean interference with their dominance of civilian markets. Both market share and corporate autonomy from government interference were at stake.[22]

Responding to the threat to their discretionary authority, many corporate representatives strategically shifted to the argument that controls should be retained on all firms until they could be dismantled all at once. Rapid and across-the-board abandonment of most government controls would ensure that prime contractors could retain the dominance they had gained during the war. With this goal in mind, WPB dollar-a-year advisors and the military's prime contractors focused their attention on clearing plants of war materials and machinery in order to return quickly to civilian production and exploit the expected boom there. Reconversion efforts therefore came to narrow in on the procedural difficulties of contract cancellations and settlements and the disposal of surplus plants, machinery, and materials.

Nelson's hospitalization shortly after the announcement of his reconversion plan also decreased its chances for success, since it left Wilson in charge of promoting the plan's implementation. Ostensibly faithful to Nelson's program, Wilson's heart was obviously not in it. In addition, almost the entire PEC (dominated by industrialists, military officials, and representatives from the WMC) vociferously opposed spot authorization. When Wilson remained at least publicly committed to Nelson's plan, military representatives rammed a resolution through the WPB postponing Nelson's orders and went over Wilson's head to complain to their friend in the OWM, James Byrnes. Likewise, Admiral William Leahy, writing on behalf of the Joint Chiefs of Staff and for public consumption, complained to Nelson on 7 July 1944, "The issuance of orders at this time which will affect our ability to produce war materials is not consistent with the all-out prosecution of the war." Nelson responded on 10 July, saying, "The [WPB] would be negligent if it did not reckon with the possibility of . . . large cutbacks in the overall war program. Whenever those cutbacks are made, it will be important to have preparations well advanced for large-scale expansion of civilian production." The WPB's two labor vice chairmen, Joseph Keenan and Clinton Golden, sprang to the defense of Nelson's orders. As they concluded in their analysis, "The duty of the [WPB] to the military is to assure that war production requirements are met. So long as this duty is performed, the military are not in any position to oppose action by the WPB for the benefit of the civilian economy."[23]

As the controversy played out in the press, Byrnes conferred with Nelson and convinced him to stagger the implementation of his orders, with "spot authorization" delayed until August 1944. But the campaign of the military representatives (including Patterson, Forrestal, and the heads of the army and navy supply commands, Somervell and Robinson) did not stop here. To counter congressional support and favorable press coverage, they publicized a Joint Chiefs of Staff letter criticizing

Nelson's orders. Moreover, they resorted to blatant propaganda timed to coincide with this broadside, whipping up public sentiment by linking decreasing military production with critical material shortages on the front line they claimed were threatening the lives of American soldiers.[24] In fact, decreasing war production stemmed more from the military's own logistical problems and contract cancellations than from workers' fleeing their war jobs to work in civilian industries. Nonetheless, the military's tactic succeeded in convincing Byrnes, who was certainly open to such blandishments, that production difficulties were for real. He issued a new directive that gave McNutt's War Manpower Commission a veto over spot authorization orders, thereby creating a very effective barrier to Nelson's program.[25]

Meanwhile, the reconversion controversy had become a reelection issue for Roosevelt. Although Nelson had lost control of the WPB and of reconversion, it was difficult for Roosevelt to cleanly cut him loose; given the publicity of Nelson's stand against "big business," it would look as though Roosevelt himself had caved in to business pressure. Roosevelt wiggled out of the dilemma by announcing on 19 August 1944 that Nelson would depart for China as his personal emissary to Chiang Kai-shek. Roosevelt planned to have Wilson take Nelson's place, but the negative publicity surrounding Nelson's exit came to rest on Wilson's shoulders. Wilson, who had been eager to leave for months, was outraged by press stories concerning his supposed conflicts of interest. He angrily resigned, blaming Nelson and his staff for press leaks. Krug, who had earlier left the WPB for the navy, was immediately named acting chairman of the WPB by Roosevelt; when Nelson resigned upon his return in September, Krug was appointed chairman.[26]

Krug soon found that even Nelson's limited reconversion program had become greatly restricted, thanks to the military's opposition. And, with Roosevelt facing a reelection battle, Krug had to avoid a public fight with the services. Still, without resorting to the dramatic tactics of the military representatives, Krug nonetheless attempted, with some success, to move spot authorization forward against the implacable resistance of military and industry representatives. Patterson and Somervell responded to Krug's steady pressure with even heavier doses of propaganda, until reconversion efforts were effectively dropped. First, the appointment of Somervell's top assistant, General Lucius Clay—"a vigorous opponent of any reconversion"—as deputy director in Byrnes's office made reconversion a de facto dead letter. Then, a few days later, on 16 December 1944, the German offensive known as the Battle of the Bulge ended any hope of reconversion. Instead of a planned rollback of production meshed with a planned phase out of controls for certain firms and areas, the emphasis shifted to the highest possible rate of military production, to cover any possible strategic contingencies, right up until V-E Day. Even for the subsequent period, with only one theater of conflict, the 14 percent cut in requirements the services projected left little opportunity for a positive reconversion program to succeed.[27]

Reconversion: Abandoning Controls and Blocking Domestic Activism

Although the war generally strengthened the U.S. national state, it bolstered its ability to intervene abroad far more than its ability to intervene domestically. The defeat of civilian-state programming was emblematic of that paradox. Planning for the postwar era might have continued as part of the mobilization effort. Civilian-state personnel had prepared substantial plans by early 1944 to guide a stable return to peacetime production. As CIO President Philip Murray argued at the time, the Office of War Mobilization and Reconversion "and its related agencies" represented "an economic general staff [that] must now . . . demonstrate how organization can maintain employment and attain full production when the great volume of war goods no longer is necessary." But military and corporate officials blocked implementation of a planned approach and ensured that the legacy of effective government regulation of prices, flows of raw materials, and production schedules would not be projected into the postwar era.[28]

With the defeat of the programming option, preparations for reconversion within the war agencies (civilian and military) came to focus on the narrower, procedural difficulties of contract cancellations and settlements, disposal of surplus plants and goods, and clearing plants of wartime machinery and materials. The very success of the 1944 Baruch-Hancock report, which addressed these "nuts and bolts" problems of getting industry quickly into civilian production, suggests how thoroughly the broader debate about reconversion had been stifled. V. O. Key, for instance, at the time judged the report "a tour de force," but he added that "it did not meet the desires of those who felt the opportunity should have been grasped for a penetrating examination of the adequacy of our institutional arrangements to prevent a recurrence of the great depression."[29]

A "penetrating examination" had become, along with the programming option, a casualty of military and corporate opposition to expanding civilian-state authority in the postwar era. Until the Brewster incident, the WPB's ability to plan reconversion had been hamstrung by the military's inability or unwillingness to share information about contract cutbacks. As a member of the WPB noted: "At the present moment one of the most important factual backgrounds for [WPB] policy and operations planning is lacking. This lack arises from the failure of the military procurement agencies to discuss with the [WPB] in advance their plans for contract terminations." Yet, even after the Brewster incident led to greater collaboration between the services and the WPB, little changed.

The predominance of the military-dominated PEC within the WPB resulted in little more than the semblance of planning for military cutbacks. The official WPB history records that, without adequate information concerning cutbacks, "much of WPB's planning for VE-day was shadow-boxing." Thus, thanks to flaws engineered into the planning process by military obstinacy or incompetence, pressure mounted to remove WPB's controls after the end of the war in Europe.[30]

When Krug took over from Nelson as chairman of the WPB in late summer 1944, a fierce debate was raging over whether to continue controls in some form to smooth the transition to a peacetime economy or to abandon them as soon as feasibly possible. On one side stood the WPB's Smaller War Plants Corporation, Planning Division, Program Bureau, Office of Civilian Requirements, Office of Manpower Requirements, and the labor vice chairmen of the Office of Labor Production; on the other, the military services and the rest of the WPB, including of course the industry advisory committees, industry divisions, and dollar-a-year advisors. Bowing to Operations Vice Chairman Boulware's argument that "WPB powers could not guarantee full employment through government action," Krug decided to retain a bare minimum of controls. Krug himself was certainly aware of the military's prowess at destroying their domestic opposition; yet he was not unsympathetic to business interests. "Neither an intellectual nor an idealist nor an evangelist preaching political theory and waving a New Deal banner," as one scholar puts it, "Krug sought the advice of businessmen, respected their desires, and frequently followed their recommendations." Moreover, given the military's penchant after the Battle of the Bulge to run up their requirements to startling heights, Krug was given very little room to maneuver. His frustration spilled forth in a plea to Fred Vinson, Byrnes's successor as OWMR director, for help in reducing the military's continued massive list of requirements: "Considerable duplication exists among the procurement plans of the several services. It appears that the Air, Naval, and Ground Forces are each developing production plans for winning the war practically single-handed." Krug could do little but complain. Accordingly, though Krug had once favored a planned route for reconversion, by mid-1945 he surrendered to the immense pressures arrayed against such a policy.[31]

WPB planners did not accept Krug's decision to abandon controls without a fight. The replacement of Byrnes with Judge Fred Vinson in early April 1945 revived the battle over reconversion one last time. Vinson brought in Robert Nathan, former head of the WPB's Planning Committee and nemesis of the military services, as deputy director for reconversion; Nathan in turn attracted other New Dealers who believed in maintaining certain controls during a postwar transition period. He and his OWMR allies provided a sharp retort to Krug's decision to lift wartime controls quickly at the end of hostilities, and they urged Vinson to take Krug to task. Nathan claimed that the alternatives Krug had presented—a "speedy blanket removal of controls" versus some kind of extreme regimentation orchestrated by Washington—amounted to a false choice, since "neither extreme alternative is necessary nor desirable."[32]

Nathan also urged Vinson to use his authority to question continuing massive military requirements, which interfered with attempts to smooth the way for reconversion: "If OWM&R has the responsibility of planning for war mobilization *and* reconversion it must assume a real and not a fictitious role in both activities. The Army and Navy cannot be permitted to fix their programs independently, free from review, with the understanding that civilian production will utilize whatever resources remain. We must be certain that military programs are *justified*." Philip Murray, CIO president, also wrote Vinson to complain about the WPB's "deliberate suicide." He argued that, because Congress had done "practically nothing . . . to provide purchasing power for the mass of people who will be unemployed when war production is cutback and cancelled," it was imperative that Vinson use the authority under the 1944 War Mobilization and Reconversion Act to further the "logistics of full employment."[33]

Nathan and his staff needed Vinson's continued sponsorship to engage in the type of effort Murray demanded. But Vinson remained director of the OWMR for only three months before leaving in July 1945. He was replaced by a relative newcomer to Washington politics, John Snyder, who gained the position because he was close to the new president, Harry Truman. Snyder, Somers reports, "regarded himself primarily as a businessman," and relations between him and those, including Nathan, who desired a more activist approach to reconversion soon soured. Nathan maintained a rearguard fight for months before finally leaving in frustration in January 1946.[34]

The Broader Reconversion Context

In any case, by late 1944 reconversion efforts had narrowed to the problems of quickly clearing industries of war-related work, tools, and materials and of quickly settling with contractors for uncompleted war work—issues that the Baruch-Hancock report, issued early in 1944, had already discussed. Baruch characteristically believed the intense anxieties over a possible return to economic depression conditions could be allayed by private decisions. So he articulated policies designed to take "the Government out of business." In October 1944, Congress, eager to reassert its prerogatives for the postwar era, had backed the Baruch-Hancock recommendations with legislation; Byrnes's OWM was granted sweeping responsibilities and a new name, the Office of War Mobilization and Reconversion (OWMR). Congress had also placed within the newly-created OWMR a Surplus Property Board and an Office of Contract Settlement—both established earlier by executive order and now granted congressional sanction. Such legislation established extremely generous reconversion provisions for wartime contractors but ignored what came to be called the "human side of reconversion," that is, the expected problems relating to the unemployment and displacement caused by war contract cutbacks.[35]

Congress's desire to play a more direct role in reconversion also contributed to the construction of a new postwar governance project, especially given the powerful conservative coalition brought to power in the 1942 midterm elections. More an expression of apathy and of barriers to voting by displaced workers and soldiers than the result of an electoral shift to the Republican Party, the 1942 election, in which Republicans gained 10 seats in the Senate and 47 in the House, allowed conservatives expanded influence over the course of wartime domestic policy and postwar planning. In 1943, the new Congress went on the offensive. It killed off the remnants of activist New Deal depression-era agencies, including the National Youth Administration, Civilian Conservation Corps, Works Progress Administration, National Resources Planning Board, and the Farm Security Administration and attacked organized labor with the passage of the Smith-Connally Act. Likewise, when Roosevelt asked for $12 billion in new taxes to hold down domestic consumption and to pay for growing war costs, Congress voted to raise only $2.3 billion, and then only by shifting the tax burden downward.[36]

The new Congress also blocked liberal proposals for the postwar period. For example, an alternative version of the legislation that established the OWMR (sponsored by Senators Kilgore, Murray, and Truman) would have granted centralized authority over reconversion for the express purpose of planning governmental solutions for expected unemployment and reemployment problems. The alternative bill's extension and expansion of unemployment benefits alongside promotion of planning measures proved too progressive to pass muster with conservatives, especially in the House of Representatives. Even after the campaign of 1944 brought Roosevelt back to the White House and 24 Democrats back into the House, a full employment bill, which would have given the president the responsibility and authority to counter economic downturns through planned governmental spending initiatives, ran into a wall of opposition in the conservative House. There, antagonistic business forces rallied to press for the watered-down alternative bill that would be signed by President Truman in February 1946.[37] So too with a bill proposed by Senators Wagner and Murray and Representative Dingell, which would have nationalized and expanded social security, disability, and unemployment insurance while nationalizing the U.S. Employment Service and creating national health insurance for war workers and returning servicemen. First proposed in 1943 (in response to the NRPB's 1943 swan song, the lengthy and controversial report, *Security, Work, and Relief Policies*), the Wagner-Murray-Dingell bill was reintroduced in 1945 after many of its provisions had been already passed as part of the G.I. Bill of Rights (the Servicemen's Readjustment Act). What Congress was willing to do for returning servicemen, however, it was unwilling to do for displaced war workers.[38]

Congress thus reinforced the WPB's desire to handle reconversion by letting business deal with the problem as it saw fit. Senator Walter George's influential Committee on Post-war Economic Policy and Planning emphasized that, "without a proper 'economic environment,' without confidence in the friendly attitude of government, . . . business will not be willing to go forward and expand." Providing business with the proper environment for expanding its investments did not necessarily mean simply reducing the role of the national government altogether, however. One legacy of the expanded national government from the war years was the huge public subsidies given those large producers who had dominated wartime prime contracting. For example, as the Smaller War Plants Corporation (SWPC) estimated, *"about $20,000,000,000 of the $26,000,000,000 wartime plant [was] usable for the production of peacetime products,* either immediately or after minor conversion." The implications of these numbers were startling: "Facility holdings of the 250 largest corporations in 1945 approximately equaled those of *all* corporations in 1939." Now, as the war came to its end, almost all of these plants were usable for postwar production. A portion of the funding for these wartime plants ($4.8 billion) had come from private sources; but since the government allowed accelerated five-year amortization privileges to prime contractors the plants were essentially publicly funded. Moreover, contractors who plowed their enormous wartime profits into expanding their plants and equipment had been able to deduct the expense from the excess-profits taxes they owed the government; the more contractors spent their own funds investing internally, the lower their tax bill.[39]

Similarly, government-financed plants—"the most massive economic resource created during the war," whose disposition, the SWPC warned, "will do more than anything else to determine the future economic destiny of this country"—tended to follow prime contracts straight into the hands of the nation's largest firms. Although Congress sought to give smaller business an opportunity to acquire these plants, the War Assets Administration reported to Congress that the 250 largest manufacturing corporations, having operated 79 percent of the plants, had acquired 70 percent of them. And government-financed plants were often disposed of for 20 cents on the dollar. Fire sale prices for top-quality, modernized plants and machinery and quick amortization of privately-financed plants amounted to a huge public subsidy to monopoly-sector firms. The resolution of these matters confirmed the preponderant economic and political leverage gained by the nation's largest firms during the war.[40]

As the foremost American Keynesian of this period, Alvin Hansen, has noted, these subsidies and others disprove the fallacy that speedy conversion can be credited to "the free operations of the private-enterprise economy." Hansen points to the incredible amounts of government monies expended for veteran benefits, the "typically generous" contract settlements for uncompleted work on terminated military contracts, the repeal of the excess-profits tax immediately after the war, and the refund of 10 percent of the excess-profits taxes paid during the war. On top of these gifts, prime contractor's wartime profits were more than double the peacetime average, even after renegotiation and taxes. The Truman Committee cited Treasury estimates that put net corporate profits at $10 billion in 1943 and $11 billion in 1944, "nearly double the average of $5,500,000,000 after taxes for the years 1936 through 1940." Labor's gains, by contrast, were primarily the result of working longer hours, since workers were subject to strict wage controls.[41] Combine the public generosity to monopoly-sector firms with the public subsidy for the huge wartime plant expansions and one can see that Congress willingly acquiesced in a particular type of government intervention—direct and indirect public subsidy of corporate profits and growth. This form of "commercial" Keynesianism, pursued by corporate liberals, would continue to be a key component of the postwar governance project to come.[42]

Corporate Liberal Planning

As noted, two interrelated concerns, both tied to fears of a postwar depression, infused the controversy over reconversion: the economic disruptions expected to accompany the transition from military to civilian production, and the challenges of long-term domestic economic stabilization. While the process of defining political solutions to these economic problems restimulated the domestic tensions left over from the New Deal, congressional conservatism thrust the initiative, at least at first, into the hands of those guiding wartime mobilization. And both military and corporate personnel prevented New Dealers and their allies from using the mobilization side of reconversion to further civilian-state planning. Corporate and military hostility to civilian-state reconversion planning proved integral to the efforts to prevent wartime regulation from continuing into the postwar era and to blunt the general effort to develop publicly guided tools for ensuring economic stability.

The defeat of the planners' agenda inspired resurgent conservatives in Congress and traditional elements of the business community with the belief that the governmental expansions of the last fifteen years could be rolled back. The postwar era would not, however, herald a return to any kind of mythic "night watchman" state, since the specter of postwar economic instability placed great pressure on national policy makers to articulate some type of publicly guided program. Yet, although ascendant conservatives helped to define the new political mood of the nation and acted to gut critical elements of a full employment bill to ensure its passage, they were institutionally incapable of taking the lead in constructing a positive governance project. The essential question thus remained, Under what governance project would the newly enlarged American state find its raison d'etre?

By the end of World War II, three broad alternatives were posed for what to do with the national state: the first, a simplistic rejection of intrusive governmental meddling in the economy; the second, an extension of the interventionist civilian-state authority of the New Deal through implementation of full employment legislation and the like; the last, an as-yet-undefined governing synthesis based on the institutional shifts of the war. Although many business traditionalists and congressional conservatives preferred the first alternative, it was hardly a real possibility. The spectacular growth of the military and economic importance of the United States, both in itself and in relation to vitiated European powers, ensured a permanently expanded role for the national state in international affairs. Moreover, the legislative accomplishments of the New Deal had expanded the national state's statutory responsibilities. Certainly, the American public looked to the national state to guarantee a measure of economic stability, and even optimists about the potential for postwar economic growth foresaw difficulties that would necessitate government intervention.[43]

Thus, for some in the corporate world, simple-minded opposition to expanding civilian-state domestic authority could only be self-defeating. Accordingly, even as WPB dollar-a-year business advisors and industry advisory committees colluded with military officials to block a civilian-state reconversion program, an influential group of corporate liberal planners developed a business-centered programmatic strategy for securing postwar economic stability. Aware that any affirmation of business's ability to shoulder responsibility for postwar economic stability would be crucial during this period of public anxieties about postwar economic instabilities, corporate planners operated through the Committee for Economic Development (CED) to promote their own alternative to expansive Keynesian interventionism. In addition to their efforts, an analogous set of corporate executives, representing the East Coast financial-internationalist establishment, were invited into the high counsels of war and foreign policy during and after the war. There they were key participants in developing a synthesis of international economic and geopolitical strategic concerns that served as the basis not only of postwar foreign policy but also of the postwar governance project.[44]

As the war wound down, the idea of expanding the national government's responsibilities to deal with a feared postwar economic crisis had gained strength in Congress and taken form in Senator James Murray's full employment bill. Defeat of the substantive elements of this bill demonstrated the political clout of those segments of the business community seeking to limit national state interventionism. Still, whereas traditional business organizations such as the U.S. Chamber of Commerce (USCOC) and the National Association of Manufacturers (NAM) tended to reject interventionist schemes altogether, the CED recognized the importance of a certain measure of national responsibility for economic stability. The USCOC and the NAM embodied traditional beliefs in "decentralized, private, competitive capitalism," free of the obstructive influences of "Big Labor and Big Government" and, during the New Deal, engaged in "negativistic opposition" to expanding government activities. Yet the American business community had not been universally hostile to New Deal expansions in national authority. The Business Advisory Council (BAC), for example, had been created in 1933 by Roosevelt's first secretary of commerce, Daniel Roper, as a semipublic organization linking the most influential members of the business community to the new Roosevelt administration. Besides allowing business leaders privileged access to the highest levels of government, the BAC provided a mechanism for major corporations to transcend narrow parochial and competitive concerns in order to consider long-range plans for economic stability and the national state's part in these plans.[45]

Despite the progress in organizing businessmen, however, one chronicler of business planning reports that, by 1941, "the lack of leadership in the private sector was depressing." Controversies over the Roosevelt administration's turn to Keynesianism in the late 1930s, along with the arrival of war, inspired a reappraisal of the BAC's relationship to the national government. Paul Hoffman (president of Studebaker and BAC vice chairman) and William Benton (a New York advertiser), together with BAC leader Marion Folsom (of Eastman Kodak), approached Commerce Secretary Jesse Jones for help in creating a new business organization designed to ready business for the economic shocks expected to follow the war. Jones, a conservative Texas banker hostile to progressive elements of the New Deal, agreed to Commerce Department sponsorship of business planning for the postwar period. Jones wrote to Roosevelt only months after Pearl Harbor to explain his intentions: "It is our plan to create a nationwide committee of business and industrial representatives to study the post-war economic situation from the standpoint of fitting business and industry into conditions that will follow the war. It is our belief that industry itself must give some thought and study to its post-war problems and obligations. At the present time business, as business, is making no national effort in this direction." Although Roosevelt tried to discourage Jones, the CED was incorporated with Jones's help in September 1942.[46]

The CED desired to transform the standard knee-jerk opposition to government by many in the U.S. business community. Unlike traditional business organizations such as the USCOC or NAM, the CED accepted the New Deal innovations in recognizing organized labor, establishing Social Security, regulating monopolistic business behavior, and promoting governmental responsibility for overall economic stability. And they hoped to lead the rest of the business community to accept the necessity and validity of some limited measure of national interventionism. As economist Gardiner Means, at the time a CED employee, telegrammed to one of the organization's trustees, "AM AWFULLY TIRED OF HEARING BUSINESS MEN DEFINE ROLE OF GOVERNMENT IN NEGATIVE TERMS STOP BIG FACT IS THAT GOVERNMENT HAS TO DO MORE THAN IN THE 1920'S STOP UP TO BUSINESS TO SAY WHAT MORE [IS] SO THAT IT [THE GOVERNMENT] WON'T TAKE ON MORE THAN IS NECESSARY. . . ."[47]

The experience of war mobilization had convinced many corporate leaders to value the compensatory role played by the national state and to appreciate a national state apparatus tamed by the wartime influx of corporate executives. Many of these men, including those who organized the CED, preferred a new era of economic growth based on a business-oriented Keynesianism to either a return to a mythic laissez-faire economy or a redistributive welfare state. Of course, the CED's endorsement of a positive role for the national state did not entail acceptance of any reduction of corporate privileges and prerogatives. The CED, while liberal, opposed any replacement of corporate control with governmental direction and, as historian Norman Markowitz notes, "remained entranced by the vision of a New Deal killed painlessly by flowing private capital and consumer goods."[48]

The founding members of the CED were driven by two concerns. First, like other business activists, they feared private corporate prerogatives would be abridged or curtailed as interventionist governmental programs were instituted or expanded to deal with postwar economic disruptions. As official CED sponsor Jesse Jones declared at the CED's first national meeting on 14 April 1943: "This much is certain, that if the business men of the country, either through the [CED] or in some other way, do not have concrete, practical suggestions for the conversion of industry from war to peace, government will have to make the decisions." Paul Hoffman also explained to the International Chamber of Commerce, "It is the encroachment of public enterprise upon the normal field of private enterprise which causes us concern."[49] Second, they realized that the U.S. business community was too disorganized, shortsighted, and unremittingly hostile to any and all forms of governmental interventionism to either deal with economic disruptions itself or actively shape national interventionism.[50] Indeed, the CED came to realize at least in part that the problems of business collective action were endemic to capitalism itself. As John Clark, a Columbia University economist, explained in a CED-sponsored monograph, forging class-conscious political action in a competitive market situation is problematic, since business executives must concern themselves first and foremost with their firm's profits and market position; yet, as Clark explained, "[A businessman] is not effectively safeguarding his individual business unless he is also working effectively to keep the system of which it is part in good working order." This lack of attention to the larger system concerned the CED, especially during wartime, because "businessmen were too busily engaged in the competitive struggle of capturing their share of the [wartime] activity financed by government funds to interest themselves in planning for the day when those funds would cease to flow."[51]

The CED hoped to counter the predatory, antistatist, and inherently anarchic character of the U.S. business community by organizing positive, business-centered solutions to imminent economic problems and by delineating and advocating a limited Keynesian role for the national state. "Business," Clark recommended, "needs to advocate sound public policies, to follow policies of its own which may support these public policies, and to adopt measures of its own which may reduce or forestall the need for public intervention." The CED therefore sponsored academic research efforts as intellectual grounding for their endeavors and operated through Jesse Jones's Department of Commerce to organize local affiliates throughout the nation through which businesses of all sizes could prepare for the difficulties of reconversion. Directing their educational efforts to national officials as well as to other businessmen, this corporate brain trust spearheaded the articulation of private remedies and a limited range of national policies to address the economic problems to come.[52]

CED leaders, for example, jumped into the national fray over reconversion as President Truman promoted the full employment bill. Paul Hoffman intervened with Truman on behalf of the CED, warning against precipitous action: "We do not yet have a clear conception of the responsibility which the Federal Government can and should assume in promoting abundant employment, nor do we have a comprehensive and coordinated program for meeting that responsibility." Hoffman recommended the creation of a "Presidential Full Employment Commission . . . to formulate a positive program which can be presented to you and the Congress at the earliest possible moment," and he reported that the CED "stands ready to make all of its facts and conclusions available, and to assist such a Commission in any way possible." Likewise, although at first the CED expressed some discomfort with what was seen as "an undue emphasis on deficit federal spending" and on governmental versus private-sector responsibility in Senator Murray's full employment bill, CED members themselves helped revise and see the bill through to passage. In the end, they were influential because they staked out a middle ground between antistatist advocates of laissez-faire and those stagnationists whose dark economic forecasts demanded more substantive governmental interventions, such as planning for public works.[53]

The CED's limited Keynesian prescriptions demonstrated a preference for reasonable, fair, and stable income taxes (as opposed to consumption or corporate taxes) alongside a flexible monetary policy (calibrated to meet the threats of recession and inflation) in contrast to the still limited but more statist fiscal policies relating to public works or public jobs programs. CED leaders feared that any but the most automatic fiscal mechanisms would progressively expand the national government's bureaucratic authority over the national economy; emphasizing tax and monetary policies, conversely, "would leave to the private sector the basic decisions about resource allocation, production, prices, and wages." As Paul Hoffman testified to the Senate committee considering the full employment bill: "I think, first of all, we ought to get this Budget made automatically stabilizing insofar as we can and only go on spending as a last resort."[54]

The CED's efforts to secure the benefits of national state interventionism while maintaining autonomous business privileges and prerogatives would, it turned out, mesh naturally with the efforts of those corporate internationalists in the executive branch who promoted postwar governance based on economic growth and international expansionism.[55] The CED successfully promoted the domestic component of this option during and after the war, thus demonstrating the ability of at least part of the U.S. business community to provide a substantive vision for the future rather than merely lobbying for or against particular measures introduced by state officials. Thus, despite its minority status within the business community, the CED devised its own alternative Keynesian program for the postwar era, organized a supportive coalition, and participated in policy formation to promote and develop a viable postwar consensus.[56]

▼ ▼ ▼

Despite public apprehensions and pressure by still-influential congressional liberals, military and corporate forces defeated WPB civilian-state reconversion planning while congressional conservatives and their business allies blocked most proposals for postwar domestic activism. The struggles over reconversion—the last battle of wartime mobilization—demonstrated the extent to which mobilization shifted the trajectory of statebuilding from the expansions in civilian-state authority begun during the New Deal to the industry-dominated corporatist tradition of the War Industries Board and the National Recovery Administration. Of course, wartime institutional shifts did not halt or reverse the development of national governance. On the contrary, the domestic military ascendancy, the successful military-corporate alliance, and the efforts of various corporate liberals provided the key ingredients for the postwar national security state. Military and corporate personnel together planned and promoted this national security rationale for expansive national state power.

Constructing Postwar Governance

• With the war, the military services assumed a central place in the national state, in many ways filling much of the space created and then vacated by the policies and personnel of New Deal domestic activism. In Samuel Huntington's words, World War II heralded "a remarkable revolution in the power and attitudes of the military" as they shouldered extensive new responsibilities and enjoyed unprecedented levels of public acclaim. Indeed, the military's domestic wartime ascendancy would be institutionalized after the war with the creation of the national security state. As Huntington relates, the military services "emerged as the supreme embodiment of national purpose." Although the ability of the military services to project their wartime power into the postwar era was partly predicated on the international ascendancy of the United States, it was also due to the strength and depth of wartime military-corporate relationships and to the dramatic expansion with the war of corporate political influence.[1]

War and the preparation for war provided the opportunity for corporate personnel to participate directly and indirectly in the formation of national policy. By exploiting increased governmental power for their own benefit and helping to block civilian-state control of mobilization, corporate executives influenced the trajectory of U.S. statebuilding. Some did so directly, through their official positions within mobilization, as they resisted civilian-state personnel and supported military-state authority instead; some, indirectly, from within their firms, by simply refusing to cooperate with civilian-state personnel during the crucial early defense period of mobilization. Still other corporate personnel from prominent industrial and financial firms gained power and position within the top levels of national civilian and military administration, learning along the way that they need not fear growing national state power, especially when that power was lodged with the military services or with themselves.

Besides the increases in military and corporate influence, the war in general initiated a conservative trend in U.S. politics, especially as the election of 1942 elevated conservative southern Democrats to key leadership positions in Congress. Retrenchment of New Dealer civilian-state authority thus proceeded during the war, reversing the expansionary political dynamics of the New Deal decade and preparing the ground, as it were, for a conservative settlement of the New Deal political stalemate. Of course, while domestic national activism was thus curtailed, wartime shifts set the stage for a new kind of national activism, founded on the military and corporate domination of mobilization.

The Turn to Internationalism

The war may have replaced the depression as the focus for governmental activity, but it neither supplanted depression-era fears of economic instability nor ended depression-era conflicts over the organization of governance. So, as the war wound down, national state officials returned to the unresolved and interrelated problems of national governance and economic stability, especially as those concerns pertained to the immediate problems of sustaining the domestic economy and rebuilding the international economy. On one side, emboldened congressional conservatives allied with conservative business and sectional forces believed economic stability could best be achieved by rolling back recent expansions in national domestic activism in order to ensure that economic decisions would be left to private business forces. On the other, congressional New Dealers allied with organized labor and a liberal intelligentsia promoted the institutionalization of some form of domestic planning through their full employment bill. Yet neither the conservative plan nor the New Dealer project proved capable of a decisive victory; instead, their relative weakness provided an opportunity for a third, more powerful, state-class alliance to harness the domestic and international shifts occasioned by the war.

Domestically, the defeat of both the peacetime use of wartime controls and a substantive extension of the New Deal via the original full employment bill left a vacuum that the military-corporate alliance, forged during the war, could now fill with an alternative governance project. Internationally, the collapse of the European powers and the ascendance of the United States as the world economic and military power provided an opportunity too attractive and dangerous not to exploit.

Still, the turn to internationalism and the establishment of the national security state represented a substantial and dramatic break with the past, despite the fact that expansion into the domestic and international "frontier" had for some time been a standing strategy for securing U.S. economic stability. Building postwar governance in terms of a national security state now emerged as a logical outgrowth of the war and offered both New Dealers and conservatives something they could support: economic growth through U.S. dominance in world markets, undergirded by a form of national activism that would pose little threat to business or sectional prerogatives.[2]

A coalition of national officials and internationally minded corporate liberals (operating within and outside of government) understood the need to reorganize U.S. governance around internationalism and national security. By the end of the war, worries about the domestic economy became merged, for these men, with concerns for the international trading system and apprehensions about U.S.-Soviet relations, all of which called for a particular type of strong interventionist state. Just as corporate liberals in the Committee for Economic Development (CED) recognized the need for some limited national fiscal/monetary countercyclical policy to stabilize the postwar domestic economy, key national officials and corporate liberals within, or in contact with, the Roosevelt and Truman administrations realized the dangers represented by any return to the statist economic autarky of the 1930s. Rebuilding an open international trading system therefore topped the agenda for these men. Yet the Bretton Woods agreements of 1945 that laid the basis for an international monetary system capable of sustaining multilateral trade represented only the beginning of what would be necessary to truly rebuild world trade. To consolidate America's new international hegemony, this beginning, however important, needed to be buttressed by a major reorientation of U.S. national governance. But an internationalist governance project remained relatively undeveloped and unarticulated in the immediate aftermath of the war; there was no functional, lockstep march from wartime institutional and political shifts to the national security state, military Keynesianism, and the military-industrial complex. Rather, a dramatically shifting domestic-political and international-strategic context made the construction of any coherent governance project extremely problematic. Still, we can easily discern a more or less steady process of political learning in the course of which national officials at the apex of U.S. politics built upon the dramatic domestic changes initiated during the war to provide a more or less coherent resolution to both the long-standing dilemma of U.S. statebuilding and the strategic problem of securing U.S. international hegemony. As it worked out, solving the second problem would pave the way for resolving the first.[3]

The most pressing strategic international problem for government officials provided the opportunity to develop this dual solution: Europe needed to be stabilized, economically and politically. Rebuilding the economies of Europe would provide both an outlet for the built-up industrial capacity of the United States and foreclose on the attractiveness of the Left in Europe. These two goals became interrelated for policy makers who feared that the postwar suffering in Europe would spawn leftist regimes that would close off national markets in an autarkic pursuit of economic stability and then eventually be incorporated within the Soviet orbit. In the face of this international policy problem, a uniquely political resolution to the problems of domestic governance was fashioned, based on the domestic-institutional and international-strategic shifts of World War II.[4]

Although traditional business interests, together with conservatives in Congress, combined to block particular policy options like the full employment bill, they were much less capable of producing positive options for future policies. Corporate internationalists serving in the executive branch, however, together with interested corporate liberals in organizations like the CED, were able to prod President Truman into making the necessary economic and military commitments to Europe. Truman, new to the presidency and in need of close support from trusted advisors, gradually replaced most of Roosevelt's staunch New Deal advisors with associates who were much less committed to any form of programmatic liberalism, although he did retain a number of conservative Roosevelt advisors who were outspoken corporate internationalists. Most of these men came from Wall Street banks or New York and Washington law firms and therefore had significant commitments to strengthening international capitalism.[5] "They were," as Kim Mc-Quaid explains, "essential to postwar policy and process." For them, economic interest and geopolitical concerns naturally meshed. Corporate bankers, Lynn Eden points out, were especially influential as political advisors, since they were "in a strategic location to take the long-range view of the requirements of American capitalism." And as a group these men saw Europe as the linchpin of their hopes and fears.[6] Truman's corporate internationalist advisors would be seconded in this view by corporate liberals from the CED, as the latter's statement on behalf of the Marshall Plan indicates:

> How important is European recovery and development to the American people? How important would a prosperous Europe be for our trade? Before the war a third of our exports went to Western Europe and a fifth of our imports came from there. Prosperity in both Europe and America will mean the reestablishment on a normal basis of this important part of our trade. We need have no fear that the development of Western Europe will reduce our markets. History clearly shows that, the greater the industrialization of a country, the larger is our trade with it. How important is a strong free Europe for our security? Where would we have been if we had

fought Hitler alone? What happens to Western Civilization if it goes down in Europe? Clearly these things cannot be measured, but equally clearly a strong free Europe is important to us.

. . . World Events will not allow us to live alone. The American people are closely tied to the maintenance of free peoples and a strong economy in Western Europe. Unless the European economy is making real progress, the basis of American freedom will be in danger.

Fashioning economic and political stability in Europe, in the context of an emerging east-west rivalry, would provide the organizing principle for a new governance project geared to international versus domestic activism and based on continuing extensive corporate autonomy, a business-friendly form of Keynesianism, and the national security state. The creators of this project neither themselves conceived it as simply one of strengthening international capitalism nor was it sold to the American public in this guise. Instead, focus was placed upon the strategic threat posed by the Soviet Union. The resulting strategic consensus served a distinct political function of ensuring internal state unity and securing societal acquiescence to the newly expanded national state.[7]

With the death of Roosevelt in March 1945, the burden for formulating postwar policy fell on President Truman's shoulders. In the immediate aftermath of the war, Truman turned his attention inward as the normal centrifugal dynamic of domestic U.S. politics began to erode the often forced harmony of wartime. Conservative and liberal-labor pressures building within his administration and in the national political scene along with his limited preparation for the job of president left Truman indecisive about the direction the country should take. But given the conservative drift of the immediate postwar period—characterized by a crisis-weary public, by the inflow of conservatives who continued to replace New Dealers in the key positions surrounding the president, and by resurgent and aggressive business conservatives fortifying an increasingly assertive conservative congressional coalition—Truman's equivocations reinforced both the trend toward conservatism and his own less-than-liberal predilections.[8]

A turning point was nonetheless reached when, at the end of 1945 and through 1946, almost five million workers went on strike demanding that the enormous corporate profits of wartime be finally translated into wage increases for workers. New Dealers, including Commerce Secretary Henry Wallace and Office of War Mobilization and Reconversion Deputy Director Robert Nathan, supported labor's call for wage increases without price hikes to reduce income inequality and help sustain the mass consumption necessary to stabilize the domestic economy. They argued that corporations could more than afford pay increases while the Office of Price Administration (OPA) held the line on price increases. Monopoly-sector, labor-intensive firms dominating the core manufacturing sector, however, would have none of this talk. Although wartime had taught them the value of responsible unionism, they wished to exploit the political and economic leverage they held in the immediate postwar period to further discipline organized labor and thereby protect themselves from labor's larger agenda: a larger national state presence in overall economic management, abridgement of management prerogatives, and redistribution of the nation's wealth.

For a time Truman wavered, caught between two powerful constituencies. In the spring of 1946, however, as congressional conservatives grew more aggressive and railroad workers and miners joined the strike wave, Truman sided with management. Despite corporate unwillingness to cooperate with the government's mediation efforts, Truman both denounced labor and relented on the issue of price control, allowing wage hikes to be paid for through price increases. As a result, OPA efforts to hold the line on prices were undermined and inflation soared, erasing much of the wage gains won in the first place.[9] Dispirited liberal forces then watched in dismay as Republicans gained control of both houses of Congress in the midterm elections of 1946. Although thereafter Truman recaptured at least a rhetorical commitment to domestic activism during the 1948 presidential campaign, his preoccupation with foreign policy matters from this point forward, together with the Republican congressional victories, spelled the end to domestic activism.[10]

Besides being pressured by conservatives on the domestic front, Truman was relentlessly harried in these initial years of his presidency by the isolationist call of both Congress and large sectors of the public to bring the troops home and demobilize the military machine. His advisors, however, presented ever more alarmist reports about the devastation in Europe and the probability that the Soviets would exploit the situation. Keen to secure his domestic base, Truman acquiesced to pressures for quick military demobilization while continuing his search for a way to promote U.S. commitments abroad. Eventually, he would escape the dilemma of domestic versus international commitments, and the yawning trap of domestic political polarization, by mobilizing both Congress and public opinion around the need to confront a new implacable enemy, the Soviet Union. Historian Melvin Leffler's assertion that "identification of the Soviet Union as the enemy eased U.S. policymaking" is something of an understatement; it also eased the burdens of governance for Truman and made it possible to develop a governance project capable of unifying the U.S. state system.[11]

The Truman Doctrine and the New Project of Anticommunism

Having lost the domestic front to the Republicans and their conservative allies in the 1946 midterm elections, Truman seemed more than happy to turn his attention to foreign policy and international politics. He did not have to wait long for an international crisis to present itself, as the British informed U.S. officials on 21 February 1947 that they would soon withdraw their military forces supporting the repressive yet pro-West Greek government in its civil war against determined leftist partisans. For Truman's advisors, it became imperative that the United States fill the vacuum created by the British withdrawal.

Truman, however, faced the exacting task of securing a huge appropriation for foreign aid from a Republican Congress committed to fiscal conservatism, economic nationalism, and political isolationism, despite their inflamed anticommunist rhetoric. Truman's advisors had themselves only recently arrived at an intellectual consensus on anticommunism with the arrival of George Kennan's famous telegram outlining the case for viewing the Soviet Union as an incorrigible threat to U.S. security. Although for Congress and the U.S. public anticommunism remained an unthinking and emotional reflex, now the ideological and geopolitical certainties of men like James Forrestal, Kennan's key sponsor and patron in Washington, had to be broadly imparted and disseminated to secure both public acquiescence and intragovernmental unity.[12]

Truman's internationalist advisors thus used the Greek crisis to transform the public's anticommunist reflex into a central motive force for a powerful new governance project.[13] Truman himself initiated the campaign by calling congressional leaders together and having his new secretary of state, George Marshall, and Marshall's under secretary, Dean Acheson, dramatize the situation for them. Republican senator Arthur Vandenberg, who personified the bipartisan approach to foreign policy and national security issues in the immediate postwar period, encouraged the president to present the issue to the American public as a matter of communist aggression that the United States as a nation must meet forcefully if it was not to suffer the fall of friendly nations. As reported by Acheson, the congressional leaders "were greatly shaken and impressed with this analysis and promised to support whatever measures should be necessary, *on the condition that* the President should explain the situation fully to Congress . . . and to the people. They felt that they could support such a program only if the public were apprised of the grim facts." Vandenberg, one participant remembered, famously instructed Truman that "the only way you are going to get this is to make a speech and scare the hell out of the country." Accordingly, Truman and his advisors immediately turned to this task:

> The President had been concerned from the beginning not so much about the decision he had to make regarding Greece and Turkey as about the extent to which Congress and the American people could be convinced that a program of aid was necessary. . . . [T]he President, Marshall, Acheson, Vandenberg, and the Cabinet as a whole had *emphasized the public approach.*

An ad hoc subcommittee of the State-War-Navy Coordinating Committee, itself an ad hoc group formed toward the end of the war to coordinate foreign and military policy, went to work on "the public approach." They sorted what was essentially a public relations task into the following objectives:

> 1. To make possible the formulation of intelligent opinions by the American people on the problems created by the present situation in Greece through the furnishing of full and frank information by the Government.
> 2. To portray the world conflict between free and totalitarian or imposed forms of government.
> 3. To bring about an understanding by the American people of the world strategic situation.[14]

State Department personnel who began work on Truman's address were informed by one of Acheson's aides that "this was certainly the most important thing that had happened since Pearl Harbor." Clark Clifford, close advisor to Truman, ignored concerns that an "all-out" speech against the Soviet Union seemed unwarranted in the absence of any recent hostile Soviet actions, instead declaring that the speech was an "opening gun in a campaign to bring people up to [the] realization that *the war isn't over by any means.*" A full-scale public relations blitz of the nation's key opinion makers preceded Truman's crusading speech, which was aimed to persuade Congress and the U.S. public that the $400 million in military, political, and economic assistance to Greece and its neighbor, Turkey, was part of a greater struggle to confront the new Soviet enemy and so protect the national security of the United States. With the pronouncement of the Truman Doctrine, the anticommunist gauntlet had been thrown down, and Congress could do little else but follow their president's lead. The Truman Doctrine in turn launched the new consensus and the new governance project.[15]

The Marshall Plan and Economic Containment

Even as Truman and his advisors prepared for his speech, planning was underway for a larger and more comprehensive initiative for European assistance. Much of what became the Marshall Plan was in the works by the time Truman gave his speech on the Greek crisis. The task of planning a comprehensive approach for European assistance required Truman's advisors to harmonize any remaining differences about policy ends and means, and this task also furthered the process of centralizing the disparate efforts of various planning agencies. In the immediate postwar period, civilian State Department and military planners had operated independently of each other in an environment marred by organizational and policy disarray. General George Marshall, appointed secretary of state in January 1947, used his impeccable credentials and commanding stature to introduce order and to strengthen the chain of command within the State Department and over foreign policy in general; he began by consolidating authority in the hands of his under secretary, Dean Acheson, and consequently established a Policy Planning Staff (PPS) under George Kennan. Acheson in turn sought to increase civilian-military coordination by proposing to Patterson and Forrestal, now secretaries of war and the navy, that the special State-War-Navy Coordinating Committee (SWNCC) be granted responsibility to frame a comprehensive foreign assistance program.[16]

The resulting SWNCC subcommittee's report, read and absorbed by Kennan's PPS, specifically linked U.S. global strategic and economic interests: "It is important to maintain in friendly hands areas which contain or protect sources of metals, oil, and other natural resources, which contain strategic objectives, or areas strategically located, which contain a substantial industrial potential, which possess manpower and organized military forces in important quantities, or which for political or psychological reasons enable the U.S. to exert a greater influence for world stability, security, and peace." The report also warned of an impending crisis in the ability of the U.S. to achieve its foreign strategic goals if Congress followed through on its intention to curtail foreign aid. A reduction in aid for 1948 and 1949 would spell disaster for Europe and would "have a depressing effect on business activity and employment in the United States."[17] Coordinated planning by the Joint Chiefs of Staff and Kennan's PPS focused primarily on Western European nations, given these nation's developed industrial, manpower, and military resources and their current exposure to direct Soviet influence and indigenous leftist forces. Kennan picked up these policy threads and gave them shape, but it was Under Secretary of State Will Clayton—conservative Democrat, former Liberty Leaguer, and "the world's richest cotton merchant"—who upon his return from Europe in May 1947 spelled out the dire situation in bold relief: "Without further prompt and substantial aid . . . economic, social, and political disintegration will overwhelm Europe. Aside from the awful implications which this political disintegration would have for the future peace and security of the world, the immediate effects on our domestic economy would be disastrous: markets for our surplus production gone, unemployment, depression, a heavily unbalanced budget on the background of a mountainous war debt."[18]

So, once the Greek crisis provided the first opportunity for Truman to dramatize to the American public the need for a coherent anticommunist policy, the Marshall (European Recovery) Plan, promoted throughout late 1947 and early 1948, took center stage in U.S. politics. Likewise, economic containment of the European Left and the Soviet Union through Marshall Plan reconstruction aid became the centerpiece of the rapidly unfolding new governance project. The plan was first and foremost an economic program designed to revive the economies of Western Europe, a principal goal for reviving world trade and facilitating American exports. The politics of growth could not be secured if Western Europe became, owing to dire economic circumstances, a series of closed national markets. Moreover, as historian David Eakins has observed, "Foreign aid [through programs such as the Marshall Plan] was . . . government compensatory spending that avoided a revived New Deal at home." But the plan was also viewed as a mechanism to influence European politics and prevent gains by leftist forces. In fact, given the reemerging isolationism of the American public and the expected opposition to such massive foreign aid in Congress, the Marshall Plan and, with it, the new governing project both had to be sold as anticommunist measures. Of course, the economic and political dimensions of the plan coalesced in the minds of its supporters. Former dollar-a-year man Philip Reed of General Electric, as a member of the CED's European Relief and Rehabilitation Subcommittee, even remarked, "As we all know, one of our objectives is to prevent Communism from infiltrating Western Europe. Another one is in our own interest to prevent Europe, if we can, from becoming an economic cesspool, which we cannot deal with and which, whether we like it or not, would certainly affect the standard of living in this country."[19]

However necessary it appeared to corporate internationalists and corporate liberals, the magnitude of the Marshall Plan roused concerns among congressional conservatives, who were quick to exploit fears of foreign aid as the proverbial wasteful "rat hole" and to pounce on the plan as a form of international New Dealism. In response, various groups of ascendant political and economic elites were mobilized to build public and congressional support, creating, in effect, a powerful coalition around the new governance project itself. Dean Acheson, for the moment a private citizen back at his Washington law firm, formed the Citizens' Committee for the Marshall Plan, chaired by former Secretary of War Robert Patterson with former Secretary of State and War Henry Stimson serving as honorary chair. The committee built a solid front among the internationalist corporate elite and drew in organized labor and agriculture as well as other important groups—support came from both the American Federation of Labor and the Congress of Industrial Organizations, from the Veterans of Foreign Wars, and from the American Farm Bureau Federation. Support also came from the Americans for Democratic Action (ADA), an influential cold war organization that had come to house most of the New Deal liberals. The ADA's support signified the extent to which the burgeoning conflict with the Soviet Union refocused the liberal intelligentsia upon international concerns and provided the occasion for many liberals to make their peace with the U.S. corporate order.[20]

These efforts were supplemented by the activities of three committees appointed by President Truman: a bipartisan President's Committee on Foreign Aid under Secretary of Commerce Averell Harriman that included financial, business, and farm leaders (almost half of its 19 members were connected to the CED), to study the broad aspects of aid and the "limits within which the U.S. may safely and wisely plan to extend such assistance"; the Nourse Committee, essentially the Council of Economic Advisors, to study the impact of U.S. aid on European nations; and the Krug Committee (headed by Interior Secretary Julius Krug, former head of the WPB) to analyze the ability of the United States to finance the Marshall Plan. Marshall himself reported, "The selling of the ERP to the American people was an exacting task and I traveled so widely that in this regard it almost seemed as though I were running for office. I had good success in enlisting the cooperation of special interest groups."[21]

Truman's advisors, taking no chances, also relied directly upon business groups for support. For example, the Washington director of the Committee for the Marshall Plan recalled:

> One of the strong supporting groups was the National Cotton Council. I remember a meeting after their board of directors had voted to go all out for it. They had a delegation in every state who knew the key financial backers of each congressman. "Don't worry," they said, "we'll give it the same treatment that we did Taft-Hartley."

In addition, Schriftgiesser and others have documented the critical role the CED and other business groups played in lobbying to secure the congressional compromises critical to the bill's passage. In turn, one of the CED's leaders, Paul Hoffman, became the first administrator of the agency specially designed to administer the plan, the Economic Cooperation Administration (ECA), and recruited other CED businessmen as his top lieutenants. The ECA was established as a concession to congressional Republicans fearful of an international New Deal; Republicans wanted to prevent the politicization of the program by the State Department and to emphasize private sector—especially corporate—management of Europe's economic recovery. These corporatist arrangements thus found their place in the long train of such arrangements from the War Industries Board to the WPB and directly connected the CED's planning efforts to the developing postwar governance project.[22]

Despite all these efforts to create and mobilize support for the Marshall Plan, the odds that the bill establishing it and setting it into motion would pass unscathed were slim. 1948 was an election year, and Truman's approval rating had plummeted. In the Senate and especially in the House, hostile amendments and delaying actions threatened Truman's timetable for European aid. In response, Secretary of State Marshall and others prepared to exploit the situation in Czechoslovakia, where on 25 February the Czech Communist Party overtly consolidated its control of the government and, two weeks later, the Czech Foreign Minister Jan Masaryk died under suspicious circumstances. Although these developments were certainly viewed as alarming, historian Frank Kofsky has persuasively argued from primary documents that "in no way" did the Truman administration regard "the Communist accession in Czechoslovakia as a prelude to war." Yet Marshall, at a press conference, alluded to the "reign of terror" unleashed by the events in Czechoslovakia, and he and Truman subsequently continued to insist in their public statements on the need for timely passage of the European Recovery Plan as a way of forestalling other such communist advances.[23]

On the heels of the Czech "crisis" came the famous telegram from General Lucius Clay, army chief of the U.S. zone in Germany, that intimated war seemed likely. Now recognized as pure contrivance, the telegram's vague warnings were immediately used by James Forrestal and others to increase the sense of emergency. Public anxiety mounted, and despite Republican Senator Robert Taft's public questioning of the administration's hysterical response the Senate hastily passed the ERP. Eventually, following Marshall's testimony before the Senate Foreign Relations Committee and an address by Truman before a joint session of Congress, the House passed the ERP as well. Moreover, despite Marshall's subsequent attempt to cool the crisis—out of fear that Congress might decide to replace economic aid with military assistance—the military services saw their opening and got into the anticommunist act themselves. Thus, as a bonus to passage of the ERP, Congress came forward with a new military draft and increased military appropriations.[24]

Of course, during the immediate postwar period, economic containment of the Soviet Union through Marshall Plan aid was certainly more acceptable to Congress and to the American public than the alternative of renewed military mobilization. First, the threat at this point was interpreted as political and not military.[25] U.S. intelligence revealed what was obvious to all observers: the Soviet Union had been terribly devastated during the war and would need a significant number of years before it could afford to engage in any type of military confrontation. Second, U.S. civilian and military officials felt fairly secure in their atomic monopoly, and Truman faced enormous domestic pressures for military demobilization both to help balance the budget and to address the fear of many business interests that continued high military expenditures combined with postwar inflation would necessitate a return to wartime economic controls. Third, military leaders remained, for a time, preoccupied with growing interservice rivalries over both decreasing military expenditures and a proposed new military establishment.[26] Fourth, corporate elites inside and outside of the Truman administration preferred economic containment to military containment at this time, since the former maximized reliance upon international corporations and minimized statist developments potentially hostile to private corporate power. Economic containment was thus viewed by a powerful bloc of state and class forces as a necessary first step to increasing the security of Western European nations plagued by political and economic woes. The battle had to be won on the economic and political front first, it was thought, or the result might be increasing statism in Europe or, worse yet, closed economic blocs under the sway of the Soviet Union. The United States, it was feared, would then be forced both to regiment its own economy as world trade withered and to cultivate militarism at home to counter growing Soviet might and influence abroad. Either alternative would disrupt what Truman's corporate advisors saw as the accepted balance of power between state and society in the United States.[27]

Still, despite the political and economic focus of official thinking, the increasingly alarmist rhetoric about an implacable communist threat prepared the American public for military remobilization and for a shift to military containment of the Soviet Union.[28] For key officials, in fact, military might went hand in hand with economic containment, as two halves of the same strategy. Secretary of the Navy James Forrestal noted this when he spoke to the House Armed Services Committee on behalf of the Marshall Plan:

> We hope to prevent a war, by creating a political and economic and social stability which will make it possible to maintain peace—but we also hope, if war should eventually come . . . that we will have in Western Europe allies instead of enemies. This part of the answer to "What do we do?" has come to be known as the "Marshall Plan." . . . As I have mentioned, it is only one part of the answer. Still another part of the answer is our military strength.[29]

Economic containment of the Soviet Union had never stood alone; military assistance to Europe had always constituted part of the aid program. U.S. officials first agreed to military assistance as part of the ERP to allay French fears about the reintegration of Germany and possible Soviet retaliation. Subsequently, the Senate Vandenberg resolution on 11 June 1948 committed the United States to a policy of mutual aid with Western European nations, who had previously organized a collective defense agreement under the Brussels Pact. The Vandenberg resolution represented a direct precursor to the North Atlantic Treaty Organization (NATO), which Truman referred to as "the first peacetime military alliance concluded by the United States since the adoption of the Constitution." The Soviet blockade of Berlin and the resulting airlift beginning 18 June 1948 then provided the impetus for the formal creation of the Western military alliance. Thus, while economic aid emerged as the first and highest priority of U.S. national officials, the way to it was paved and purchased by an anticommunist fervor that sanctioned first an ongoing state of high military readiness and ultimately a return to military mobilization.[30]

National Security Act of 1947

Remobilization and rearmament, when they came, would find new national security organizational structures already in place as a result of the National Security Act of July 1947. The end of the war brought a reassessment of the wartime military structure. Obviously, an overhaul was needed. Army and navy wartime reorganizations had served, in effect, as short-term solutions to longer-term problems. Even Ferdinand Eberstadt's sympathetic 1945 evaluation of the military's wartime performance concluded that the services' record on procurement, logistics, and strategic planning left much to be desired. Besides these problems, issues related to the wartime Joint Chiefs of Staff and to the emergence of an independent and forceful Army Air Corps needed attention. It became clear to many that the military's entire organizational structure would need serious reevaluation once the war ended. Army Chief of Staff George Marshall and other forces in the army began in 1943 to identify the need for improved interservice cooperative relations, joint control, and unified command. Fearing as well postwar budgetary constraints and the inevitable interservice competition, Marshall became an early proponent of military unification. As Forrestal recorded in his diary on 9 May 1945, "Marshall continued to express his fear of the starvation of the Army in another period of peace." After the humbling demobilization of the army after the First World War, Marshall wanted to unite the services both for improved coordination and cooperation during the postwar period and to limit interservice competition for congressional favor in order to protect the army's budgetary position.[31]

In response to Marshall's proposal to unify the War and Navy Departments into a single military department, James Forrestal, then secretary of the navy, appointed his close friend Ferdinand Eberstadt to produce an alternative unification plan respectful of navy prerogatives. Thanks to both his connection to Forrestal and the growing navy resistance to Marshall's plan, Eberstadt came to exercise enormous influence over military unification. Forrestal and the navy hierarchy worried that under the army unification plan the navy would be subordinated and weakened.[32] Given the promotion of the air force and strategic bombing as an efficient and economical alternative to a large postwar navy, they particularly feared the increasing political influence of an independent air force within a unified command structure. Eberstadt, moreover, remained deeply concerned about the larger questions of state power and New Deal statism, fearing both that the plan offered by Marshall concentrated too much power in the military and that Truman would use unification to promote New Deal civilian-state authority. Either way, for Eberstadt the plans under consideration entailed a dangerous centralization of state power. Viewing the defense reorganization fight as a continuation of the wartime struggle between New Dealers and corporate dollar-a-year advisors over the future organization of U.S. governance, Eberstadt saw an opportunity to institutionalize the wartime corporate-government partnership and so anchor expanding state power to a knowledgeable and trustworthy corporate elite.[33]

For Eberstadt and Forrestal as well as for most of the corporate internationalists operating within the top levels of the Truman administration, there was no question but that the extensive military-corporate partnership that operated so effectively during the war would continue to play a large role in the postwar period. For it to do so, however, foreign policy had to be reconstructed in terms of new national security precepts linking U.S. international hegemony to the righteous labor of resisting Soviet communism. U.S. national officials developed "a sense of mission, historical necessity, and evangelical fervor" that posited the United States as the champion of freedom and democracy—a role that implied a readiness to intervene with force anywhere and anytime that these values were threatened. Such a militarization of foreign policy required in its turn a comprehensive and permanent mobilization for war, given both the nature of modern, total war and the aggressive, hostile, and untrustworthy intentions of the new Soviet enemy.[34]

Thus wartime corporatism continued into the postwar period as an apparently permanent precondition for U.S. international hegemony, and the struggle over postwar military unification came to embody this larger project. Forrestal, echoing Eberstadt's sentiments, wrote to Truman aide Clark Clifford on 7 September 1946, emphasizing: "Unification is *not* merely a matter of Army and Navy and Air Forces—it is the whole complex of our national, economic, military and political power."[35] U.S. national security required full-scale reconstruction of the national administration based upon the new international mission of the United States and upon the successes and acknowledged weaknesses of the recent mobilization experience. As the release prepared to accompany Eberstadt's final report avowed: "Our present situation calls for action far more drastic and far-reaching than unification of the military services. It calls for *a complete realignment of our governmental organization to serve our national security* in the light of our new world power and position, our new international commitments and the epochal new scientific discoveries." For Eberstadt and Forrestal, the touchstone for this "complete realignment" would be the recent corporatist experience of the war; the postwar reconstruction of the national state meant institutionalizing successful and effective working relationships but also rectifying the "serious weaknesses both between and within the services and in their relationships to other important elements concerned with national security [that] were revealed during World War II." And for Eberstadt and Forrestal national security required that military policy be coordinated and integrated with intelligence, scientific, economic, and diplomatic policies to sustain U.S. international hegemony. As Eberstadt's report puts it:

The question of the form of organization of our military forces must be viewed in its proper perspective as only one part of a much larger picture encompassing many elements, military and civilian, governmental and private, which will contribute to our national security and defense. . . .

Our goal should be to bind them together in such a way as to achieve the most productive and harmonious whole. . . .

The necessity of integrating all these elements into an alert, smoothly-working and efficient machine is more important now than ever before.[36]

For Eberstadt and many others in the top echelons of the corporate and political elite, to strengthen the national state for a worldwide confrontation with communism without upsetting the balance of power between state and society meant formalizing the lessons of the War Industries Board and extending the military-corporate partnership of World War II. These experiences and this partnership had demonstrated that a strong national state and various corporate elites could reinforce and augment their shared and separate powers. Eberstadt and others wanted a strong, rationalized national administrative apparatus able to coordinate and promote corporate internationalism and U.S. international hegemony. But they wanted this apparatus insulated from the pluralistic competition and popular control that might dilute its strength and undercut its effectiveness. The strong national security coordinating apparatus they called for would thus be linked to private corporate power but insulated from other parts of state and society. For example, Eberstadt envisioned a permanent system of coordinating agencies staffed whenever possible by skilled corporate managers reliant upon advisory committees representative of major economic sectors. As historian Jeffrey Dorwart concludes, "Eberstadt's plan would create paths through which business could dominate national security."[37]

Thanks to his experiences chairing the Senate special committee investigating wartime mobilization, President Truman remained highly skeptical of the industry-dominated corporatist arrangements of World War II and feared for presidential prerogatives under Eberstadt's corporatist schemes. As protectors of presidential authority, Truman's two directors of the Bureau of the Budget, Harold Smith and James Webb, resisted many of Eberstadt's proposals, particularly the proposal for a Council of Common Defense, or what would come to be called the National Security Council. For example, Smith, a proponent of a "single [military] department under a single Secretary," protested the Eberstadt report's tendencies toward "divesting the President of authority and responsibility" and toward giving "the military an undue control . . . over foreign policy." "The great danger in the whole approach," he declared, "is that the formulation of basic national policy will be dominated by the military under the guise of a civilian committee structure."[38]

Actually, as Dorwart has pointed out, Smith's interpretation of the unification controversy in terms of a military-civilian conflict was misleading insofar as proponents of both the army (Marshall) and navy (Eberstadt) plans argued for strong civilian stewardship.[39] Yet Eberstadt's plan so completely reconstructed U.S. governance in terms of military necessities and so emphatically placed military concerns at the top of the national agenda that Smith's misinterpretation was understandable. As Huntington and just about every other observer would recognize, the new pattern was clear: "Military requirements . . . became a fundamental ingredient of foreign policy and military men and institutions acquired authority and influence far surpassing that ever previously possessed by military professionals on the American scene." Still, just as the military's domestic wartime ascendancy was underpinned by corporate support, so too was the extensive influence Eberstadt planned for the military in postwar governance closely tied to a corporate-dominated corporatism. Indeed, in Eberstadt's view, the risks of expanding military authority would be minimized by the business-dominated corporatist arrangements to which such authority would be anchored within the national state.[40]

With his own administration divided over military unification, Truman, in his Special Message to Congress on 19 December 1945, acceded to some aspects of Eberstadt's plans, including the argument that unification be taken up together with the larger issues of science, mobilization, and foreign policy. Although he accepted the broader goals of unification, however, he rejected the corporatist arrangements Eberstadt had elucidated. Angered and disappointed, Eberstadt, Forrestal, and other supporters of Eberstadt's plan continued to promote these arrangements throughout the next year and a half of legislative and bureaucratic trench warfare—including bitter interservice feuds over the division of military responsibilities, a single secretary of defense, the role of supportive, coordinating agencies, and presidential power and responsibility. In the end, to salvage his demand for a single defense secretary, Truman would have to accept most of the arrangements called for in the original Eberstadt report.[41]

The resulting National Security Act of 1947 emphasized the broader aspects of unification, specifically calling for close and constant integration of domestic, military, and foreign policies at the highest levels of the national state. Enacting legislatively the majority of the corporatist arrangements Eberstadt espoused, the act went a long way in attempting to institutionalize the mobilization experience of World War II. Title I provided for a National Security Council (NSC) with advisory authority to organize and coordinate this top-level integration (in essence picking up where the State-War-Navy Coordinating Committee left off).[42] Specifically, the NSC would "assess and appraise the objectives, commitments, and risks of the United States in relation to our actual and potential military power" and "to consider policies on matters of common interest to the Department of State, the National Military Establishment and the National Security Resources Board [NSRB]." Also called for was a Central Intelligence Agency to provide the NSC with timely and adequate intelligence regarding the political intentions and military capabilities of other nations. The act drew heavily on the experience of wartime mobilization. Title I created the NSRB, designed to advise the president concerning the integration of military, industrial, and civilian mobilization. The NSRB would plan for military and civilian mobilization and, in the event of an emergency, take charge of domestic mobilization. Title II created the National Military Establishment (NME), consisting of three military departments (the air force now being elevated to department status), and a War Council to coordinate these departments under the direction of a single secretary of defense. The NME also included the Joint Chiefs of Staff to serve as professional military advisors to the president. Originally created during World War II and now given legal status, the Joint Chiefs enjoyed a status similar to the secretary of defense. Title II also provided for a Munitions Board (exercising responsibilities similar to the wartime Army-Navy Munitions Board) and the Research and Development Board (exercising responsibilities similar to the wartime Office of Scientific Research and Development).[43]

While requiring amendments in 1949 and operational changes to correct flaws that showed up in various crises to come, the National Security Act modernized the U.S. military establishment and created a permanent apparatus for top-level coordination of national security. Creation of this domestic-institutional apparatus, largely based on lessons taken from the experience of World War II, would be the first step in refitting the national state to meet the evolving security needs identified by national state officials and defined by the Truman Doctrine. In a reversal of the 1930s template, the national state reoriented its energies from domestic to international activism, reducing domestic employment, relief, and planning commitments while building a powerful national state apparatus around military and foreign policy commitments.[44]

The Truman Doctrine, asserting the right of the United States to intervene anywhere threatened by communist aggression, provided the ideological justification for the new internationalism at the heart of the Marshall Plan and the security justification for the passage of the National Security Act.[45] Likewise, it provided the strategic justification for the shift from economic to military containment. The recession of 1948–1949 raised fears about the continuing ability of Europe to absorb the U.S. domestic productive surplus. This, in turn, triggered concerns that the aid flowing under the Marshall Plan would not stabilize Europe by the time of its expected termination in 1952. The resolution to this dilemma was provided by the "massive U.S. and European rearmament" justified by the expanding cold war, by domestic anticommunist hysteria, and by the Korean War.[46] After NATO was formed, Acheson wrote

Truman to report on the "political and economic success in Europe and successful containment of Communist expansion elsewhere." But he warned: "Much of the impetus behind this movement derives from the belief abroad . . . that these moves would be further supported by the provision of military assistance. An inadequate program would be interpreted by our friends as a withdrawal of our support and leadership, and by the Soviet Union as a weakening of our will to resist its expansion." Although Congress would allocate less than administration officials had requested, the amount of aid appropriated was still $1 billion above regular military appropriations. A few years later the Korean War accelerated the shift from economic to military aid in Europe and sped up domestic rearmament. Rearmament provided a mechanism for continuing aid to Western Europe, allowing both economic and political stabilization to be financed by U.S. dollars.[47]

Meanwhile, any fear that the extensive military remobilization would disrupt the balance of power between state and society was resolved by the very premises of military Keynesianism. Rearmament nourished the domestic economy on terms decidedly favorable to the U.S. monopolysector firms, who were its prime beneficiaries. Military spending would pump capital into the U.S. economy without the national state interfering with market relationships or with corporate managerial prerogatives. As Gunnar Myrdal observed in 1944, "Armament as well as the methods of carrying it through are accepted by business as being a prudent and necessary national policy—which cannot be said regarding the New Deal, despite its moderation." *Business Week* lauded the potential of military Keynesianism in early 1949, before the Korean War began, by comparing it to an altogether more invidious social Keynesianism:

> Military spending doesn't really alter the structure of the economy. It goes through the regular channels. As far as business is concerned, a munitions order from the government is much like an order from a private customer.
>
> But the kind of welfare and public-works spending that Truman plans [through the Fair Deal] does alter the economy. It makes new channels of its own. It creates new institutions. It redistributes income.[48]

Although military Keynesianism and the military-industrial complex did not come into full flower until the early 1950s, these keystones of the postwar U.S. economy and polity were rooted in the institutional, programmatic, and ideological outcomes of wartime mobilization and reconversion struggles.

Conclusion

The Warfare-Welfare State

Calvin Coolidge would be utterly bewildered by the Washington scene today. American government has become a global operation. We have troops stationed in Germany in peacetime. The fleet is in the Mediterranean. United States military bases ring the world. All has been done in spite of a strong isolationist political tradition, in spite of intense opposition to the expansion of governmental functions, in spite of strenuous opposition to high taxes and in spite of a labyrinthine governmental structure almost perfectly designed for obstruction. As a matter of fact, the changes in the regime could hardly have been greater if we had had a violent revolution. *How did it happen?*

—E. E. Schattschneider, 1960[1]

• The national security "warfare" state, which forty years ago evoked such wonder from E. E. Schattschneider, today remains at the core of U.S. national governance. Established in the wake of World War II's wartime mobilization effort, this conservative consolidation of national authority resolved the New Deal political stalemate by limiting the democratic challenge to private corporate power. This study has offered an answer to Schattschneider's question by focusing on the successful wartime military-corporate alliance—the basis of the national security state that would later be built. This focus, of course, has meant expanding upon accepted institutionalist accounts of U.S. statebuilding, which tend to disregard the interplay of state and class forces. In general, we have seen that, while state officials are often the central agents in orchestrating resolutions to governance crises, these crises increase both intragovernmental and state-societal tensions, ensuring that the support or resistance of class forces will be crucial to successfully completing and legitimizing any reconstruction of the political order.

Through this broader understanding of statebuilding, the strengths and weaknesses of the New Deal are understood not only in terms of a vast internal governmental reconstruction but also in terms of the degree to which powerful state and class forces converged around specific institutional innovations and broader governance alternatives. Overall, the New Deal as an ongoing political project was successful in mediating for a time the economic and political crises of the 1930s. It was also successful in beginning a progressive redirection of U.S. political development through the passage of the National Labor Relations Act and the Social Security Act. Still, the New Deal failed to resolve either intragovernmental turmoil or the state-societal tensions caused by expanding national state power because too many of its innovations roused too much antagonism among powerful class forces (including business interests and the southern planter elite). Despite the many ongoing connections between national officials and representatives of various economic sectors during the 1930s, and despite the myriad ways that New Deal programs provided substantial benefits for both business and sectional interests, growing national state power appeared threatening to these class forces. Displeasure with the potentially democratizing and equalizing thrust of the New Deal reached a crescendo in the late 1930s, manifesting itself in executive-congressional conflicts and business-government tensions.

We have seen how business antagonisms combined with isolationism to limit Roosevelt's options as war increasingly displaced the depression as the central focus of governmental action. The shift to war and the necessities of mobilization enhanced the leverage of corporate executives from industry and finance who opposed New Dealer civilian-state control of wartime mobilization and supported the domestic military ascendancy. These executives, operating both from within their firms and industries and within military and civilian mobilization agencies, offered crucial support for military control of mobilization. Preoccupied with profits—especially after years of economic stagnation—and with the fear that New Dealers would exploit the war emergency to expand and extend national authority over corporate firms and the national economy, they resisted the extension of civilian-state authority. They also fought to retain as much authority as possible in their firms and trade associations and either acquiesced to or actively supported implementation of the relatively weaker and compliant version of mobilization authority promoted by the military services. Likewise, the corporate advisors dominating the top posts of the civilian and military agencies preferred military stewardship of mobilization because military plans called for extensive de facto reliance on the private capacities of corporate America. These combined corporate forces and efforts led to a significant shift in national authority as the military services displaced many of the New Deal interventionist agencies at the heart of the newly empowered national state apparatus.

As the war drew to a close, an increasingly influential and savvy military-corporate alliance defeated attempts to utilize wartime economic controls to stabilize the postwar economy. Meanwhile, a leading segment of corporate America also engaged in a deliberate effort to build upon the political and institutional shifts of wartime. The Committee for Economic Development (CED) organized a business-centered alternative to increasing domestic national interventionism. And corporate internationalists, as key advisors to Roosevelt and especially Truman, complemented the CED's work by helping to organize and construct postwar U.S. governance in terms of internationalism and a national security state. Thus, by playing such a key role in the statebuilding struggles of wartime, influential corporate personnel helped to pour the foundation for a national security state whose superstructure it subsequently helped to build.

To move now from *how* to *why* the U.S. consolidated national state authority around the national security state brings us back to the profound difficulties of constructing positive national governance in the United States. In general, expanding national state power threatened to disrupt relations of power in two interrelated ways: On the one hand, a strengthened national state tended to invigorate the presidency and displace Congress while strengthening the hold of the national government over the states; on the other, it threatened to disrupt or even displace the private prerogatives of powerful class forces. Given the stakes involved, any such proposed or attempted expansion of national governance was bound to ignite conflicts within, and over, the state system, providing a political flash point for conflicts between private power and democratic accountability. As we can now see, in the course of World War II these intragovernmental and state-societal tensions were contingently resolved as wartime mobilization enabled a military-corporate alliance to usher in the warfare state.

In hindsight, this resolution proves instructive as to the barriers to progressive and democratic governance in the United States. While the difficulties of formulating any stable governance are pronounced, the obstacles confronting the formulation of socially progressive projects are especially large and forbidding. Ironically, the fragmentation of the U.S. state system (horizontally in terms of the separation of powers and vertically in terms of federalism) does not prevent the use of state power, but it does help to block its democratization. Likewise, institutional fragmentation militates against progressive governance projects insofar as the difficulties of orchestrating intragovernmental unity often force state officials into alliances or compromises with powerful class forces to stabilize governance. These effects of fragmentation are, moreover, exacerbated in the United States by a dominant ideology that tends to restrict the legitimate exercise of state power to narrow parameters, which thereby further weakens the predisposition for initiating national programs that might interfere with business or sectional prerogatives. Add to these factors the traditional weakness of a labor force riven by ethnic, racial, and religious divisions, and we begin to see the difficulties for constructing progressive governance projects in the United States.

Then there is the factor of corporate-capitalist power. The institutional and ideological limitations noted above enhance the conspicuous leverage already enjoyed by U.S. corporations as a consequence of state officials' dependence upon private economic activity. Despite, or even because of, their conspicuous autonomy in the United States, corporate capitalists often resist expansions of state power that might impinge upon their prerogatives. They typically oppose various elements of the welfare state and other progressive regulatory policies insofar as these policies pose a democratic challenge to corporate prerogatives: by expanding political control of the economy and so subverting free market ideologies; by politicizing economic conflicts and thereby increasing the leverage of popular class forces; and, potentially, by redistributing income and wealth.

Realizing the direct and indirect threat posed by welfare and other progressive state policies, many business interests have resisted or sought to contain the extension of political-economic rights. Yet during the depression national state interventionism in market processes could not simply be resisted, especially considering the inability of the private economy to contain crises of social disruption and profitable accumulation. The war thus offered a crucial opportunity for national state officials, in close cooperation and collaboration with prominent corporate capitalists, to channel national interventionism into military and national security institutions. Nationally prominent corporate executives welcomed expanding military/national security institutional authority, because growth in this sector of the state neither directly threatened private corporate prerogatives nor enhanced, as did the New Deal, the political influence of popular class forces. In fact, national authority centered in national security institutions more often than not supplemented rather than threatened corporate autonomy.

Economic mobilization thus resulted in a paradoxical strengthening and weakening of the U.S. national state as it simultaneously diminished the threat of an expansive welfare state and channeled national state power into warfare state policies and institutions. Likewise, the military-state alternative that supplanted the New Deal substantially increased the capacity of the national state to intervene internationally while containing its ability to intervene domestically. The resulting warfare state was qualitatively different from the welfare and regulatory state undergoing construction during the New Deal. There was no simple transfer of New Deal state power to the national security state; it was, after all, precisely the democratizing elements of the New Deal that corporate executives involved in war mobilization hoped to defeat by fighting the expansion of civilian-state authority during the war.

Popular class forces certainly secured some basic gains in the immediate aftermath of the war, even though these gains themselves proved contradictory, containing weaknesses that would prevent further breakthroughs. The rudiments of a welfare state remained in place from the Social Security Act, although the bifurcation of social insurance from social welfare (which emphasized the distributive versus redistributive nature of the welfare state) and the decentralization of responsibility for social welfare programs weakened subsequent attempts to expand and universalize these programs. Similarly, though hemmed in by the postwar Taft-Hartley Act's revisions of the Wagner Act, organized labor would benefit from a limited postwar accord with management that tied wage gains and benefits to productivity increases, but the accord also formalized a less militant and more oligarchical union movement wedded to the maintenance of existing corporate prerogatives and to the warfare state. Finally, fears about postwar unemployment resulted in the G.I. Bill of Rights (the Servicemen's Readjustment Act), which secured housing, employment, and education benefits for a special class of Americans, and in a national commitment to employment embodied in the Employment Act, which remained significant despite having lost its institutional and programmatic teeth. Still, domestic policy logic in the postwar years remained biased against redistributive and nationally interventionist domestic policies as a truncated, bifurcated, and weak welfare state was vastly overshadowed by a strong warfare state that wedded economic security to national security (a trend that even survived the welfare state expansions and anti–Vietnam War protests of the 1960s and early 1970s). Of course, corporate participation in wartime and postwar statebuilding struggles accounts for the impressive ability of this national security state to encompass both the profit-making goals of corporate executives and the strategic goals of national officials in a governance project capable of uniting a fragmented and internally competitive state system and of solidifying the allegiances of a class-divided society to expansive national state power. In this sense, then, promoting a national security focus for U.S. national state power was integral to resolving both the depression-era intragovernmental and state-societal tensions and depression-era legitimation and accumulation dilemmas.

The national security warfare state became the preeminent legitimating institution of the postwar growth of national state power. Its ideological, programmatic, and institutional mechanisms—anticommunism, the defense establishment, the military-industrial complex, and military Keynesianism—absorbed much of the energies of postwar national state development. The warfare state accentuated the state's ideological and military capabilities while minimizing the need for popularly responsive regulatory and redistributive capabilities. Anticommunism provided cover for America's new international hegemonic role, supplied the political and ideological glue that unified, in a particular and peculiar way, the disparate and clashing elements of the U.S. state system and society, and laid the groundwork for an expanded state that both liberals and conservatives could accept. The state capabilities unleashed by anticommunism silenced or bought off most domestic critics. And most segments of the business community also accepted high military expenditures, some because they understood how a strong military could help secure access to foreign markets and government subsidies, others simply because they themselves were roused by the anticommunist crusade.

The construction of a warfare-dominated, warfare-welfare governance project strengthened, without democratizing, U.S. national state power, and this deployment of national authority has uniquely delimited, skewed, and distorted postwar U.S. national policy making and political development up to the present time. It is not simply a matter of trading military investments for social investments. Institutions and ideas matter. And the institutions and ideologies of the warfare-welfare governance project have imposed a distinctive, restrictive logic onto U.S. national political development as the major sectors of state and society settled into the rhythms and routines of anticommunism and national security. As a result, the welfare state became a weak adjunct to a powerful warfare state and a subordinate and controversial part of postwar U.S. governance. Grounded upon the twin goals of national security and profitable accumulation, the strong warfare–weak welfare state secured a powerful governance consensus for a particular type of extensive state intervention, one whose chillingly high degree of effectivity has often been masked by the weaknesses and incoherence of the domestic interventionist state. Thus, a nation that argues endlessly and often fruitlessly over controversial domestic policies—that appears to Stephen Skowronek as a "hapless administrative giant"—easily manages to mobilize itself for military adventures abroad and for huge military expenditures at home. Certainly, the military capabilities of the United States constitute one of the most impressive state capacities the world has seen.[2]

It may have been inevitable that U.S. national officials would exploit U.S. postwar international hegemony to resolve its domestic problems and so avoid the controversies associated with building domestic interventionism. But the choice to construct and rely on the internationally interventionist national security state reflects both the heavy influence of corporate power within the fragmented U.S. political order and the limits of political interventionism and democratic government in a capitalistic society. The national security state evolved according to its own internal rhythms and its own pathologies, but these rhythms and pathologies often intersected those of corporate America. This intersection can be traced to the wartime military-corporate alliance and to the restrictive statebuilding logic imposed by this alliance. Overcoming that logic will mean confronting both military and corporate predominance within the processes of U.S. national state power. Ultimately, it will also mean confronting the dilemmas of trying to reconcile assertive democratic national governance with private corporate power.

List of Abbreviations

AFL	American Federation of Labor
ANMB	Army-Navy Munitions Board
ASF	Army Service Forces (US Army)
BAC	Business Advisory Council
BOB	Bureau of the Budget
CED	Committee for Economic Development
CIO	Congress of Industrial Organizations
CND	Council of National Defense
IAC	Industry Advisory Committee
IMP	Industrial Mobilization Plan
NAM	National Association of Manufacturers
NDAC	National Defense Advisory Committee
NDMB	National Defense Mediation Board
NIRA	National Industrial Recovery Act
NLRB	National Labor Relations Board
NME	National Military Establishment
NRA	National Recovery Administration
NRPB	National Resources Planning Board
NSC	National Security Council
NWLB	National War Labor Board

NWMB	National War Mediation Board
OASW	Office of the Assistant Secretary of War
OCS	Office of Civilian Supply
OEM	Office of Emergency Management
OES	Office of Economic Stabilization
OPA	Office of Price Administration
OPACS	Office of Price Administration and Civilian Supply
OPD	Operations and Plans Division (US Army)
OPM	Office of Production Management
OP&M	Office of Procurement & Material (US Navy)
OUSW	Office of the Under Secretary of War
OWM	Office of War Mobilization
OWMR	Office of War Mobilization and Reconversion
PEC	Production Executive Authority
RFC	Reconstruction Finance Corporation
SOS	Services of Supply (US Army)
SPAB	Supply Priorities and Allocation Board
SWPC	Smaller War Plants Corporation
TNEC	Temporary National Economic Committee
USCOC	United States Chamber of Commerce
WIB	War Industries Board
WLB	War Labor Board
WMC	War Manpower Commission
WPB	War Production Board
WRB	War Resources Board

Notes

Introduction

1. C. Wright Mills certainly provided some analysis of the military-corporate alliance, although his analysis focused on the postwar implications of that alliance. See *The Power Elite* (New York: Oxford University Press, 1959). Recent studies of wartime statebuilding that downplay the impact of corporate power on wartime outcomes include Gregory Hooks, *Forging the Military-Industrial Complex: World War II's Battle of the Potomac* (Urbana: University of Illinois Press, 1991); Bartholomew Sparrow, *From the Outside In: World War II and the American State* (Princeton, N.J.: Princeton University Press, 1996).

2. Recent work that does acknowledge the importance of the national security state is Benjamin Fordham, *Building the Cold War Consensus: The Political Economy of U.S. National Security Policy, 1949–51* (Ann Arbor: University of Michigan Press, 1998).

3. Theda Skocpol, *States and Social Revolutions: A Comparative Analysis of France, Russia, and China* (New York: Cambridge University Press, 1979), 31; quotations from Fred Block, "Beyond Relative Autonomy: State Managers as Historical Subjects," 87, and Block, "The Ruling Class Does Not Rule: Notes on the Marxist Theory of the State," 66, in Block, *Revising State Theory: Essays in Politics and Postindustrialism* (Philadelphia: Temple University Press, 1987). On the origins of national states, see Charles Tilly, ed., *The Formation of National States in Western Europe* (Princeton, N.J.: Princeton University Press, 1975).

4. Harland Prechel, "Conflict and Historical Variation in Steel Capital-State Relations: The Emergence of State Structures and a More Prominent, Less Autonomous State," *American Sociological Review* 56 (1991): 693–98; Clyde Barrow, *Critical Theories of the State* (Madison: University of Wisconsin Press, 1993). 144. On the necessity to induce rather than force concessions from society, see Charles Tilly, "Reflections on the History of European State-Making," in Tilly, ed., *Formation of National States,* 35; Benjamin Ginsburg, *The Captive Public: How*

Mass Opinion Promotes State Power (New York: Başic, 1986).

5. Bob Jessop, *State Theory: Putting the Capitalist State in Its Place* (University Park: Penn State University Press, 1990), 362.

6. Hooks, *Forging the Military-Industrial Complex,* argues that wartime exigencies enhanced the autonomy of state (military) officials.

7. David Truman, *The Governmental Process: Political Interests and Public Opinion* (New York: Alfred A. Knopf, 1951), 12–13, 34–35. For a particularly helpful analysis of these issues and a review of the debates, see Jeffrey Isaac, *Power and Marxist Theory: A Realist View* (Ithaca, N.Y.: Cornell University Press, 1987). Direct versus indirect power is discussed in Colin Hay, "Divided by a Common Language: Political Theory and the Concept of Power," *Politics* 17 (1997): 45–52.

8. See for example Truman, *Governmental Process,* 506–15. For criticism of the pluralist argument, see Ralph Miliband, *The State in Capitalist Society* (New York: Basic, 1969), chap. 1, quotation on 2; E. E. Schattschneider, *The Semisovereign People: A Realist's View of Democracy in America* (1960; rpt., Hinsdale, Ill.: Dryden Press, 1975).

9. The debate among neo-Marxists directly involved Ralph Miliband and Nicos Poulantzas. See reviews and citations of relevant materials in Jeffrey Isaac, *Power and Marxist Theory;* Clyde Barrow, *Critical Theories of the State.* For pluralist dismissals of neo-Marxist theory, see, for example, Gabriel Almond, "The Return to the State," *American Political Science Review* 82 (1988): 853–74. Jeffrey Isaac notes, "Pluralist theorists have never taken Marxism very seriously, except insofar as it seemed to them to represent a manifestly unscientific, and thus clearly illegitimate, intellectual exercise" (*Power and Marxist Theory,* 193). See also John Manley in "Neo-Pluralism: A Class Analysis of Pluralist I and Pluralist II," *American Political Science Review* 77 (1983): 368–83.

10. The state-centered approach is outlined in Theda Skocpol, "Bringing the State Back In: Strategies In Current Research," in Peter B. Evans, Dietrich Reuschmeyer, and Theda Skocpol, eds., *Bringing the State Back In* (New York: Cambridge University Press, 1985); Theda Skocpol, "Political Response to Capitalist Crisis: Neo-Marxist Theories of the State and the Case of the New Deal," *Politics and Society* 10 (1980): 155–201; Margaret Weir, Ann Schola Orloff, and Theda Skocpol, eds., *The Politics of Social Policy in the United States* (Princeton, N.J.: Princeton University Press, 1988). On the sui generis nature of state autonomy, see Skocpol, *States and Social Revolution.*

11. Margaret Levi, *Of Rule and Revenue* (Berkeley: University of California Press, 1988), 197; Stephen Skowronek, *Building a New American State: The Expansion of National Administrative Capacities, 1877–1920* (New York: Cambridge University Press, 1982).

12. Skowronek, *Building a New American State,* 13.

13. Skowronek asserts the centrality of state officials because of "the state's claim to control the use of coercion within the territory," and because state officials must "vindicate this distinctive claim" (*Building a New American State,* 12, 14).

14. Skowronek, *Building a New American State,* 13. Skowronek even writes, "Focusing on institutional politics will not exclude these private interests from consideration" (*Building a New American State,* 14).

15. Isaac makes this point in *Power and Marxist Theory.* See esp. 156–59.

16. Stephen D. Krasner, "Approaches to the State: Alternative Conceptions and Historical Dynamics," *Comparative Politics* 16 (1984): 244. See also Jessop,

State Theory, 30; Block, *Revising State Theory*, 21.

17. Frances Fox Piven and Richard Cloward, *The New Class War: Reagan's Attack on the Welfare State and Its Consequences* (New York: Pantheon, 1982), 52; Nicos Poulantzas, *State, Power, Socialism* (London: New Left, 1978), 17 (emphasis in original). See also Isaac, *Power and Marxist Theory*, 165; Jessop, *State Theory*, 361.

18. Claus Offe and Volker Ronge, "Theses on the Theory of the State," *New German Critique* 6 (1975): 140; Miliband, *The State in Capitalist Society*, 149–50. Stan Luger examines the structural dimension of corporate power and its implications for public policy in *Corporate Power, American Democracy, and the Automobile Industry* (New York: Cambridge University Press, 2000).

19. Charles Lindblom, *Politics and Markets: The World's Political Economic Systems* (New York: Basic, 1977), 205. See Miliband, *The State and Capitalist Society*, 162 and chap. 5.

20. Poulantzas, *State, Power, Socialism*, 133; Block, *Revising State Theory*, 173–76; Claus Offe and Volker Ronge, "Theses on the Theory of the State," 126; Isaac, *Power and Marxist Theory*, 182.

21. Schattschneider, *Semisovereign People*, 70; Jessop, *State Theory*, 10, 260. See also Claus Offe, "Structural Problems of the Capitalist State," *German Political Studies* 1 (1974): 31–57. Statists offered a similar argument; as Skocpol writes, "Directly or indirectly, the structures and activities of states profoundly condition . . . class capacities." But in the statist framework this is a one-way determinism of states over classes ("Bringing the State Back In," 25).

22. Schattschneider, *Semisovereign People*, 40 (emphasis in original); Jurgen Habermas, *Legitimation Crisis* (Boston: Beacon Press, 1975), 36, 52; see in particular the discussion beginning on 33.

23. This formulation originated with Gosta Esping-Anderson, Roger Friedland, and Erik Olin Wright, "Modes of Class Struggles and the Capitalist State," *Kapitalistate* 4–5 (1976): 186–220. See also Isaac, *Power and Marxist Theory*, 184; Jessop, *State Theory*, 256, 361.

24. Jessop, *State Theory*, 161, 362.

25. This term relies upon Jessop, who proposes the terms *state project* and *hegemonic project*, respectively, for the intrastate and broader state-societal accommodations formed to stabilize political rule (*State Theory*, 161, 181, 208–10, 217, 346, 362).

26. Colin Hay, "Political Time and the Temporality of Crisis," *Contemporary Political Studies* (1997): 1097. See also Peter A. Hall, "Policy Paradigms, Social Learning, and the State," *Comparative Politics* 25 (1993): 175–96. Actually Schattschneider understood the importance of ideology; as he put it, *"the definition of the alternatives is the supreme instrument of power . . ."* (*Semisovereign People*, 66 [emphasis in original]).

27. Robert Lynd, "Power in American Society as Resource and Problem," in Arthur Kornhauser, ed., *Problems of Power in American Democracy* (Detroit: Wayne State University Press, 1957), 20; John R. Bowman, "The Politics of the Market: Economic Competition and the Organization of Capitalists," *Political Power and Social Theory* 5 (1985): 64; Bowman, *Capitalist Collective Action* (New York: Cambridge University Press, 1989), esp. 62–68; Colin Crouch, "The State, Capital, and Liberal Democracy," in Colin Crouch, ed., *State and Economy in Contemporary Capitalism* (New York: St. Martin's Press, 1979); David Vogel, "Why Businessmen Distrust Their State: The Political Consciousness of American Corporate Executives,"

British Journal of Political Science 8 (1978): 50; Mills, *The Power Elite,* 170.

28. See Poulantzas, *State, Power, Socialism,* 133; James O'Connor, *The Fiscal Crisis of the State* (New York: St. Martin's Press, 1973), 13–16; Adolf A. Berle and Gardiner Means, *The Modern Corporation and Private Property,* rev. ed. (New York: Harcourt, Brace and World, 1968), 18–19. Figures for the concentration of military contracts are available in Senate, Report of the Smaller War Plants Corporation to Special Committee to Study Problems of American Small Business, *Economic Concentration and World War II,* 79th Congress, 2d sess., 1946, S. Doc. 206. An indicator of the overwhelming presence of monopoly-sector personnel in military and civilian mobilization agencies is the prominence congressional committees (especially Truman's Senate investigative committee) gave to feared conflicts of interest involved in employing "dollar-a-year" and "without compensation" corporate officials; see chap. 2.

29. G. William Domhoff, *The Power Elite and the State* (New York: Aldine de Gruyter, 1990), 33–39; Harland Prechel, "Steel and the State: Industry Politics and Business Policy Formation, 1940–1989," *American Sociological Review* 55 (1990): 648–68. Barrow provides a skillful articulation of Domhoff's perspective in *Critical Theories of the State,* esp. 39–40.

30. Howell John Harris, *The Right to Manage: Industrial Relations Policies of American Business in the 1940s* (Madison: University of Wisconsin Press, 1982), 178. For a theoretical discussion of historical shifts in business-government relations, see Stan Luger, *Corporate Power, American Democracy, and the Automobile Industry* (New York: Cambridge University Press, 2000).

1: The Crisis of Modern U.S. Governance

1. See Skowronek, *Building a New American State,* esp. 166; Martin Sklar, *The United States as a Developing Country: Studies in U.S. History in the Progressive Era and the 1920s* (New York: Cambridge University Press, 1992), 65ff.; Sklar, *The Corporate Reconstruction of American Capitalism, 1890–1916* (New York: Cambridge University Press, 1988), 429; R. Jeffrey Lustig, *Corporate Liberalism: The Origins of Modern American Political Theory, 1890–1920* (Berkeley: University of California Press, 1982), 22, 251–60, quotation on 22.

2. Richard Hofstadter, *The Age of Reform* (New York: Alfred A. Knopf, 1955), 226–27; Arthur S. Link, *Woodrow Wilson and the Progressive Era, 1910–1917* (New York: Harper and Row, 1954), 74–78, 229; Richard Hofstadter, *The American Political Tradition and the Men Who Made It* (New York: Vintage, 1954), 249–50, 258–60; Gabriel Kolko, *The Triumph of Conservatism: A Re-Interpretation of American History, 1900–1916* (Chicago: Quadrangle, 1963), 206ff., 255ff.; Donald Brand, *Corporatism and the Rule of Law* (Ithaca: Cornell University Press, 1988), 66–68; Sklar, *Corporate Reconstruction,* 383ff.

3. Sklar, *Corporate Reconstruction,* quotation on 393.

4. See Skowronek, *Building a New American State,* 246–47, 283–84, 286. Robert D. Cuff, *The War Industries Board: Business-Government Relations during World War I* (Baltimore: Johns Hopkins University Press, 1973), is indispensable, and it is relied upon extensively here. On the relationship between corporate personnel and government under Wilson, see Cuff, *War Industries Board,* 5; Jordan A. Schwarz, *The Speculator: Bernard M. Baruch in Washington, 1917–1965*

(Chapel Hill: University of North Carolina Press, 1981), 102ff.; Sklar, *Corporate Reconstruction*, 20ff.

5. Cuff, *War Industries Board*, 49, 55, 60, 70, 83, quotation on 49. See also Bernard M. Baruch, *American Industry in the War* (Paramus, N.J.: Prentice Hall, 1941), 18–19, 109–10, 117; Paul A. C. Koistinen, *Mobilizing for Modern War: The Political Economy of American Warfare, 1865–1919* (Lawrence: University Press of Kansas, 1997), 154, 160–65, 169–74; Schwarz, *The Speculator*, 48; also 49, 56, 65.

6. See in particular Koistinen, *Mobilizing for Modern War*, 175ff.

7. For the problems caused by disorganized army procurement, see Cuff, *War Industries Board*, 33, 66, 72, 87–88, 110, 115, 117–18, 121, 135–37; Baruch, *American Industry in the War*, 31–33, 397–98; Paul Y. Hammond, *Organizing for Defense: The American Military Establishment in the Twentieth Century* (Princeton, N.J.: Princeton University Press, 1961), 36–38; Koistinen, *Mobilizing for Modern War*, 182–87. See also Daniel R. Beaver, *Newton D. Baker and the American War Effort, 1917–1919* (Lincoln: University of Nebraska Press, 1966), 6, 71.

8. See Cuff, *War Industries Board*, 268; Skowronek, *Building a New American State*, 237; Paul A. C. Koistinen, *The Military-Industrial Complex: A Historical Perspective* (New York: Praeger, 1980), 36.

9. Skowronek, *Building a New American State*, quotation on 238; Cuff, *War Industries Board*, 10, 147, 168; Koistinen, *Mobilizing for Modern War*, 166–67; Samuel Huntington, *The Soldier and the State* (New York: Vintage, 1957), 267–68.

10. Koistinen, *Mobilizing for Modern War*, 198–216; Cuff, *War Industries Board*, 80–85, 103–6; Baruch, *American Industry in the War*, 20; Beaver, *Newton D. Baker*, 72–74.

11. Cuff, *War Industries Board*, 153–62, 272, 274n. 12; Koistinen, *Military-Industrial Complex*, 33–34; Baruch, *American Industry in the War*, 391–93; Grant McConnell, *Private Power and American Democracy* (New York: Vintage, 1966), 61; Ellis Hawley, *The New Deal and the Problem of Monopoly* (Princeton, N.J.: Princeton University Press, 1966), 11.

12. Cuff, *War Industries Board*, 113–15, 132–42; Koistinen, *Mobilizing for Modern War*, 225–29; Skowronek, *Building a New American State*, 239–40; Schwarz, *The Speculator*, 61; Beaver, *Newton D. Baker*, 93–95.

13. Cuff, *War Industries Board*, 165. See also Schwarz, *The Speculator*, 76; Baruch, *American Industry in the War*, 23–9; Koistinen, *Mobilizing for Modern War*, 230ff., 292; Beaver, *Newton D. Baker*, 106–9; Skowronek, *Building a New American State*, 241.

14. Baruch, *American Industry in the War*, 116; Cuff, *War Industries Board*, 173; Schwarz, *The Speculator*, 79ff.; Koistinen, *Mobilizing for Modern War*, 279–81; George Soule, *Prosperity Decade: From War to Depression, 1917–1929* (New York: Harper and Row, 1968), 78–80. Certainly, some degree of compromise with the antitrust laws was necessary during the exigencies of total war. Yet, just as certainly, business advisors such as Baruch were more than willing to countenance an administrative and regulatory experimentation beyond the tolerances of the general public.

15. Melvyn Dubofsky, *The State and Labor in Modern America* (Chapel Hill: University of North Carolina Press, 1994), 61–63, 65–69; Soule, *Prosperity Decade*, 164–65, 188; Rhonda Levine, *Class Struggle and the New Deal: Industrial Labor, Industrial Capital, and the State* (Lawrence: University Press of Kansas, 1988), 35–40; Beaver, *Newton D. Baker*, 66–67, 234–35; David Brody, *Workers in Industrial America:*

Essays on the 20th Century Struggle (New York: Oxford University Press, 1980), 37–40, 42–43; Colin Gordon, *New Deals: Business, Labor, and Politics in America, 1920–1935* (New York: Cambridge University Press, 1994), 68.

16. Dubofsky, *State and Labor*, 62–63, 66, 69–74; Soule, *Prosperity Decade*, 70.

17. Soule, *Prosperity Decade*, 200; Mike Davis, *Prisoners of the American Dream: Politics and Economy in the History of the U.S. Working Class* (London: Verso, 1986), 51. See also Dubofsky, *State and Labor*, 74–77; Soule, *Prosperity Decade*, 165, 188, 190–94; Brody, *Workers in Industrial America*, 44–45; William Scheuerman, "The Politics of Protest: The Great Steel Strike of 1919–20 in Lackawanna, New York," *International Review of Social History* 31 (1986): 121–46; Richard Edwards, *Contested Terrain: The Transformation of the Workplace in the Twentieth Century* (New York: Basic, 1979), 61–65; Irving Bernstein, *The Lean Years: A History of the American Worker, 1920–1933* (New York: Penguin, 1960); Gordon, *New Deals*, 89–91.

18. Gabriel Kolko, *Main Currents in Modern American History* (New York: Pantheon, 1984), 19. See also Robert Himmelberg, *The Origins of the National Recovery Administration: Business, Government, and the Trade Association Issue, 1921–1933* (Bronx, N.Y.: Fordham University Press, 1976), 9–10.

19. Brody, "The Rise and Decline of Welfare Capitalism," in *Workers in Industrial America*; Gordon, *New Deals*, 123; Soule, *Prosperity Decade*, 131–33; Levine, *Class Struggle and the New Deal*, 42–43.

20. Smaller War Plants Corporation Report, *Economic Concentration and World War II*, 13; Soule, *Prosperity Decade*, 127–33, 138–40; Kolko, *Main Currents*, 101–5; Gordon, *New Deals*, 36–37; Levine, *Class Struggle and the New Deal*, chap. 2; Himmelberg, *National Recovery Administration*, 7–14, 20, 35–37.

21. Quoted in Arthur M. Schlesinger, *The Crisis of the Old Order, 1919–1933* (Boston: Houghton Mifflin, 1957), 238; Himmelberg, *National Recovery Administration*, 11; Ellis W. Hawley, "Herbert Hoover, the Commerce Secretariat, and the Vision of an 'Associative State,' 1921–1928," *Journal of American History* 61 (1974): 116–40. For views concerning the importance of Hoover's contribution to American political development, see Hofstadter, "Herbert Hoover and the Crisis of American Individualism," in *American Political Tradition*; Kolko, *Main Currents*, 105–11; William Appleman Williams, *The Contours of American History* (Cleveland: World Publishing, 1961), 425–38.

22. Hawley, "Hoover and the 'Associative State,'" quotation on 118; Schwarz, *The Speculator*, 223–24, 253; Albert U. Romasco, *The Poverty of Abundance: Hoover, the Nation, the Depression* (New York: Oxford University Press, 1965), 13–15; Himmelberg, *National Recovery Administration*, 11, 16–21, 26–27, 65–67; Bernard Bellush, *The Failure of the NRA* (New York: W. W. Norton, 1975), 4.

23. The Anti-Trust Division of the Justice Department capitalized on sympathetic Supreme Court decisions to promote the cooperative efforts of trade associations. The FTC, after reorganization under Coolidge in 1925, sponsored a series of conferences on trade practices, wherein industries created codes of behavior to regulate their competition. See Himmelberg, *National Recovery Administration*, 11, 48, 61–63, 94; Soule, *Prosperity Decade*, 134–38; Hawley, "Hoover and the 'Associative State,'" 136.

24. Williams, *Contours of American History*, 426–28.

25. Gordon, *New Deals*, 129–39; Hawley, *New Deal and the Problem of Monopoly*, quotation on 11.

26. Romasco, *Poverty of Abundance,* 96.

27. Jordon A. Schwarz, *The Interregnum of Despair: Hoover, Congress, and the Depression* (Chicago: University of Illinois Press, 1970), 88, 89, 93; Peter Fearon, *War, Prosperity, and Depression: The U.S. Economy, 1917–45* (Oxford: Philip Allan, 1987), 143; Hofstadter, *American Political Tradition,* 303, 305–8; Romasco, *Poverty of Abundance,* 188, 223–26. It must be noted that, under the New Deal, banks, railroads, insurance companies, and major industries continued to receive huge infusions of government monies while the unemployed made do with very little. See Romasco, *The Politics of Recovery: Roosevelt's New Deal* (New York: Oxford University Press, 1983), 63–64.

28. William Leuchtenburg, *FDR and the New Deal* (New York: Harper and Row, 1963), 57; Leuchtenburg, "The New Deal and the Analogue of War," in John Braeman, Robert Bremner, and Everett Walters, eds., *Change and Continuity in Twentieth-Century America* (Columbus: Ohio State University Press, 1964); Himmelberg, *National Recovery Administration,* 135, 145, 162, 169, 176, quotation on 221–22.

29. Schattschneider, *Semisovereign People,* 84; Frances Fox Piven and Richard Cloward, *Poor People's Movements: Why They Succeed, How They Fail* (New York: Vintage, 1979).

30. Mills, *The Power Elite,* 273; Schattschneider, *Semisovereign People,* 84.

31. Piven and Cloward, *Poor People's Movements,* 67. See also Leuchtenburg, *FDR and the New Deal,* 121; Romasco, *Politics of Recovery,* 64–65.

32. Sources on the National Industrial Recovery Act include Hawley, *New Deal and the Problem of Monopoly,* 19–34; Himmelberg, *National Recovery Administration,* 195–208; Bellush, *Failure of the NRA,* 6–15; J. Joseph Huthmacher, *Senator Robert F. Wagner and the Rise of Urban Liberalism* (New York: Atheneum, 1971), 143–44; Kolko, *Main Currents,* 124–26; Levine, *Class Struggle and the New Deal,* 68–69; Gordon, *New Deals,* 167–71.

33. Schwarz, *The Speculator,* 280, 286–89; Hawley, *New Deal and the Problem of Monopoly,* 23; Bellush, *Failure of the NRA,* 9–10; Gerald D. Nash, "Experiments in Industrial Mobilization: WIB and NRA," *Mid-America* 45 (1963): 170–74; Hawley, *New Deal and the Problem of Monopoly,* 24; Himmelberg, *National Recovery Administration,* 201–2; Steve Fraser, *Labor Will Rule: Sidney Hillman and the Rise of American Labor* (Ithaca, N.Y.: Cornell University Press, 1993), 282–88; Theodore Rosenof, *The Failure to Develop a Democratic-Left Synthesis, 1933–1950* (New York: Garland, 1983), 62–63.

34. Himmelberg, *National Recovery Administration,* 212. See also Hawley, *New Deal and the Problem of Monopoly,* 56–66; Kim McQuaid, *Big Business and Presidential Power* (New York: William Morrow, 1982), 30; Bellush, *Failure of the NRA,* 45–48.

35. Huthmacher, *Senator Wagner,* quotation on 147; Hawley, *New Deal and the Problem of Monopoly,* 57; Bellush, *Failure of the NRA,* 13, 38–39; Levine, *Class Struggle and the New Deal,* 74–82, 109; Piven and Cloward, *Poor People's Movements,* 29, 108–15.

36. Levine, *Class Struggle and the New Deal,* 90; McQuaid, *Big Business and Presidential Power,* 24–25, 50–51; Brand, *Corporatism and the Rule of Law,* 119; Schwarz, *The Speculator,* 291–93. Enforcement was, however, problematic at best. See, for instance, Gordon, *New Deals,* 187.

37. Robert M. Collins, *The Business Response to Keynes, 1929–1964* (New York: Columbia University Press, 1981), 32–35, quotation on 35. See also

Romasco, *Politics of Recovery*, 207–9, 218–22; Gordon, *New Deals*, 173, 187–94; Schwarz, *The Speculator*, 292; Hawley, *New Deal and the Problem of Monopoly*, 30, 75–90, 98, 102, 112, 130, 143; Brand, *Corporatism and the Rule of Law*, 89–94, 120–24, 269; Bellush, *Failure of the NRA*, 62–71.

38. Stanley Vittoz, "The Economic Foundations of Industrial Politics in the U.S. and the Emerging Theory of the State in Capitalist Society: The Case of the New Deal Labor Policy," *Amerikastudien* 27 (1982): 373; McQuaid, *Big Business and Presidential Power*, 34–49; Bellush, *Failure of the NRA*, 97–106; Huthmacher, *Senator Wagner*, 153, 160–64; Dubofsky, *State and Labor*, 116–21.

39. Piven and Cloward, *Poor People's Movements*, 119–21, quotation on 130; Romasco, *Politics of Recovery*, 25–26, 205. For Roosevelt's preemption of the Wagner labor bill, his indecisiveness, and the 1934 election, see Huthmacher, *Senator Wagner*, 168–82, 190. Generally, see Irving Bernstein, *Turbulent Years: A History of the American Worker, 1933–1941* (Boston: Houghton Mifflin, 1970), 199–205, 331.

40. Fraser, *Labor Will Rule*, quotation on 326; Huthmacher, *Senator Wagner*, 182–98; Hawley, *New Deal and the Problem of Monopoly*, 69–70; Himmelberg, *National Recovery Administration*, 116, 221; Gordon, *New Deals*, 180, 187–94; Michael A. Bernstein, *The Great Depression: Delayed Recovery and Economic Change in America, 1929–1939* (New York: Cambridge University Press, 1987), 194–95, 200–3; Williams, *Contours of American History*, 442; Michael Goldfield, "Worker Insurgency, Radical Organization, and New Deal Labor Legislation," *American Political Science Review* 83 (1989): 1257–82; Piven and Cloward, *Poor People's Movements*, esp. 130–33; Levine, *Class Struggle and the New Deal*, 16–17, 94ff.

41. David Vogel, "Why Businessmen Distrust Their State," 65. See Leuchtenburg, *FDR and the New Deal*, 162–66, quotation on 132–33.

42. Contemporary accounts of the emergence and coalescing of a new group of New Dealers can be found in Joseph Alsop's interview notes from meetings with Leon Henderson, Isador Lubin, Lauchlin Currie, Robert Jackson, and Thomas Corcoran ("Interviews by Joseph Alsop" in Box 65, Joseph Lash Papers, Franklin D. Roosevelt Library [hereafter cited as FDRL]). John W. Jeffries has also used this term in his "The 'New' New Deal: Franklin D. Roosevelt and American Liberalism, 1939–1945," *Political Science Quarterly* 105 (1990): 397–418.

43. "Thomas G. Corcoran: Autobiographical Notes," in Box 61, Lash Papers, FDRL. Sectional forces, like many business constituencies, came to be threatened by the increasing scope of national power (James T. Patterson, *Congressional Conservatism and the New Deal: The Growth of the Conservative Coalition in Congress, 1933–1939* [Lexington: University of Kentucky Press, 1967], 128–36).

44. Fraser, *Labor Will Rule*, 399–400; Corcoran, 27 July 1938, interview with Joseph Alsop, copy in Box 65, Lash Papers, FDRL. Lauchlin Currie expresses similar views to Corcoran in his "Draft of Autobiography," Box 62, Lash Papers, FDRL, 97.

45. Barry Dean Karl, *The Uneasy State: The United States from 1915 to 1945* (Chicago: University of Chicago Press, 1983), 128, 155–56, quotation on 128; similar sentiment is found in McQuaid, *Big Business and Presidential Power*, 16.

46. Stephen Hess, *Organizing the Presidency* (Washington, D.C.: Brookings Institution, 1976), 36. Brand sees this strategy as leading to "ad-hocracy" (*Corporatism and the Rule of Law*, 72). The Roosevelt quotation is from Leuchtenburg, *FDR and the New Deal*, 41.

47. See Levine, *Class Struggle and the New Deal*, 170; Louis Brownlow, *A*

Passion for Anonymity: The Autobiography of Louis Brownlow, vol. 2 (Chicago: University of Chicago Press, 1958), 318–23; A. J. Wann, *The President as Chief Administrator: A Study of Franklin D. Roosevelt* (Washington, D.C.: Public Affairs Press, 1968), 50–65; Barry Dean Karl, *Executive Reorganization and Reform in the New Deal: The Genesis of Administrative Management, 1900–1939* (Cambridge, Mass.: Harvard University Press, 1963), 196–98, 248; Hess, *Organizing the Presidency,* 28–36; Richard Polenberg, *Reorganizing Roosevelt's Government: The Controversy over Executive Reorganization, 1936–1939* (Cambridge, Mass.: Harvard University Press, 1966).

48. Steve Fraser, "The 'Labor Question,'" in Gary Gerstle and Steve Fraser, eds., *The Rise and Fall of the New Deal Order, 1930–1980* (Princeton, N.J.: Princeton University Press, 1989), 70, 72; Fraser, *Labor Will Rule,* 262–64, 284–85, 327–29, 349–52, 375, 391–92, 409; McQuaid, *Big Business and Presidential Power,* chap. 2; Alan Brinkley, *The End of Reform: New Deal Liberalism in Recession and War* (New York: Alfred A. Knopf, 1995), 40–42, 291–92n. 32; Collins, *Business Response to Keynes,* 56ff. These authors are among many who discuss the limited but important alliance between so-called "corporate liberals" and New Dealers.

49. These concepts are developed in Alvin Hansen's Keynesian analysis of the Great Depression, *Full Recovery or Stagnation?* (New York: W. W. Norton, 1938). For a concise statement of the mature economy thesis, see Richard Gilbert et al., *An Economic Program for American Democracy* (New York: Vanguard, 1938). See also Dean L. May, *From New Deal to New Economics* (New York: Garland, 1981), 55–56, 84–86; Rosenof, *Failure,* 39.

50. Romasco, *Politics of Recovery,* 227; Rosenof, *Failure,* 49.

51. The Eccles quotation is from May, *From New Deal to New Economics,* 130. See also Brinkley, *The End of Reform,* 61–64, 73–86, 97, 105; Rosenof, *Failure,* 71–73. Lauchlin Currie remembers that Eccles "was 'with' the New Dealers but not 'of' them" (Currie, "Draft of Autobiography," Lash Papers, 56).

52. Earlier New Deal initiatives embodied in such measures as the Securities Act of 1933 and the Securities Exchange Act of 1934, designed to reign in the speculative abuses of the 1920s by oversight and self-regulation of the financial industry, and the Banking Act of 1935, designed to strengthen the hand of the Federal Reserve chairman in determining monetary policy, were relatively passive tools of national intervention.

53. See Rosenof, *Failure,* 48–49, 106–8; Brinkley, *End of Reform,* 104–5. Gilbert et al., *Economic Program for American Democracy,* discusses this shift from "extensive" to "intensive" investment (18ff.). May reports that the work by Gilbert et al., published in 1938 by a group of "7 Harvard and Tufts Harvard economists," promoted the administration's turn to domestic spending and gave it intellectual credibility. In fact, May calls it "a bible of the New Dealers" (*From New Deal to New Economics,* 147–49).

54. Robert Lekachman, *The Age of Keynes* (New York: Random House, 1966), 142; "Personal Statement of Isador Lubin and Leon Henderson Supplementing the Report of the Temporary National Economic Committee," 29 March 1941, copy in Box 69, "Temporary National Economic Committee," Lash Papers, FDRL.

55. Lekachman, *Age of Keynes,* 139; Brinkley, *End of Reform,* 105.

56. Collins, *Business Response to Keynes.* See Fraser, *Labor Will Rule,* 416; Davis, *Prisoners of the American Dream,* 69–71.

2: From Depression to War

1. One official contemporary account reports that even the first six months (May–December 1940) of active defense period mobilization "were sufficient to set a pattern that was to have profound influence throughout the war" ("Relations Between the Armed Services and the Advisory Commission to the Council of National Defense," memorandum from James Fesler, Chief of the Policy Analysis and Records Branch, to G. Lyle Belsley, War Production Board [WPB] Executive Secretary, 5 November 1943, James Fesler Papers, Yale University, 43). U.S. Civilian Production Administration (hereafter cited as USCPA), *Industrial Mobilization for War* (Washington, D.C.: Government Printing Office, 1947), quotation on xiii.

2. For the military reliance upon corporate leaders within their ranks, see esp. Jeffrey M. Dorwart, *Eberstadt and Forrestal: A National Security Partnership, 1909–1949* (College Station: Texas A&M University Press, 1991), 8. John Brigante, *The Feasibility Dispute* (Washington, D.C.: Committee on Public Administration Cases, 1950), quotation on 2.

3. See Paul A. C. Koistinen, "The Interwar Years," in *The Military-Industrial Complex,* for a succinct summary of military-business cooperation. Other sources relied upon for this section include Paul A. C. Koistinen, *The Hammer and the Sword: Labor, the Military, and Industrial Mobilization, 1920–1945* (New York: Arno Press, 1979), 11ff.; Koistinen, *Planning War, Pursuing Peace: The Political Economy of American Warfare, 1920–1939* (Lawrence: University Press of Kansas, 1998), 10ff.; John D. Millett, *The Organization and Role of the Army Service Forces* (Washington, D.C.: U.S. Department of the Army, 1954), 14–19; Skowronek, *Building a New American State,* 244–46; R. Elberton Smith, *The Army and Economic Mobilization* (Washington, D.C.: U.S. Department of the Army, 1959), 35–47, 73–81; Robert H. Connery, *The Navy and the Industrial Mobilization in World War II* (Princeton, N.J.: Princeton University Press, 1951), 34–39.

4. The navy, maintained as the nation's first line of defense, remained at a greater state of readiness than the army and so foresaw less need for in-depth planning. Thus, most of the planning activities during the 1920s and into the 1930s became the army's responsibility. See Connery, *Navy and Industrial Mobilization,* 37–39; Smith, *Army and Economic Mobilization,* 41, 45.

5. Millett, *Army Service Forces,* 19; Koistinen, *Hammer and Sword,* 16–20; Schwarz, *The Speculator,* 336–37; Smith, *Army and Economic Mobilization,* 74.

6. Smith, *Army and Economic Mobilization,* 75; Koistinen, *Hammer and Sword,* 47–54; Koistinen, *Planning War, Pursuing Peace,* chap. 14; Millett, *Army Service Forces,* 19; Matthew Coulter, "The Franklin D. Roosevelt Administration and the Special Committee on Investigation of the Munitions Industry," *Mid-America* 67 (1985): 23–35.

7. Testimony before U.S. House, Select Committee Investigating National Defense Migration (hereafter cited as Tolan Committee), *Third Interim Report,* 77th Congress, 2d sess., 1942, 84.

8. "Industrial Mobilization Plan: Revision of 1939," reprinted as S. Doc. 134, 76th Congress, 2d sess., 1939, 7, copy in Box 301, "Organization of NDAC," Harry Hopkins Papers, FDRL; Smith, *Army and Economic Mobilization,* 75, 79–80; Koistinen, *Hammer and Sword,* 52–53, Baruch quotation on 54. For Baruch's sentiments, see also Schwarz, *The Speculator,* 335.

9. For Stimson and Patterson testimony, see Senate, Special Committee Investigating the National Defense Program (hereafter cited as Truman Committee), *Hearings,* 77th Congress, 1st sess., 1941, Part 1, esp. 11, 23. Robert Nathan quotation from "Summary of Statements of Robert R. Nathan, formerly Chairman of the Planning Committee of the War Production Board," WPB Policy Analysis and Records Branch Staff Meeting, 4 August 1945, Box 2, Fesler Papers. Fesler's memoranda and reports represent a rich source of information about the evolution of mobilization authority. He was secretary to the WPB Planning Committee before taking charge of the WPB Policy Analysis and Research Branch. See "Abandonment of the Industrial Mobilization Plan," memorandum sent under his signature to J. A. Krug, 10 September 1945, 2–3 (copy provided by James Fesler), 4. See also the very critical "Comments on our Industrial War Plans," Lauchlin Curry to Roosevelt, 20 May 1940, Box 132, "Lauchlin Currie," President's Secretary's Files [hereafter cited as PSF], FDRL; Harry Magdoff letter to author, 22 November 1994; Millett, *Army Service Forces,* 186.

10. Koistinen, *Planning War, Pursuing Peace,* 315–17.

11. "Fortune Survey," *Fortune* (November 1941): 200; Albert A. Blum, "Birth and Death of the M-Day Plan," in Harold Stein, ed., *American Civil-Military Decisions: A Book of Case Studies* (University: University of Alabama Press, 1963), 65–70, quotation on 69. See also Koistinen, *Hammer and Sword,* 817.

12. Fesler to Krug, "Abandonment of the Industrial Mobilization Plan," Fesler Papers.

13. Truman Committee, *Hearings,* 77th Congress, 1st sess., 1941, Part 6, 1516. See Keith Eiler, *Mobilizing America: Robert P. Patterson and the War Effort, 1940–1945* (Ithaca, N.Y.: Cornell University Press, 1997), 84–87, 162–63, 207; Dorwart, *Eberstadt and Forrestal,* 32, also 34–48. One employee of the War Production Board recalled a daily car pool from Alexandria, Virginia, to Washington in the company of dollar-a-year executives who continually cursed Roosevelt and the New Deal in the harshest terms imaginable (Edythe First, interview by author, New York, N.Y., 4 October 1994). In general, see also Townsend Hoopes and Douglas Brinkley, *Driven Patriot: The Life and Times of James Forrestal* (New York: Alfred A. Knopf, 1992), 165–67; Eiler, *Mobilizing America,* 94–96.

14. Ferdinand Eberstadt, "Diary Entries, October 31, 1941," emphasis added, Box 12, "ANMB Files," Eberstadt Papers, Seeley G. Mudd Manuscript Library, Princeton University.

15. Michael S. Sherry, *Preparing for the Next War: American Plans for Postwar Defense, 1941–45* (New Haven, Conn.: Yale University Press, 1977).

16. David Brody, "The New Deal and World War II," in John Braeman, Robert H. Bremner, and David Brody, eds., *The New Deal: The National Level* (Columbus: Ohio University Press, 1975), 268. Bruce Catton, a participant in mobilization, articulates a very similar position in *The War Lords of Washington* (New York: Harcourt, Brace, 1948), 121–22. See also Schwarz, *The Speculator,* 401–8.

17. See Fesler to Krug, "Abandonment of the Industrial Mobilization Plan," Fesler Papers; Harold Ickes, *The Secret Diary of Harold Ickes,* vol. 3, *The Lowering Clouds, 1939–1941* (New York: Simon and Schuster, 1955), 357; Mark Skinner Watson, *Chief of Staff: Prewar Plans and Preparations* (Washington, D.C.: U.S. Department of the Army, 1950), 164–66.

18. Many commentators have noted this propensity of Roosevelt's. In relation to defense mobilization, see Herman Miles Somers, *Presidential Agency:*

OWMR, the Office of War Mobilization and Reconversion (Cambridge, Mass.: Harvard University Press, 1950), 1–10; Eliot Janeway, *The Struggle for Survival: A Chronicle of Economic Mobilization in World War II* (New Haven, Conn.: Yale University Press, 1951), 51–52; USCPA, *Industrial Mobilization for War,* 9–10.

19. Most telling perhaps is Ickes's criticism of Roosevelt's irresolution: "I do know that in every direction I find a growing discontent with the President's lack of leadership. He still has the country if he will take it and lead it. But he won't have it very much longer unless he does something. It won't be sufficient for him to make a speech and then go into a state of innocuous desuetude again" (Ickes, *Secret Diary,* 3:511).

20. Koistinen, *Hammer and Sword,* 560.

21. As it was, many argued that existing agencies and departments, for example, the Departments of Commerce and Labor, would be able to handle war-related tasks. See Somers, *Presidential Agency,* 10; Harold Smith to Roosevelt, "Memorandum On Defense Organization," Records, Council of National Defense, Advisory Commission, Box 9, "Bureau of Budget," FDRL.

22. Koistinen, *Hammer and Sword,* quotation on 580; Smith, *Army and Economic Mobilization,* 456–57.

23. Smith, *Army and Economic Mobilization,* quotations on 456–57 (emphasis added); "Fortune Survey," *Fortune* (November 1941): 200; I. F. Stone, *Business as Usual: The First Year of Defense* (New York: Modern Age, 1940), 162.

24. USCPA, *Industrial Mobilization for War,* 91; Janeway, *Struggle for Survival,* 111, quotations on 44–45. See also Walter Millis, with Harvey Mansfield and Harold Stein, *Arms and the State: Civil-Military Elements in National Policy* (New York: Twentieth Century Fund, 1958), 44; Holley, *Buying Aircraft,* 213. For the development of presidential authority during the war, see Louis William Koenig, *The Presidency and the Crisis: Powers of the Office from the Invasion of Poland to Pearl Harbor* (New York: King's Crown Press, 1944). For the view that executive reorganization was made possible by the approach of war, see John Millett's comments in Frederick C. Mosher, *"The President Needs Help": Proceedings of a Conference Held on January 15, 1987 . . .* (Lanham, Md.: University Press of America, 1988), esp. 28.

25. Ickes, *Secret Diary,* 3:182, 210–11, 289–90, esp. 295–96; Koistinen, *Hammer and Sword,* 583, quotation on 579; Smith, *Army and Economic Mobilization,* 215–21, 242–47, 267, quotation on 221; Stone, *Business as Usual,* 165–66. See McQuaid, *Big Business and Presidential Power,* 77–85; Clifford Durr, "The Defense Plant Corporation," in Harold Stein, ed., *Public Administration and Policy Development: A Case Book* (New York: Harcourt, Brace, 1952); Gerald T. White, *Billions for Defense: Government Financing by the Defense Plant Corporation* (University: University of Alabama Press, 1980).

26. Stone, *Business as Usual,* 159–69, quotation on 167. See also Ickes, *Secret Diary,* 3:290. Edward Stettinius Jr., chairman of the board of U.S. Steel, appointed by Roosevelt to facilitate the procurement of raw material, verifies much of what Stone surmised. The issue of amortization and excess profits were a central issue of Stettinius's diary notes from this period, and they report how he and other members of the National Defense Advisory Committee worked to convince Roosevelt to back off from a demand that 5-year amortization be passed only alongside a stringent excess-profits taxes (Stettinius diary notes, Box 90, Stettinius Papers, University of Virginia).

27. Catton, *War Lords of Washington,* 29–30.

28. For Riskin's plans, see his testimony before the Truman Committee, *Hearings*, 77th Congress, 2d sess., 1942, Part 10, 3731–802, and Appendix, 4203–22.

29. For an overview, see Nelson Lichtenstein, *Labor's War at Home: The CIO in World War II* (New York: Cambridge University Press, 1983), 12–13; Joshua Freeman, "Delivering the Goods: Industrial Unionism during World War II," *Labor History* 19 (1978): 580; Fraser, "The 'Labor Question,'" 71; Dubofsky, *State and Labor*, 170–71.

30. Policy Analysis Staff, WPB Policy Analysis and Records Branch, "Minutes of Staff Meeting, June 15, 1945" (digest of discussion with George W. Brooks, an assistant to Hillman from NDAC to OPM and after), Box 2, Fesler Papers; Koistinen, *Hammer and Sword*, 106–7, 145; Fraser, *Labor Will Rule*, 453. On the misleading portrayal of strikes, see, for example, Lichtenstein, *Labor's War at Home*, 95–97.

31. Freeman, "Delivering the Goods," 589; Fraser, "The 'Labor Question,'" 70; Lichtenstein, *Labor's War at Home*, 45, 79–80.

32. Christopher Tomlins, *The State and the Unions: Labor Relations, Law, and the Organized Labor Movement in America, 1880–1960* (New York: Cambridge University Press, 1985), 247–57; Koistinen, *Hammer and Sword*, 279–82; Lichtenstein, *Labor's War at Home*, esp. chaps. 7 and 10, "The Social Ecology of the Shop-Floor Conflict" and "The Bureaucratic Imperative." Not all wildcat strikes had to do directly with shop-floor grievances; Freeman also cites "a national wave of racist wildcats that began in the spring of 1943" ("Delivering the Goods," 574, quotation on 584–85).

33. Edythe First, *Industry and Labor Advisory Committees in the National Defense Advisory Commission and Office of Production Management, May 1940 to January 1942*, USCPA Special Study No. 24 (Washington, D.C.: Government Printing Office, 1946), quotation on 207. See also William J. Schuck, "Industry and Labor Advisory Committees in the [WPB], January 1942 to November 1945," USCPA Special Study No. 34, unpublished typescript, Historical Records of the War Production Board, RG 179, Box 3, National Archives (hereafter cited as NA), Washington, D.C., 10; Richard J. Purcell, *Labor Policies of the National Defense Advisory Commission and Office of Production Management, May 1940 to April 1942*, USCPA Special Study No. 23 (Washington, D.C.: Government Printing Office, 1946), 32; Koistinen, *Hammer and Sword*, 145–46, 352–55; Fraser, *Labor Will Rule*, 453, 474–76.

34. Purcell, *Labor Policies of the NDAC and OPM*, 34–69, quotation on 47; Koistinen, *Hammer and Sword*, 127–45, quotation on 136–37; Fraser, *Labor Will Rule*, 455–58; Eiler, *Mobilizing America*, 155–64; Fesler to Belsley, "Relations Between the Armed Services and the Advisory Commission," Fesler Papers, 32–33.

35. Schuck, "Industry and Labor Advisory Committees in the WPB," RG 179, NA, 24–30. The Murray Plan is outlined in "Report of President Philip Murray to the Fourth Constitutional Convention of the [CIO]," Detroit, Michigan, 17 November 1941, copy in Official File 2546, FDRL; Nelson Lichtenstein, "From Corporatism to Collective Bargaining: Organized Labor and the Eclipse of Social Democracy in the Postwar Era," in Gerstle and Fraser, eds., *Rise and Fall of the New Deal Order*, quotation on 126; Stone, *Business as Usual*, quotation on 228, emphasis in original.

36. Janeway, *Struggle for Survival*, 223.

37. "War is Horsepower," *Fortune* (November 1941): 86.

38. Stone, *Business as Usual*, 239. See also Nelson Lichtenstein, *The Most Dangerous Man in Detroit: Walter Reuther and the Fate of American Labor* (New York: Basic, 1995), 162–68. For a review of the Reuther plan, and the importance of converting the auto industry, see J. Carlyle Sitterson, *Aircraft Production Policies*, USCPA Special Study No. 21 (Washington, D.C.: Government Printing Office, 1946); Purcell, *Labor Policies of the NDAC and OPM*, 151ff.; Lichtenstein, *Most Dangerous Man in Detroit*, chap. 8; Stone, *Business as Usual*, 223–41.

39. Truman Committee, *First Annual Report*, 77th Congress, 2d sess., 1942, Report No. 480, Part 5, 34 (emphasis added); Janeway, *Struggle for Survival*, 227.

40. Policy Analysis Staff, "Minutes of Staff Meeting of June 15, 1945," Fesler Papers; First, *Industry and Labor Advisory Committees*, quotation on 178; Fraser, *Labor Will Rule*, 477.

41. First, *Industry and Labor Advisory Committees*, 196, quotation on 190. See also Schuck, "Industry and Labor Advisory Committees in the WPB," RG 179, NA, 31–32; Koistinen, *Hammer and Sword*, 354.

42. As Isador Lubin wrote to Henry Wallace on 18 November 1941: "Strike statistics have given a false impression of the seriousness of the situation. A plant may be tied up for eight or ten hours, and one gets the idea from the press and the army that the World is going to pieces. With the exception of the coal difficulty, there is really nothing in the labor picture today that justifies our being more excited about strikes than in normal times" (Box 126, "Henry Wallace," Isador Lubin Papers, FDRL).

43. Koistinen, *Hammer and Sword*, 106; U.S. Bureau of the Budget (hereafter cited as USBOB), *The United States at War: Development and Administration of the War Program by the Federal Government* (Washington, D.C.: Government Printing Office, 1947), 190; Lichtenstein, *Most Dangerous Man in Detroit*, 177ff.

44. Lichtenstein, *Labor's War at Home*, 49.

3: Building the Wartime State

1. Somers, *Presidential Agency*, 6–7; Janeway, *Struggle for Survival*, 53–72; US-BOB, *United States at War*, 22–23; Brownlow, *Passion for Anonymity*, 2:424–26; Blum, "Birth and Death of the M-Day Plan," 74, 84–87; "Report of the War Resources Board," 3–4, 7, copy in Box 173, "War Resources Board," PSF, FDRL. For the importance of Bernard Baruch's input, see Koistinen, *Planning War, Pursuing Peace*, 305–10; Janeway, *Struggle for Survival*, 66–67, 74–96; Schwarz, *The Speculator*, 357–62.

2. Koistinen, *Hammer and Sword*, 72.

3. First, *Industry and Labor Advisory Committees*, 10; Stone, *Business as Usual*, 141.

4. See James A. McAleer, *Dollar-A-Year and Without Compensation Personnel Policies of the War Production Board and Predecessor Agencies, August 1939 to November 1945*, USCPA Special Study No. 27 (Washington, D.C.: Government Printing Office, 1947).

5. Fesler to Belsley, "Relations Between the Armed Services and the Advisory Commission," Fesler Papers, 3. This detailed memorandum describes the head start gained by military agencies, through the Army-Navy Munitions Board,

over civilian mobilizers because of the lack of formal civilian authority.

6. USCPA, *Industrial Mobilization for War,* 22–23, quotation on 18; Koistinen, *Planning War, Pursuing Peace,* 312–13.

7. USCPA, *Industrial Mobilization for War,* quotation on 19. William Batt, chairman of the Business Advisory Council Business Advisory Council, explained to members of the WPB Policy Analysis and Records Branch (PARB) staff that "Stettinius drew the first members of his staff from the [BAC] of the Department of Commerce" (WPB-PARB "Minutes of Staff Meeting, May 4, 1945," Box 2, Fesler Papers). See also Stettinius diary notes, 24 and 29 May 1940, Stettinius Papers.

8. Ickes, *Secret Diary,* 3:195–96.

9. See Donald Nelson, *Arsenal of Democracy* (New York: Harcourt, Brace, 1946); "Don Nelson: The Man from Sears Goes to War," *Fortune* (November 1941): 86ff.

10. Harold Smith, Roosevelt's director of the Bureau of Budget, in fact reported to the president in December that despite the advisory status of the NDAC "the trend of activity . . . is distinctly in the direction of operations" (Smith to Roosevelt, 2 December 1940, "Memorandum On Defense Organization," Records, Council of National Defense, Advisory Commission, Box 9, "Bureau of Budget," Smith Papers).

11. USCPA, *Industrial Mobilization for War,* 56. See Smith to Roosevelt, 2 December 1940, "Memorandum On Defense Organization," Records, Council of National Defense, Advisory Commission, Box 9, "Bureau of Budget," Smith Papers.

12. See Fesler to Belsley, "Relations Between the Armed Services and the Advisory Commission," Fesler Papers, 5ff.; Koistinen, *Hammer and Sword,* 564–67; Connery, *Navy and Industrial Mobilization,* 92–95.

13. Eberstadt, "Interview with Christman," 18 July 1969, Eberstadt Papers; Millis, *Arms and the State,* 56.

14. Janeway, *Struggle for Survival,* 125–45; Hoopes and Brinkley, *Driven Patriot,* 128–31; Eiler, *Mobilizing America,* 33–41. Stimson and Knox directly recruited a group of corporate personnel, including Patterson, Forrestal, Robert Lovett, John Lord O'Brian, and John J. McCloy, who would figure prominently in mobilization and postwar military and political strategy.

15. The Office of Production Management was created by Executive Order No. 8629. For the organization and powers of the OPM, see USCPA, *Industrial Mobilization for War,* 93–102; Nelson, *Arsenal of Democracy,* 117.

16. USCPA, *Industrial Mobilization for War,* 98, 102–3.

17. Priorities power was authorized under section 2(a) of the National Defense Act of 28 June 1940. Compulsory manufacturing orders were authorized under section 9 of the Selective Training and Service Act of 1940.

18. Executive Order No. 8629, reprinted in Truman Committee, *Hearings,* Part 1, 374–83. See also USCPA, *Industrial Mobilization for War,* 95–96; Knudsen in Truman Committee, *Hearings,* Part 1, 104; Reed in Truman Committee, *Hearings,* Part 10, 3837, 3832; Nelson, *Arsenal of Democracy,* 124.

19. Somers, *Presidential Agency,* quotation on 16; USCPA, *Industrial Mobilization for War,* 96; Truman Committee, *Third Annual Report,* 78th Congress, 2d sess., 1944, Report No. 10, Part 16, 2–10.

20. Truman Committee, *First Annual Report,* 77th Congress, 2d sess., 1941, Report No. 480, Part 5, 7; McAleer, *Dollar-A-Year and Without Compensation Personnel Policies,* 9; "Report of President Philip Murray," Official File 2546, FDRL;

Ickes, *Secret Diary*, 3:530, 533, esp. 591.

21. Truman Committee, *First Annual Report*, quotations, in order, on 2, 8, 9, 6–7, emphasis added.

22. Janeway, *Struggle for Survival*, 272–73.

23. USCPA, *Industrial Mobilization for War*, quotation on 24. See "Memorandum: Summary of Remarks of John P. Gregg before Policy Analysis Staff, October 20, 1944," Edythe W. First to James W. Fesler, 21 October 1944, Box 1, "October, 1944," Fesler Papers.

24. Minutes of National Defense Advisory Committee, quoted in Fesler to Belsley, "Relations Between the Armed Services and the Advisory Commission," Fesler Papers, 29–30. See also USCPA, *Industrial Mobilization for War*, 144–45. Eiler refers to the "bottleneck-or-rubber-stamp dilemma" that faced civilians in charge of reviewing burgeoning military contracting (*Mobilizing America*, 85–86).

25. USCPA, *Industrial Mobilization for War*, 141–45, quotation on 145; Koistinen, *Hammer and Sword*, 574.

26. Nelson Testimony before Truman Committee, *Hearings*, 77th Congress, 1st sess., 1941, Part 5, 1340–41, Eccles quotation on 1658. See USCPA, *Industrial Mobilization for War*, 57–58, 61–63, 171; Nelson, *Arsenal of Democracy*, 150; Fesler to Belsley, "Relations Between the Armed Services and the Advisory Commission," Fesler Papers, 28–30, 34–41.

27. USCPA, *Industrial Mobilization for War*, 31–32, 58, 63. See Truman Committee, *Report concerning Priorities and the Utilization of Existing Facilities*, 77th Congress, 2d sess., 1942, Report No. 480, Part 3, reprinted in *First Annual Report*, Appendix II, esp. 193–94. The Senate reported that 100 corporations held 70 percent of war and essential civilian contracts. See Senate Special Committee to Study the Problems of American Small Business (hereafter cited as Murray Committee), *Additional Report*, 77th Congress, 2d sess., 1942, Report No. 479, Part 2, 6–7. Also see Smaller War Plants Corporation Report, *Economic Concentration and World War II*.

28. USCPA, *Industrial Mobilization for War*, 117–18; Koistinen, *Hammer and Sword*, 566; Janeway, *Struggle for Survival*, 195.

29. See Murray Committee, *Additional Report*, Report No. 479, Part 2, section entitled "New Facilities Versus Existing Capacity," 7ff.; testimony of Floyd Odlum, director of the OPM's Contract Distribution Division, in Truman Committee, *Hearings*, 77th Congress, 1st sess., 1941, Part 8, 2455–91, 2591–2614.

30. Truman Committee, *First Annual Report*, 36; Truman Committee, *Hearings*, Part 8, Mead quotation on 2478, Odlum quotation on 2591. See USCPA, *Industrial Mobilization for War*, 146–47.

31. James Fesler memorandum of 2 December 1944, "Comments of Thomas C. Blaisdell, Jr., Director, Bureau of Program and Statistics, WPB, on my November 29 memorandum and attachments concerning annual report of WPB for 1944," Box 1, Fesler Papers. See also Millett, *Army Service Forces*, 283, 290; Smith, *Army and Economic Mobilization*, 111, 224; I. F. Stone, *The War Years: 1939–1945* (Boston: Little, Brown, 1988), 117–18, 151–52.

32. USCPA, *Industrial Mobilization for War*, 106.

33. First, *Industry and Labor Advisory Committees*, quotations on 1, 20.

34. First, *Industry and Labor Advisory Committees*, 73–88, 139–47, quotation on 144; Truman Committee, *Hearings*, 77th Congress, 1st sess., 1941, Part 3, Truman quotation on 771–72. See also Truman Committee, *Interim Report on Steel*,

78th Congress, 1st sess., 1943, Report No. 10, Part 3, 1–3. Stone, *Business as Usual,* analyzes the steel and aluminum industries. USCPA, *Industrial Mobilization for War,* 153–54, examines the resistance of the steel industry to expansions. See also Nelson, *Arsenal of Democracy,* 143–44.

35. First, *Industry and Labor Advisory Committees,* quotation on 145; USCPA, *Industrial Mobilization for War,* quotation on 32. See also Catton, *War Lords of Washington,* 88–90; Ickes, *Secret Diary,* 3:509; Koistinen, *Hammer and Sword,* 584.

36. Luther Gulick, *Administrative Reflections from World War II* (University: University of Alabama Press, 1946), 46. See also USCPA, *Industrial Mobilization for War,* 193–94; USBOB, *United States at War,* 60, 80; Nelson, *Arsenal of Democracy,* 143; Schwarz, *The Speculator,* 373.

37. Stettinius's diary from 1940 records many instances of exasperation with Thurmond Arnold. See particularly 23 July 1940, Stettinius diary notes, Stettinius Papers, 72. See also First, *Industry and Labor Advisory Committees,* 17–19, 70–73.

38. See "Summary of Remarks of John Lord O'Brian Before Policy Analysis Staff, December 15, 1944," Edythe First to James Fesler, 16 December 1944, Box 2, Fesler Papers, 4; First, *Industry and Labor Advisory Committees,* 67–68, 91–93; Catton, *War Lords of Washington,* 104–5.

39. First, *Industry and Labor Advisory Committees,* 114.

40. The OPACS was created by Executive Order No. 8734 on 11 April 1941. For a review of OPACS's organization and authority, see USCPA, *Industrial Mobilization for War,* 102–5; Drummond Jones, *The Role of the Office of Civilian Requirements in the Office of Production Management and the War Production Board, January 1941 to November 1945,* USCPA Special Study No. 20 (Washington, D.C.: Government Printing Office, 1946), 6–9. On the OPM-OPACS dispute, see USCPA, *Industrial Mobilization for War,* 103; V. O. Key to Sydney Stein, 24 February 1943, "Attached Report on Civilian Supply," Box 2, "Bureau of Budget: Miscellaneous Reports," Wayne Coy Papers, FDRL, 2–3.

41. Koistinen, *Hammer and Sword,* 585–86; Henderson to Knudsen, 30 June 1941, Box 36, "SPAB—Formation of," Leon Henderson Papers, FDRL.

42. Jones, *Office of Civilian Requirements,* quotation on 25.

43. See Janeway, *Struggle for Survival,* 266; USCPA, *Industrial Mobilization for War,* 113; Somers, *Presidential Agency,* 21–22; Nelson, *Arsenal of Democracy,* quotation on 159.

44. In a memorandum to one his primary assistants, Wayne Coy, Roosevelt worried over the lack of movement on aid to the Soviets and tells Coy, "Please get out the list [of materiel the Soviets requested] and please, with my full authority, use a heavy hand—act as a burr under the saddle and get things moving!" He closes with the exhortation, "Step on it!" ("Memorandum for Wayne Coy," 2 August 1941, Box 132, "Wayne Coy," PSF, FDRL). See also USCPA, *Industrial Mobilization for War,* 110; Koistinen, *Hammer and Sword,* 626; Theodore Wilson, *The First Summit: Roosevelt and Churchill at Placentia Bay, 1941,* rev. ed. (Lawrence: University Press of Kansas, 1991), 40–42, 213–19.

45. Actually, the successes of the SPAB and its planners have been attributed to the fact that the agency was not burdened by operating responsibilities. See USCPA, *Industrial Mobilization for War,* 110–11; USBOB, *United States at War,* 79; Nelson, *Arsenal of Democracy,* 156; Somers, *Presidential Agency,* 21, 22.

46. SPAB Executive Order, quoted in USCPA, *Industrial Mobilization for War,*

110; Wilson, *First Summit,* quotation on 60. It was obvious that Chief of Staff George Marshall and other military chiefs found it difficult to wrench themselves from the interwar experience of low military budgets and vigilant civilian oversight. In fact, Congress, as late as May 1940—a week before the German army overran the Low Countries—rejected increases in military spending.

47. See Brigante, *Feasibility Dispute,* 23–26, for the most comprehensive overview of the planners' activities. See also Koistinen, *Hammer and Sword,* 627–28; Nelson, *Arsenal of Democracy,* 160ff.; USCPA, *Industrial Mobilization for War,* 133–40.

48. Koenig, *Presidency and the Crisis,* 96; Fesler to Belsley, "Relations Between the Armed Services and the Advisory Commission," Fesler Papers. For similar sentiments, see First, *Industry and Labor Advisory Committees,* 2; Catton, *War Lords of Washington,* 27.

49. Section 1, Executive Order No. 9040, quoted in USCPA, *Industrial Mobilization for War,* 208. See also documents, including letters from Roosevelt to Nelson, in Official File 4735, Box 1, "War Production Board, January–March, 1942," FDRL; Nelson, *Arsenal of Democracy,* 196.

50. Fesler to Belsley, "Relations Between the Armed Services and the Advisory Commission," Fesler Papers, 43. See also Donald H. Riddle, *The Truman Committee: A Study in Congressional Responsibility* (New Brunswick, N.J.: Rutgers University Press, 1964), 69.

51. USCPA, *Industrial Mobilization for War,* 972.

52. Ibid., 209–12, 581, quotation on 211; Riddle, *Truman Committee,* 68.

53. Nelson, *Arsenal of Democracy,* 199–201. Also see Nelson's statements to the Truman Committee, *Hearings,* Part 8, 2449; Truman Committee, *Hearings,* 77th Congress, 2d sess., 1942, Part 12, esp. 5089, 5227–31; USCPA, *Industrial Mobilization for War,* 972, 981–82.

54. See Nelson, *Arsenal of Democracy,* 369–71. Also see Nelson's optimistic statements to the Truman Committee concerning his ability to control military procurement by placing production men alongside military procurement heads (Truman Committee, *Hearings,* Part 12, 5229–31); W. L. Batt's comments in "Minutes of WPB Policy Analysis and Records Branch (PARB) Staff Meeting," 4 May 1945, Fesler Papers; USCPA, *Industrial Mobilization for War,* 524–25; Catton, *War Lords of Washington,* 201. Herman Somers discerns, "For one reason or another the military establishments were thus involved in every facet of the home front war program" (*Presidential Agency,* 110).

55. Nelson Testimony before Truman Committee, *Hearings,* Part 12, 5079–89. See Truman letter to Nelson, reproduced in Nelson, *Arsenal of Democracy,* 335–36.

56. Koistinen, *Hammer and Sword,* 161. See also USCPA, *Industrial Mobilization for War,* 319–20.

57. Truman Committee, *Hearings,* Part 12, 5019–20. Nelson, by contrast, resigned his position with Sears and earned $15,000 as a top-level government employee. See both Guthrie and Reed comments in Truman Committee, *Hearings,* Part 12, 4959ff., Knowlson quotation on 5001.

58. Nathan memorandum of 16 March 1942, reprinted in Truman Committee, *Hearings,* Part 12, 4997; Nathan testimony before Truman Committee, *Hearings,* Part 12, 5037; Truman quoted in Truman Committee, *Hearings,* Part 12, 5066.

59. First, *Industry and Labor Advisory Committees,* 85, 92, 95–96, quotation on 114. See also Koistinen, *Hammer and Sword,* 587; Knowlson quoted in Schuck, "Industry and Labor Advisory Committees in the WPB," RG 179, NA, 186.

60. First, *Industry and Labor Advisory Committees,* 141. See also Schuck, "Industry and Labor Advisory Committees in the WPB," RG 179, NA, 107.

61. First, *Industry and Labor Advisory Committees,* 123–24, 150–51, quotation on 155. Similar points are made in Schuck, "Industry and Labor Advisory Committees in the WPB," RG 179, NA, 127–29. See also Koistinen, *Hammer and Sword,* 588; Truman Committee, *Interim Report on Steel,* 8.

4: The Politics of Wartime Mobilization

1. Murray Committee, *Additional Report,* Report No. 479, Part 2, 13. See also Truman Committee, *Priorities and Utilization,* in *First Annual Report,* Appendix II, 191–94; W. L. Batt's comments in "Minutes of WPB Policy Analysis and Records Branch (PARB) Staff Meeting," 4 May 1945, Box 2, Fesler Papers.

2. Truman Committee, *Priorities and Utilization,* in *First Annual Report,* Appendix II, quotation on 193; USBOB, *United States at War,* 112–13.

3. Truman Committee, *Priorities and Utilization,* in *First Annual Report,* Appendix II, quotation on 193–94; USCPA, *Industrial Mobilization for War,* 981; Tolan Committee, *Third Interim Report,* 83.

4. Millett, *Army Service Forces,* 27; Smith, *Army and Economic Mobilization,* 111.

5. Smith, *Army and Economic Mobilization,* quotation on 111. Brigante, *Feasibility Dispute,* quotation on 63; Millett, *Army Service Forces,* quotation on 283. See also the extremely critical assessment of military capabilities by the Truman Committee in *Priorities and Utilization,* in *First Annual Report,* Appendix II, 192.

6. Truman Committee, *Hearings,* Part 8, 2449; Koistinen, *Hammer and Sword,* 695–98.

7. The War Department's defense of its procurement responsibilities, entitled *Military Responsibility for Equipping the Armed Forces* (19 February 1943) is reviewed and summarized in Smith, *Army and Economic Mobilization,* 238ff., quotations on 239, 211 (emphasis added). Clay quoted in Jean Edward Smith, *Lucius D. Clay: An American Life* (New York: Henry Holt, 1990), 114. See also USBOB, *United States at War,* 130–31; Janeway, *Struggle for Survival,* 204.

8. USCPA, *Industrial Mobilization for War,* 151–52.

9. Hammond, *Organizing for Defense;* Millett, *Army Service Forces,* 18–26. The Office of the Assistant Secretary of War (OASW) was replaced by the Office of the Under Secretary of War (OUSW) on 12 December 1940 to ensure unified civilian command. Under the National Defense Act of 1920 the secretary and assistant secretary of war had separate command authority, and this had led to difficult quarrels during 1939 between Stimson's and Patterson's predecessors.

10. As noted, because procurement duty was considered beneath most career army officers, Patterson recruited lawyers from prominent New York firms. See Smith, *Army and Economic Mobilization,* 111.

11. Smith, *Army and Economic Mobilization,* 106–9, quotation on 106; Hammond, *Organizing for Defense,* 113–14, 116; Millett, *Army Service Forces,* 25–36, quotations on 6, 34; Koistinen, *Hammer and Sword,* quotation on 199–200.

Somervell, during his army career, had served as New York City director of the Works Projects Administration.

12. Hammond, *Organizing for Defense,* 123–28, quotation on 123; Millett, *Army Service Forces,* 38–39; Koistinen, *Hammer and Sword,* 199.

13. Hoopes and Brinkley, *Driven Patriot,* 111, 142. See also Connery, *Navy and Industrial Mobilization,* 143–52; Hammond, *Organizing for Defense,* 146–50.

14. Hammond, *Organizing for Defense,* 140ff., quotation on 139; Connery, *Navy and Industrial Mobilization,* 146, 150–51; Hoopes and Brinkley, *Driven Patriot,* 135–38, 174–75.

15. For a list of those chosen to serve alongside Forrestal and their business affiliations, see Dorwart, *Eberstadt and Forrestal,* 34–35. See also Hammond, *Organizing for Defense,* 145, 150–57.

16. Robert Albion and Robert Connery, *Forrestal and the Navy* (New York: Columbia University Press, 1962), quotation on 108. The War Department spent just under $180 billion of the $316 billion designated as wartime national defense expenditure; the navy spent just under $84 billion. Total U.S. wartime expenditures reached $337 billion. Numbers derived from USCPA document *The Production Statement,* cited in Smith, *Army and Economic Mobilization,* 6. See also Connery, *Navy and Industrial Mobilization,* 160; USCPA, *Industrial Mobilization for War,* 523.

17. USCPA, *Industrial Mobilization for War,* 214, Nelson quotation on 216. See the text of agreement between Nelson and War Department in Nelson, *Arsenal of Democracy,* 372–76. See also Koistinen, *Hammer and Sword,* 639; Connery, *Navy and Industrial Mobilization,* 142; Millett, *Army Service Forces,* 190–93, 221, 225. An agreement with the army was signed 12 March 1942 and with the navy on 22 April.

18. Bureau of the Budget Director Harold Smith wrote Roosevelt on 5 January 1942 warning about any more expansions in military authority. See "Memorandum for the President," Official File 3716, "ANMB—1939–42," FDRL.

19. Dorwart, *Eberstadt and Forrestal,* quotations on 32, 2; Connery, *Navy and Industrial Mobilization,* 160; Huntington, *Soldier and the State,* 339; Connery, *Navy and Industrial Mobilization,* 157–61; Hoopes and Brinkley, *Driven Patriot,* 166–68; Schwarz, *The Speculator,* 430–33.

20. USCPA, *Industrial Mobilization for War,* 215, quotation on 218; Connery, *Navy and Industrial Mobilization,* 168–69; 173–75; USBOB, *United States at War,* 111; Dorwart, *Eberstadt and Forrestal,* 43–48; Huntington, *Soldier and the State,* 340. For Eberstadt's understanding of the role of the ANMB, see his "Interview with Christman," 15; "Remarks of Ferdinand Eberstadt to Policy Analysis Staff," 5 October 1945, Box 163, "Policy Analysis and Records Branch"; and "Notes on Certain Phases of Procurement Planning and Purchasing Between the Services," 20 July 1945, Box 7, all in Eberstadt Papers.

21. Hooks, *Forging the Military-Industrial Complex.*

22. USCPA, *Industrial Mobilization for War,* 151–52, Somervell quotation on 274.

23. Planning Committee Recommendation No. 3, "Planning Committee Activities, February 20 to September 9, 1942," and Robert Nathan to James Fesler, 9 September 1942, WPB-PARB, "Staff Meeting, August 4, 1945," both in Box 2, Fesler Papers.

24. Somervell's "Memorandum for Mr. Nathan," 12 September 1942, Box

234, "WPB Planning Committee," Hopkins Papers. See Brigante, *Feasibility Dispute*, 41–46; G. R. Holden to Leon Henderson, memorandum of 12 December 1941, "Subject: Feasibility of the Victory Program," Box 33, "Feasibility," Henderson Papers.

25. Millett, *Army Service Forces*, quotation on 214; USCPA, *Industrial Mobilization for War*, 364; Brigante, *Feasibility Dispute*, quotation on 53–54. Fesler reports that the U.S. dedicated up to 75 percent of its productive capability to military production. The British managed to commit only 50 percent of their total to military production (unpublished draft of James Fesler autobiography, personal copy). See also figures offered by Isador Lubin in a memorandum to Harry Hopkins "WPB Meeting, October 13, 1942," Box 229, "WPB," Hopkins Papers. As Albert Speer, Hitler's minister of armaments and war production, reports, "It remains one of the oddities of this war that Hitler demanded far less from his people than Churchill and Roosevelt did from [theirs]" (*Inside the Third Reich: Memoirs* [New York: Macmillan, 1970], 214).

26. WPB-PARB memorandum, "Remarks by Commander Milton Katz, August 31, 1945," Box 2, Fesler Papers; Smith, *Army and Economic Mobilization*, 173, 255; Fesler, unpublished autobiography, 87–88. See also Brigante, *Feasibility Dispute*, 46–53, 56–61; Koistinen, *Hammer and Sword*, 645; USCPA, *Industrial Mobilization for War*, 283–84, 363.

27. Nelson Testimony before Tolan Committee, *Third Interim Report*, 82.

28. See WPB Planning Committee Recommendation No. 15, "Feasibility of the Production Program" (19 September 1942); Policy Recommendation No. 3, in "Planning Committee Activities, February 20 to September 9, 1942" (9 September 1942), 5; WPB Planning Committee Doc. 170, "Consideration of the Program Objectives by the War Production Board" (30 September 1942), all in Box 1, Fesler Papers. See also Brigante, *Feasibility Dispute*, 66–70; USCPA, *Industrial Mobilization for War*, 286; unpublished chap. draft for USCPA, *Industrial Mobilization for War*, "The Shift in Emphasis," 12 August 1943, 2–3 (emphasis added), Box 1, Fesler Papers.

29. One observer has concluded that Somervell was most disturbed by the recommendation to increase civilian participation in the determination of military requirements. Somervell had sought authority to coordinate supply and procurement with strategy for his own organization. In May 1942, he went so far as to propose a reorganization of the WPB that would place control of WPB, and thus of the wartime economy, under the Joint Chiefs of Staff (Brigante, *Feasibility Dispute*, 78–81; USBOB, *United States at War*, 129). See Nelson's spirited retort to Somervell in Nelson to Somervell, 21 May 1942, Box 171, "Donald Nelson," PSF, FDRL.

30. Somervell, "Memorandum for Mr. Nathan," Hopkins Papers. See also Nathan's four-page, single-spaced reply dated 17 September 1942, in Box 234, "WPB Planning Committee," Hopkins Papers; USCPA, *Industrial Mobilization for War*, 287. It should be noted that, although Somervell dismissed the work of the Planning Committee, the committee correctly estimated 1942 production totals to within $1 billion, out of a $90 billion total. See Brigante, *Feasibility Dispute*, 68.

31. "Digest of minutes from WPB meeting of October 6, 1942," in Box 234, "Digest of Minutes," Hopkins Papers. See also Brigante, *Feasibility Dispute*, 88–96; USCPA, *Industrial Mobilization for War*, 288–89; Millett, *Army Service Forces*, 216–18. First and third quotations in Brigante, *Feasibility Dispute*, 95. Henderson's

comments recorded in Thomas Blaisdell's notes of the meeting, "Memorandum regarding Meeting of the [WPB], October 6, 1942," Box 6, "War Production Board, Misc. Correspondence," Thomas Blaisdell Papers, Harry S. Truman Presidential Library (HSTL). See also Box 33, "Feasibility," Henderson Papers.

32. As the official history of mobilization reports, "By the end of 1942, the Joint Chiefs of Staff had revised the 1943 military program downward, from $92.9 billion to $80.15 billion" (USCPA, *Industrial Mobilization for War*, 365, also 289, 356); Millett, *Army Service Forces*, 218–19; Brigante, *Feasibility Dispute*, 100–104.

33. David Novick, Melvin Anshen, and W. C. Truppner, *Wartime Production Controls* (New York: Columbia University Press, 1949), 32, 193, 195; USCPA, *Industrial Mobilization for War*, 533.

34. USCPA, *Industrial Mobilization for War*, 461–62, 477–78, 509–11, 517, quotation on 510. See Planning Committee Recommendation No. 15, "Feasibility of the Production Program" (9 September 1942), Fesler Papers; USBOB, *United States at War*, 302–3.

35. USCPA, *Industrial Mobilization for War*, 513; Millett, *Army Service Forces*, 111–23.

36. Millett, *Army Service Forces*, 114; Smith, *Army and Economic Mobilization*, 173.

37. See USBOB, *United States at War*, 112–15, 129, 299–302; Tolan Committee, *Sixth Interim Report*, 77th Congress, 2d sess., 1942, Report No. 2589, 22; USCPA, *Industrial Mobilization for War*, 462–63; Nelson to Somervell, 21 May 1942, Box 171, "Donald Nelson," PSF, FDRL (with handwritten note from Roosevelt to Hopkins "read and return for my confidential file").

38. Even the Planning Committee investigated alternatives to the plan, since Nathan realized that any viable material-control system would have to accommodate the military's de facto control of procurement and scheduling. See Planning Committee Recommendation No. 17, "Control of the Flow of Materials," in 9 September 1942 memorandum, "Planning Committee Activities," Box 1, Fesler Papers; USCPA, *Industrial Mobilization for War*, 456–59; Smith, *Army and Economic Mobilization*, 555–64.

39. Novick, Anshen, and Truppner, *Wartime Production Controls*, 128–37 (David Novick was the principle author of the PRP); USBOB, *United States at War*, 306. James Knowlson, who administered the PRP, wrote to WPB historians immediately after the war to say "the [PRP] did not fail. . . . It *apparently* failed, to be sure, but . . . no plan could succeed as long as the Services' requirements were so greatly in excess of the production possibilities" (USCPA, *Industrial Mobilization for War*, 446–49, 472). For military hostility to the PRP, see Millett, *Army Service Forces*, 208; Smith, *Army and Economic Mobilization*, 562.

40. Novick, Anshen, and Truppner, *Wartime Production Controls*, quotation on 136; Tolan Committee, *Sixth Interim Report*, 22. See Smith, *Army and Economic Mobilization*, 561; USCPA, *Industrial Mobilization for War*, 472, 523.

41. USCPA, *Industrial Mobilization for War*, 220–21, 259, 473; Eberstadt quotation from "Remarks of Ferdinand Eberstadt to Policy Analysis Staff," Eberstadt Papers. Other quotations from James Fesler to J. A. Krug, memorandum of 24 September 1945, "Origins of the Production Executive Committee [PEC]," and "Memo to JWF's Personal Files: Interview with Milton Katz, formerly Solicitor of the WPB," 13 July 1946, both in Box 2, Fesler Papers; USCPA, *Industrial Mobiliza-*

tion for War, 260–62, 485–91, 505–17, quotations on 260–61.

42. Charles Wilson of General Motors wrote to Eberstadt in October 1942 to recommend the auto industry plan (Wilson to Eberstadt, 16 October 1942, Box 163, "WPB: Correspondences, 1941–1942," Eberstadt Papers). A form of the CMP was also under consideration by the WPB's Planning Committee. See USCPA, *Industrial Mobilization for War,* 478–92, quotation on 476; Connery, *Navy and Industrial Mobilization,* 173; Smith, *Army and Economic Mobilization,* 567; Calvin Lee Christman, "Ferdinand Eberstadt and Economic Mobilization for War, 1941–1943" (Ph.D. diss., Ohio State University, 1971), 197–98; USBOB, *United States at War,* 317.

43. Millett, *Army Service Forces,* 210.

44. USCPA, *Industrial Mobilization for War,* 483, other quotations on 632, 629; "Remarks by Commander Milton Katz, August 31, 1945," Fesler Papers. See USCPA, *Industrial Mobilization for War,* 669–70; Novick, Anshen, and Truppner, *Wartime Production Controls,* 195.

45. USCPA, *Industrial Mobilization for War,* 484; Victor Perle and Charles Kramer to Leon Henderson, memorandum of 19 October 1942 (emphasis added), Box 33, "Feasibility," Henderson Papers.

46. USBOB, *United States at War,* 305, quotation on 306; USCPA, *Industrial Mobilization for War,* 261, 446, 488–91, quotation on 630. See also Christman, "Ferdinand Eberstadt," 225, 232–33.

47. Colonel C. F. Robinson, Mr. Livingston, and L. Short to F. Eberstadt, 3 October 1942, Box 163, "WPB: Correspondence, 1941–1942," Eberstadt Papers; Eberstadt quoted in Schuck, "Industry and Labor Advisory Committees in the WPB," RG 179, NA, 113; O'Brian's sentiment is reported in ibid., 139–40.

48. Nelson, *Arsenal of Democracy,* 209 (emphasis in original); Tolan Committee, *Sixth Interim Report,* 35; Smaller War Plants Corporation Report, *Economic Concentration and World War II,* 37, quotation on 27; Novick, Anshen, and Truppner, *Wartime Production Controls,* quotation on 181.

49. What follows is based on James W. Fesler, "Reflections of a Public Servant," *Bureaucrat* (summer 1987), 3–5; Fesler, unpublished autobiography. The Truman Committee reported: "The representatives and employees of big steel companies dominated the Iron and Steel Branch of the [WPB]" (*Interim Report on Steel,* 2). See Fesler, unpublished autobiography, 89. Eberstadt's aides warned him about the potential for prime contractors to abuse the CMP system even more than they were the existing system (Robinson and Short to Eberstadt, 3 October 1942, Eberstadt Papers).

50. USCPA, *Industrial Mobilization for War,* 616–17. See Robinson and Short to Eberstadt, 3 October 1942, Eberstadt Papers.

51. Fesler, "Origins of the PEC," Fesler Papers, quotation on 2. See also USCPA, *Industrial Mobilization for War,* 505–7.

52. "Memorandum for Mr. Wilson," 16 November 1942, copy in Box 36, "Production Controls," Henderson Papers; USCPA, *Industrial Mobilization for War,* 513–17; Millett, *Army Service Forces,* 220–26; Fesler to Krug, "Origins of the PEC," Fesler Papers.

53. USCPA, *Industrial Mobilization for War,* 518–19, 578–82; Christman, "Ferdinand Eberstadt," 281–87.

54. Fesler, "Interview with Milton Katz," provides great detail of these events; see also Eberstadt's memorandum to himself about the events of 21

February 1943, Box 167, "WPB: Charles Edward Wilson," and "Eberstadt's Interview with Policy Analysis Staff," all in Eberstadt Papers; USCPA, *Industrial Mobilization for War*, 580–87; Nelson, *Arsenal of Democracy*, 387–90; Christman, "Ferdinand Eberstadt," 291–310.

55. See Robert Nathan's comments before WPB Policy Analysis and Records Branch Staff Meeting, 4 August 1945, in Box 2, Fesler Papers. When Knudsen, former president of General Motors and then OPM cochair, left the employment of the civilian agencies with the creation of the War Production Board, the army offered him a commission of lieutenant general, which he accepted. Nathan, upon his resignation from the WPB, lost his deferment status and was inducted into the army as a private (USCPA, *Industrial Mobilization for War*, 587).

56. Fesler, "Interview with Milton Katz," Fesler Papers. See also Koistinen, *Hammer and Sword*, 662; Fesler, unpublished autobiography, 94.

57. Hooks, *Forging the Military-Industrial Complex*, 107, 171; Fesler, unpublished autobiography, 94. See also James Fesler, "Mobilization of Industry for War," *Public Administration Review* 5 (1945): 261.

5: Reconversion Politics

1. See USCPA, *Industrial Mobilization for War*, 721, 731–32; Koistinen, *Hammer and Sword*, 698–703; J. Carlyle Sitterson, *Development of the Reconversion Policies of the War Production Board, April 1943 to January 1945*, USCPA Special Study No. 15 (Washington, D.C.: Government Printing Office, 1946), 44.

2. See Somers, *Presidential Agency*, 35–38; Riddle, *Truman Committee*, 79–81; USCPA, *Industrial Mobilization for War*, 554.

3. Byrnes, for example, wrote Roosevelt concerning one instance in which Roosevelt left Byrnes out of the loop on an important issue: "Heretofore, when heads of agencies have brought to me their controversies, they have accepted my decision only because they believed I would have your unqualified support. They cannot have that view now. I know they will feel that if I am not consulted about matters in my own office, I certainly will not have much influence about matters in their offices. Therefore, I cannot be of service to you . . . I want to leave." Roosevelt, of course, declined to let Byrnes go, but pleading of this sort from Byrnes to Roosevelt ensured that Byrnes would continue to exercise substantial authority (Byrnes to Roosevelt, 26 January 1944, Box 132, "J. Byrnes," PSF, FDRL).

4. See USCPA, *Industrial Mobilization for War*, 554–56, 721–22. Also, Nelson spells out his understanding of the WPB-OWM relationship in a letter to Byrnes dated simply "June 1944" that contains the handwritten notation "Not sent as letter, but used at a meeting by OWM" (Box 14, "WPB-Organization," Milton Katz Papers, HSTL). For Byrnes's background, see Philip H. Burch Jr., *Elites in American History*, vol. 3, *The New Deal to the Carter Administration* (New York: Holmes and Meier, 1980), 81–82; Millett, *Army Service Forces*, quotation on 228.

5. See Sitterson, *Reconversion Policies*, 3–8, 21, 40–42, 50, 71–73; see also section entitled "Programming and Controls Before and After V-E Day," 128ff.; USCPA, *Industrial Mobilization for War*, 622, 731–32, 797–98; Jack Peltason, "The Reconversion Controversy," in Stein, ed., *Public Administration and Policy Development*, 228, 231; Koistinen, *Hammer and Sword*, 705; Catton, *War Lords of Washing-*

ton, 247; Kanzler's report "Economic Demobilization and Reconversion: The Problems and Some Recommendations," copy in G. Lyle Belsley Papers, HSTL, quotation on 30.

6. USCPA, *Industrial Mobilization for War,* 909, quotation on 814. See Sitterson, *Reconversion Policies,* 22, 49–50, 110–13; Koistinen, *Hammer and Sword,* 725–26.

7. Bernard M. Baruch and John Hancock, *Report on War and Post-War Adjustment Policies* (Washington, D.C.: Government Printing Office, 1944); Max Lerner quoted in Schwarz, *The Speculator,* 460.

8. Peltason, "Reconversion Controversy," 229–30; Sitterson, *Reconversion Policies,* 13–14; Jones, *Office of Civilian Requirements,* 275.

9. Nelson elaborated his viewpoint of reconversion in a letter to Senator Francis Maloney on 7 March 1944, copy in Box 6, "Reconversion," Office Files of Bernard Gladieux, RG 250, NA. In the same file, see "Considerations For the Job Ahead," Raymond T. Bowman to B. L. Gladieux and C. E. Craine, memorandum of 8 March 1944, which spells out in detail the stages of reconversion and the need for programming. See also Peltason, "Reconversion Controversy," 224–27; Sitterson, *Reconversion Policies,* 25–26, 65–70; USCPA, *Industrial Mobilization for War,* 791.

10. USCPA, *Industrial Mobilization for War,* 732–36, quotation on 733; Sitterson to Fesler, "Interview with Bernard Gladieux," memorandum of 15 November 1944, in Box 1, Fesler Papers; Sitterson, *Reconversion Policies,* 71–76; Catton, *War Lords of Washington,* 245–49; Somers, *Presidential Agency,* 181; Peltason, "Reconversion Controversy," 230–40.

11. Clay's plan was prepared by J. Anthony Panuch. A detailed, day-by-day account of this controversy was produced at the time under the title "Organization of Army-Navy-WPB Machinery for Administration of Cut-Backs and Industrial Reconversion: Daily Log of Activities," Box 6, "PPAC Plan on Reconversion," J. Anthony Panuch Papers, HSTL.

12. USCPA, *Industrial Mobilization for War,* 736; Sitterson to Fesler, "Interview with Bernard Gladieux," Fesler Papers; Peltason, "Reconversion Controversy," 239.

13. USCPA, *Industrial Mobilization for War,* 791–95; Nelson, *Arsenal of Democracy,* 395–96; Sitterson, *Reconversion Policies,* 41–46; Jones, *Office of Civilian Requirements,* 278–79; Eiler, *Mobilizing America,* 391–96. Generally, see George Q. Flynn, *The Mess in Washington: Manpower Mobilization in World War II* (Westport, Conn.: Greenwood Press, 1979).

14. USCPA, *Industrial Mobilization for War,* quotation on 737; Sitterson, *Reconversion Policies,* 38; Catton, *War Lords of Washington,* 261. Some sources place the number of displaced workers at 9,000, although a union official writing the president cited 13,000 jobs lost (Official File 526, "Brewster Aeronautical Corporation," FDRL).

15. Sitterson to Fesler, "Interview with Bernard Gladieux," Fesler Papers. See also USCPA, *Industrial Mobilization for War,* 737–39; USBOB, *United States at War,* 486; Sitterson, *Reconversion Policies,* 77–79; V. O. Key Jr., "The American Road to Peace, A Symposium: The Reconversion Phase of Demobilization," *American Political Science Review* 38 (1944): 1139–42.

16. Somers, *Presidential Agency,* 84–91, quotations on 78, 65. See Byrnes's prepared comments to the Senate committee considering OWMR legislation in

a memorandum to Roosevelt, 10 June 1944, Box 132, "J. Byrnes, 1942–1945," PSF, FDRL.

17. Byrnes to Nelson, 31 March 1944, quoted in Sitterson, *Reconversion Policies*, 77, 85–86; USCPA, *Industrial Mobilization for War*, 784–86, 887–88.

18. See Catton, *War Lords of Washington*, 250–56; Sitterson, *Reconversion Policies*, 90–94.

19. The plan was released through Wilson's office. See "Memo from C. E. Wilson" to members of WPB, 1 July 1944, Box 6, "Reconversion," Gladieux Office Files. Briefly, the steps included: first, lifting aluminum and magnesium restrictions for essential civilian end products; second, allowing orders for surplus or new machine tool equipment; third, allowing in some cases test models of civilian goods; and, fourth, developing a "spot authorization" plan.

20. See Barton J. Bernstein, "The Removal of War Production Board Controls on Business," *Business History Review* 39 (1965): 244, 251; Richard Polenberg, *War and Society: The United States, 1941–1945* (Philadelphia: J. B. Lippincott, 1972), 230; Sitterson, *Reconversion Policies*, 69, 77.

21. See esp. Barton J. Bernstein, "The Debate on Industrial Reconversion— The Protection of Oligopoly and Military Control of the Economy," *American Journal of Economics and Sociology* 26 (1967): 159–72; Sitterson, *Reconversion Policies*, quotation on 54. For official numbers on economic concentration during World War II, see Murray Committee, *Additional Report*, Report No. 479, Part 2, 6–7. Also see Smaller War Plants Corporation Report, *Economic Concentration and World War II*.

22. Sitterson, *Reconversion Policies*, quotations on 134, 50; Catton, *War Lords of Washington*, 245–48; USCPA, *Industrial Mobilization for War*, 816; Nelson, *Arsenal of Democracy*, 398–99. See also Nelson to Senator Francis Maloney, 7 March 1944, Gladieux Papers.

23. Leahy and Nelson letters in FDR's Official File 4735, Box 2, "WPB, July–August 1944"; Byrnes, "Memorandum for the President," 29 July 1944, Official File 4735, Box 2, "WPB, July–August 1944," FDRL; Keenan and Golden in WPB Doc. 305, 4 July 1944, Box 6, "Reconversion," Gladieux Papers.

24. Nelson, *Arsenal of Democracy*, 410; USCPA, *Industrial Mobilization for War*, 739, 802–3; Sitterson, *Reconversion Policies*, 94–98; Peltason, "Reconversion Controversy," 245. Ostensibly, military spokesmen were only trying to play down optimistic reports of the war's imminent end. However, they had themselves promoted optimism, with Patterson's declaration in August 1944 that Germany would collapse within four months one of the more egregious examples. See Eiler, *Mobilizing America*, 409; Peltason, "Reconversion Controversy," 246, 251–55, 260; Koistinen, *Hammer and Sword*, 714–20; Catton, *War Lords of Washington*, 266–68; Millett, *Army Service Forces*, 229–30; Sitterson, *Reconversion Policies*, 98–99.

25. See Truman Committee, *Fourth Annual Report*, 79th Congress, 1st sess., 1945, Report No. 110, Part 4, 6; Nelson, *Arsenal of Democracy*, 408; USCPA, *Industrial Mobilization for War*, 806. The services had canceled $13 billion worth of contracts by March 1944 (see Truman Committee, *Third Annual Report*, 27). See excerpts of Byrnes's directive entitled "To Provide Adequate Manpower for Essential War Production," in Sitterson, *Reconversion Policies*, 117–18.

26. For an analysis of the whole affair, see Peltason, "Reconversion Controversy," 256–60. For Nelson's viewpoint, see Nelson, *Arsenal of Democracy*, 412–16.

See also USCPA, *Industrial Mobilization for War,* 739–41. C. E. Wilson to Roosevelt, 23 August 1944, and Roosevelt to Krug, 25 August 1944, Official File 4753, Box 2, "WPB, July–August, 1944," FDRL; files containing materials concerning Nelson's removal in Box 171, "WPB: D. Nelson," PSF, FDRL; Hopkins's files on the events in Box 335, Book 9, "Explosion in WPB," Hopkins Papers.

27. Peltason, "Reconversion Controversy," 260–70; Sitterson, *Reconversion Policies,* 125, 155–57; USCPA, *Industrial Mobilization for War,* quotation on 863; USBOB, *United States at War,* 489–90. See Budget Bureau Director Harold Smith's formal complaint to Roosevelt about too high military procurement in Smith to Roosevelt, 31 August 1944, Box 2, Smith Papers; USCPA, *Industrial Mobilization for War,* 902.

28. "CIO Reconversion Statement," 1 May 1945, Philip Murray, president of the Congress of Industrial Organizations to Judge Fred Vinson, director, OWMR, Box 230, "CIO," Robert Nathan Papers, RG 250, NA.

29. Key, "Reconversion Phase of Demobilization," 1137. George Baldanzi, a vice president of the Textile Workers Union of America, and a member of the executive board of the Congress of Industrial Organizations, called the Baruch Plan a "Beveridge Plan for Millionaires." See his "Organized Labor and the State," in Arnold Zurcher and Raymond Page, eds., *Postwar Economic Society: Addresses Delivered at the Series of Conferences of the Institute on Postwar Reconstruction,* 4 vols. (New York: New York University Press, 1944), 1:99.

30. WPB quotation from "Considerations of the Job Ahead," Raymond T. Bowman to B. L. Gladieux and L. E. Craine, memorandum of 8 March 1944, Box 6, "Reconversion," Gladieux Papers; USCPA, *Industrial Mobilization for War,* quotations on 815–16, 905.

31. Krug's justifications found in "War Production and Reconversion," by J. A. Krug, chairman, [WPB], WPB Doc. 328, 19 May 1945, copy in Box 230, "Controls," Nathan Papers; Boulware quoted in USCPA, *Industrial Mobilization for War,* 814–18, 861–62, 951–52, esp. 817; Sitterson, *Reconversion Policies,* 131–41, 142–46; Koistinen, *Hammer and Sword,* 744; Bernstein, "Removal of Controls," quotation on 245; Krug to Vinson, 24 April 1945, letter quoted in USCPA, *Industrial Mobilization for War,* 902. Ferdinand Eberstadt also has claimed that Krug was "one of my men" ("Interview with Christman," Eberstadt Papers).

32. See Nathan's comments in a draft letter to be sent by Vinson to Krug protesting his decision to release controls (6 June 1945, Box 230, "Controls," Nathan Papers).

33. Undated memorandum from Nathan to Vinson (probably late May 1945), Box 232, "Military Programs," Nathan Papers; Murray in "CIO Reconversion Statement," Murray to Vinson, Nathan Papers.

34. Somers, *Presidential Agency,* 88.

35. Ibid., 76–80; Sitterson, *Reconversion Policies,* 149–53, Baruch quotation on 29; USBOB, *United States at War,* 475–78. For an overview of the congressional process resulting in the OWMR legislation, see Steven Kemp Bailey, *Congress Makes a Law: The Story behind the Employment Act of 1946* (New York: Columbia University Press, 1950), 30–35.

36. Apathy was pronounced in 1942 as Roosevelt essentially ignored the election. Yet exacerbating the low level of campaign activity was the fact that many voters became disenfranchised as they changed districts because of war work, or because of their service in the armed forces. Republican voters, older

and less likely to have been uprooted by the war, represented a larger percentage of those who voted than would have otherwise been true. See Torbjorn Sirevag, *The Eclipse of the New Deal and the Fall of Vice-President Wallace, 1944* (New York: Garland, 1985), 180–81, 204–9; James Boylan, *The New Deal Coalition and the Election of 1946* (New York: Garland, 1981), 5–7; Richard E. Darilek, *A Loyal Opposition in Time of War: The Republican Party and the Politics of Foreign Policy from Pearl Harbor to Yalta* (Westport, Conn.: Greenwood Press, 1976), 53–57; Thomas Eliot and Samuel Grafton, "The Meaning of the Elections" *New Republic* (16 November 1942): 623–42.

37. The final product, the Employment Act of 1946, provided for the creation of a Council of Economic Advisors and the rhetorical commitment to "maximum" versus "full" employment alongside its commitment to "free competitive enterprise." Very little of the original bill's commitment to active governmental fiscal intervention in the event of economic downturn remained. See Bailey, *Congress Makes a Law.*

38. Huthmacher, *Senator Wagner,* 292–96; Bailey, *Congress Makes a Law,* 30–35; Koistinen, *Hammer and Sword,* 759–65; Roland Young, *Congressional Politics in the Second World War* (New York: Columbia University Press, 1956), 207–11.

39. Senate Special Committee on Post-war Economic Policy and Planning, *Post-War Economic Policy and Planning,* 78th Congress, 2d sess., 1944, Report No. 530, Part 4, 7; Smaller War Plants Corporation Report, *Economic Concentration and World War II,* 46–47, quotations on 39 and 46, emphasis in original. See also Truman Committee, *Third Annual Report,* 36–37. The SWPC was created by the Small Business Act of 11 June 1942. The Smaller War Plants Division of the WPB was also created by Nelson under authority granted him by the act. These agencies were to help spread war work to smaller firms by helping these firms gain financing and contracts. See USCPA, *Industrial Mobilization for War,* 527–32.

40. Smaller War Plants Corporation Report, *Economic Concentration and World War II,* 48. See Walter Adams and Horace M. Gray, *Monopoly in America: The Government as Promoter* (New York: Macmillan, 1955), 120; these authors go on to show how most wartime constructed steel plants were sold to wartime operators. For the strengthening of oligopoly in the steel industry by these sales, see Walter Adams, *The Structure of American Industry: Some Case Studies,* 4th ed. (New York: Macmillan, 1971), 158–59; Alvin H. Hansen, *The Postwar American Economy: Performance and Problems* (New York: W. W. Norton, 1964), 29.

41. Hansen, *Postwar American Economy,* quotations, in order, on 29, 10–11. See also Truman Committee, *Third Annual Report,* 37. Wage controls limited labor's gains while speedup conditions combined with the influx of inexperienced workers to produce a massive number of factory casualties. The 1947 *Handbook of Labor Statistics* reported that 88,100 workers were killed and 11,112,6000 were injured during five years of war, a total that surpassed battlefield casualties (Richard O. Boyer and Herbert M. Morais, *Labor's Untold Story* [New York: United Electrical, Radio and Machine Workers of America, 1955], 336). Work-related casualties were substantial even before war was declared. Industrial accidents in 1940 resulted in four times the loss of man-hours on the job as work stoppages, and this does not include the losses resulting from some 11,000 deaths (Purcell, *Labor Policies of the NDAC and OPM,* 171).

42. "Commercial" Keynesianism is Robert Lekachman's term (*Age of Keynes,* 287).

43. See Fred Block, *The Origins of International Economic Disorder: A Study of United States International Monetary Policy from World War II to the Present* (Berkeley: University of California Press, 1977), 33–35; David Eakins, "The Development of Corporate Liberal Policy Research in the United States, 1885–1965" (Ph.D. diss., University of Wisconsin, 1966), 334–38; William Steinert Hill Jr., "The Business Community and National Defense: Corporate Leaders and the Military, 1943–1950" (Ph.D. diss., Stanford University, 1980), 49–53, 56–69, 112ff.

44. David Eakins analyzes the contribution of other corporate liberal research groups in "Corporate Liberal Policy Research." For more on this topic, see chap. 7.

45. Karl Schriftgiesser, *Business Comes of Age: The Story of the Committee for Economic Development and Its Impact upon the Economic Policies of the United States, 1942–1960* (New York: Harper and Brothers, 1960), 93; Francis X. Sutton et al., *The American Business Creed* (Cambridge, Mass.: Harvard University Press, 1956), quotations on 33, 42; Robert M. Collins, *The Business Response to Keynes, 1929–1964* (New York: Columbia University Press, 1981), 49–58, quotation is title of chap. 2; McQuaid, *Big Business and Presidential Power,* 29–32, 111. Collins also notes that BAC personnel "would fill many of the top positions in mobilization agencies" (*Business Response to Keynes,* 62).

46. Schriftgiesser, *Business Comes of Age,* 17, 24. Hoffman and Benton came in contact early in 1941 (Hoffman to Benton, 12 May 1941, Box 40, "CED, 1941–1942," Paul Hoffman Papers, HSTL). See also Jones to Roosevelt, 12 June 1942, Official File 4351, Box 1, "Postwar Problems, 1942," FDRL. Before Roosevelt responded, he wrote Cordell Hull asking for advice, saying, "I think there is real danger in having Jesse Jones expand his thought as contained in this letter." Roosevelt finally responded to Jones on 15 July 1942 and discouraged Jones from proceeding: "I hope . . . that on all domestic issues, these studies by each agency of the government should be coordinated through Mr. Frederic Delano [of the National Resources Planning Board] . . . there is great danger of confusion if several committees of this kind are set up." Jones went ahead nonetheless. For the connections between BAC and CED, see McQuaid, *Big Business and Presidential Power,* 114–17; William Benton, "Speech Before Citizens Board of the University of Chicago," 26 October 1943, Box 40, "CED Correspondence 1948–'62," Hoffman Papers.

47. Jesse Jones, "Secretary of Commerce Jesse H. Jones to the Conference of the Committee for Economic Development, Waldorf Astoria," Box 40, "CED First Meeting," Hoffman Papers; Gardiner Means to Jay C. Hormel, president, Hormel and Company, 29 May 1945, Box 21, "Correspondences, G-H," Gardiner Means Papers, FDRL.

48. Norman D. Markowitz, *The Rise and Fall of the People's Century: Henry A. Wallace and American Liberalism, 1941–1948* (New York: Free Press, 1973), 63. See also Charles S. Maier, "The Politics of Productivity: The Foundations of American International Economic Policy after World War II," *International Organization* 31 (1977): 607–33.

49. "Jones to the Conference of the Committee for Economic Development," Hoffman Papers; Hoffman, "Expansion of Private Enterprise and World Markets," speech before International Chamber of Commerce, London, 17 August 1945, Box 108, "Speech File, 1945," Hoffman Papers.

50. Historian Robert Collins does show that the U.S. Chamber of Commerce

under Eric Johnston's leadership warmed to "Keynesianism in its most attenuated and conservative form" before retreating to a knee-jerk form of laissez-faire with Johnston's departure in 1946 (*Business Response to Keynes*, 88, 117–19).

51. Hoffman, "Expansion of Private Enterprise and World Markets," Hoffman Papers; John Maurice Clark, *Demobilization of Wartime Economic Controls* (New York: McGraw-Hill, 1944), quotation on 202. See also Clark to "Gardiner and Howard," in Box 21, "Correspondence: John M. Clark," Means Papers; Schriftgiesser, *Business Comes of Age*, quotation on 16.

52. Clark, *Demobilization*, 201, emphasis added; Schriftgiesser, *Business Comes of Age*, 17–27; Hoffman, address to the National Retail Dry Goods Association, 13 January 1944, copy in Box 21, "Correspondences, G–H," Means Papers.

53. Hoffman to Truman, 4 August 1945, Box 230, "C.E.D.," Nathan Papers; Howard B. Myers to CED Research Committee, "The Murray 'Full Employment' Bill," memorandum of 5 February 1945, copy and other relevant materials in Box 25, "High Employment—Study," Means Papers. See also Schriftgiesser, *Business Comes of Age*, 90–99; Bailey, *Congress Makes a Law*, 138.

54. Collins, *Business Response to Keynes*, 86, 130–41, quotation on 139; Schriftgiesser, *Business Comes of Age*, 81–82, 95–99, 104–16; Hoffman testimony before Senate Subcommittee of the Committee on Banking and Currency, *Hearings*, 79th Congress, 1st session, Part 10, 30 August 1945, 940.

55. Early on, some members of the CED went out of their way to de-emphasize foreign trade as a factor in stabilizing the U.S. domestic economy. See Flanders to Robert H. Patchin, vice president, W. R. Grace and Company, cc's to other CED directors and staff, 2 February 1945, Box 21, "Correspondence—Flanders, Ralph," and Means to Brady, 8 January 1944, Box 20, "Correspondence—Brady, Robert," both in Means Papers. The committee later forcefully revised its thinking in its deliberations over the Marshall Plan. See materials in Box 31, "Marshall Plan," Means Papers.

56. Gary Mucciaroni, "Political Learning and Economic Policy Innovation: The United States and Sweden in the Post–World War II Era," *Journal of Policy History* 1 (1989): 398, 406.

6: Constructing Postwar Governance

1. Huntington, *Soldier and the State*, 315.

2. See, for example, Williams, *Contours of American History*.

3. William Appleman Williams, *The Tragedy of American Diplomacy* (New York: Dell Publishing, 1962), 232–37, 270–71; David Eakins, "Business Planners and America's Postwar Expansion," in David Horowitz, ed., *Corporations and the Cold War* (New York: Monthly Review Press, 1969), 150–53; Lynn Eden, "Capitalist Conflict and the State: The Making of United States Military Policy in 1948," in Charles Bright and Susan Harding, eds., *Statemaking and Social Movements* (Ann Arbor: University of Michigan Press, 1984), 236–39; David A. Baldwin, *Economic Development and American Foreign Policy, 1943–62* (Chicago: University of Chicago Press, 1966), 14–15, 52.

4. See Block, *Origins of International Economic Disorder*, 35–36, 77–79; Williams, *Tragedy of American Diplomacy*, 173, 268; Melvin P. Leffler, *A Preponderance of Power: National Security, the Truman Administration, and the Cold War* (Stan-

ford, Calif.: Stanford University Press, 1992), 13–21, 36, 107, 162–63.

5. These men included W. Averell Harriman, Dean Acheson, James Forrestal, Robert Lovett, Robert Patterson, John McCloy, and Paul Nitze. See Eden, "Capitalist Conflict," 236–37, 240–41; Hoopes and Brinkley, *Driven Patriot,* 260–64, 293–95, 301–3; Leffler, *Preponderance of Power,* 14, 26ff.; Block, *Origins of International Economic Disorder,* 70. For the background of Truman's advisors, see Burch, *New Deal to the Carter Administration,* 84–87, 98–102. In general see Dorwart, *Eberstadt and Forrestal;* Walter Isaacson and Evan Thomas, *The Wise Men: Six Friends and the World They Made, Acheson, Bohlen, Harriman, Kennan, Lovett, Mc-Cloy* (New York: Simon & Schuster, 1986).

6. McQuaid, *Uneasy Partners: Big Business in American Politics, 1945–1990* (Baltimore: Johns Hopkins University Press, 1992), 42, and chap. 2; Eden, "Capitalist Conflict," 236. See also McQuaid, *Big Business and Presidential Power,* 150; Leffler, *Preponderance of Power,* 14.

7. Draft of the CED's "An American Program of European Economic Cooperation," 14 January 1948, Box 31, "Marshall Plan," Means Papers.

8. See Alonzo Hamby, "The Mind and Character of Harry S. Truman," in Michael J. Lacey, ed., *The Truman Presidency* (New York: Cambridge University Press, 1989), 36.

9. See Lichtenstein, *Most Dangerous Man in Detroit,* 220–47; Lichtenstein, "Labor in the Truman Era," in Lacey, ed., *Truman Presidency,* 128–55; Fraser, *Labor Will Rule,* 560–68; Dubofsky, *State and Labor,* 193–95; Howell John Harris, *The Right to Manage: Industrial Relations Policies of American Business in the 1940s* (Madison: University of Wisconsin Press, 1982), 139ff.

10. See, for example, Fordham, *Building the Cold War Consensus.*

11. Leffler, *Preponderance of Power,* 121. Military spending, of course, remained very high for peacetime and very high in relation to domestic expenditures. See, for example, Michael J. Hogan, *A Cross of Iron: Harry S. Truman and the Origins of the National Security State, 1945–1954* (New York: Cambridge University Press, 1998), 83–84.

12. Clark Clifford, a top Truman aide, remembers how the top-level consensus formed. He was asked by Truman in the summer of 1946 to "produce a record of Soviet violations of International agreements." Clifford and his aide George Elsey, however, decided to go further and after conferring with Truman's top-level international advisors they argued in their report that "as a matter of the highest national security the nation urgently needed to create an integrated policy and a coherent strategy to resist the Soviet Union" (Clifford, *Counsel to the President: A Memoir* [New York: Random House, 1991], 109–28, quotations on 110, 124).

13. See Leffler, *Preponderance of Power,* 107–8, 145. For Forrestal's sponsorship of Kennan, see Hoopes and Brinkley, *Driven Patriot,* 270–81. Of course, the threat of communism had already been employed successfully to obtain passage of a large loan to Britain from a reluctant Congress in 1945.

14. Joseph Jones, "The Drafting of the President's Message to Congress on the Greek Situation," emphasis in original, memorandum of 12 March 1947, Box 1, "Drafts of the Truman Doctrine," Joseph Jones Papers, HSTL; Isaacson and Thomas, *Wise Men,* 395; "Chronology—The Drafting of the President's Message of March 12, 1947" (emphasis added), Box 1, "Drafts of the Truman Doctrine," Jones Papers.

15. Jones, "Drafting of the President's Message," Jones Papers; Robert J. Donovan, *Conflict and Crisis: The Presidency of Harry S Truman, 1945–1948* (New York: W. W. Norton, 1977), 282 (emphasis added). Joseph Jones even remarked upon the cohesiveness and purpose that Truman's speech evoked: "The message was in my opinion momentous not only for it[s] content, but for the *way* in which the Government functioned in the crisis: fast, brave, and clean. It seemed to me as though it marked our passing into adulthood in the conduct of foreign affairs" (Jones, "Drafting of the President's Message," Jones Papers, emphasis in original).

16. Clifford, *Counsel to the President,* 129. See U.S. Department of State, *Foreign Relations of the United States: 1947,* vol. 3 (Washington, D.C.: Government Printing Office, 1972), 197ff.; Leffler, *Preponderance of Power,* 40–44, 104, 142, 147; Michael J. Hogan, *Marshall Plan: America, Britain, and the Reconstruction of Western Europe, 1947–1952* (New York: Cambridge University Press, 1987), 40–45; Block, *Origins of International Economic Disorder,* 82–83; Donovan, *Conflict and Crisis,* 286–87.

17. "Report of the Special 'Ad Hoc' Committee of [SWNCC], April 21, 1947," in State Department, *Foreign Relations,* 3:209, 211. See also materials in Box 1, "Committee on Extension of U.S. Aid to Foreign Governments: RE: State-War-Navy-Coordinating Committee," Jones Papers. For an analysis of the connection between fears for a vigorous export market and U.S. foreign policy after World War II, see Thomas G. Paterson, "The Quest for Peace and Prosperity: International Trade, Communism, and the Marshall Plan," in Barton J. Bernstein, ed., *Politics and Policies of the Truman Administration* (Chicago: Quadrangle, 1970).

18. Richard Barnet, *The Roots of War: The Men and Institutions behind U.S. Foreign Policy* (New York: Penguin, 1973), quotation on 139. See also McQuaid, *Uneasy Partners,* 41–42; Gregory A. Fossedal, *Our Finest Hour: Will Clayton, the Marshall Plan, and the Triumph of Democracy* (Stanford, Calif.: Hoover Institute, 1993), 203, 210–16, 225–32, quotations from Clayton memorandum on 228–229. Marshall reported, "Kennan's [memo] was the most succinct and useful—this was during the embryo period of State's policy planning staff" ("Interview with General George C. Marshall, October 30, 1952," Harry Price Papers, HSTL).

19. David Eakins, "Corporate Liberal Policy Research," 386–87. See Williams, *Tragedy of American Diplomacy,* 239–41, 270; Block, *Origins of International Economic Disorder,* 83–87; Leffler, *Preponderance of Power,* 144–46; Hill, "Business Community and National Defense," 239–44. Reed quoted in CED, "Detailed Discussion Notes: Meeting of the European Relief and Rehabilitation Subcommittee of the Research and Policy Committee, December 12, 1947, Waldorf-Astoria Hotel," Box 31, "Marshall Plan," Means Papers, 13. See also "Summary of Findings—Report of the Harriman Committee on European Recovery and United States Aid," Box 106, Eberstadt Papers.

20. Of course, the Truman Doctrine and the Marshall Plan split liberals, with many opting to join former administration star Henry Wallace in opposition to the growing Cold War consensus. The majority of liberals, however, joined the anticommunist crusade. See Markowitz, *Rise and Fall of the People's Century,* 232, 237, 246–47; Federico Romero, *The United States and the European Trade Union Movement, 1944–1951* (Chapel Hill: University of North Carolina Press, 1992), 27, 101.

21. "Interview with General George Marshall," Price Papers; "Report on the Activities of the Committee for the Marshall Plan to Aid European Recovery,

April 5, 1948," Box 3, "Committee for the Marshall Plan—Correspondences, 1947–48," Dean Acheson Papers, HSTL; Marshall quotation in "Chronology of the Marshall Plan," by Thorstein V. Kalijarvi, 5 November 1947, in Box 106, Eberstadt Papers. See also Alan Brinkley, *End of Reform,* 267–71; Isaacson and Thomas, *Wise Men,* 428–29; Paterson, "Quest for Peace and Prosperity," 97–98; Eakins, "Corporate Liberal Policy Research," 382; Hogan, *Marshall Plan,* 55–58; Charles L. Mee, *The Marshall Plan: The Launching of the Pax Americana* (New York: Simon and Schuster, 1984), 217ff.

22. "Interview with Harold Stein," 7 August 1952, Price Papers. See Mc-Quaid, *Big Business and Presidential Power,* 151–59; Eakins, "Corporate Liberal Policy Research," 371–77, 385–87; Hill, "Business Community and National Defense," 148–50; Hogan, *Marshall Plan,* 97–98. On the ECA, see Hoffman to E. R. Carpenter, 28 April 1948, Box 1, "Chronological File, 1946–48," Hoffman Papers. See also Eakins, "Corporate Liberal Policy Research," 384–85; Hogan, *Marshall Plan,* 105, 108–9, 139–40; Michael Hogan, "American Marshall Planners and the Search for a European Neocapitalism," *American Historical Review* 90 (1985): 54–56. On the related issues of the World Bank and the International Monetary Fund, CED support also proved crucial. See Schriftgiesser, *Business Comes of Age,* 122, also 127–34.

23. See Box 1, "Executive Committee for the Marshall Plan—Minutes and Agendas," Committee for the Marshall Plan Papers, HSTL; Eden, "Capitalist Conflict," 248–53; Frank Kofsky, *Harry S. Truman and the War Scare of 1948: A Successful Campaign to Deceive the Nation* (New York: St. Martin's Press, 1993), 92ff., 124ff., quotations on 97, 125.

24. Besides Kofsky, *Truman and the War Scare of 1948,* see Isaacson and Thomas, *Wise Men,* 440, 444; Paterson, "Quest for Peace and Prosperity," 99; Leffler, *Preponderance of Power,* 203–5.

25. See Leffler, *Preponderance of Power,* 180; Isaacson and Thomas, *Wise Men,* 446.

26. In fact, interservice conflict would continue until the Korean conflict ended the zero-sum scramble by institutionalizing huge military budgets.

27. David Eakins, "Business Planners and America's Postwar Expansion"; Dorwart, *Eberstadt and Forrestal,* 105–6; Leffler, *Preponderance of Power,* 163, 200; Block, *Origins of International Economic Disorder.*

28. For insights into the economic containment thrust of U.S. foreign policy, see Robert A. Pollard, *Economic Security and the Origins of the Cold War, 1945–1950* (New York: Columbia University Press, 1985). For insights into the shift from economic to military containment, see Hogan, *Marshall Plan,* 336ff.; Leffler, *Preponderance of Power,* 209.

29. Forrestal's prepared remarks (emphasis added) for delivery to House Armed Services Committee on 8 January 1948, copy in Box 106, "Marshall Plan: Forrestal, James," Eberstadt Papers. Forrestal also made the connections between economic and military containment clear in his remarks before the president's Air Policy Commission, 3 November 1947, copies of various drafts in Box 2, "1947–1952," Felix Larkin Papers, HSTL. See also Clifford, *Counsel to the President,* 128.

30. Isaacson and Thomas, *Wise Men,* 450; Harry S Truman, *Memoirs,* vol. 2, *Years of Trial and Hope* (New York: Doubleday, 1956), 240ff.; Leffler, *Preponderance of Power,* 216–18.

31. "Summary of Report to Hon. James Forrestal, Secretary of the Navy,

from Mr. F. Eberstadt, on Unification of the War and Navy Departments and Postwar Organization for National Security," 12, 18 October 1945, Box 7, Eberstadt Papers; Walter Millis, ed., *Forrestal Diaries* (New York: Viking, 1951), 166, quotation on 60. For the development and workings of the Joint Chiefs of Staff, see Hammond, *Organizing for Defense,* 159ff. For Marshall and military planning for postwar unification, see Hammond, *Organizing for Defense,* 190, 194, 227; Hogan, *Cross of Iron,* 24–27; Eiler, *Mobilizing America,* 428.

32. See Forrestal to Eberstadt, 19 June 1945, and Forrestal to Stimson, 25 July 1945, both in Box 7, "Correspondences, Armed Services Unification Files," Eberstadt Papers. The navy feared that the Marine Corps and Naval Aviation would be stripped from them under the army plan. For navy fears and views on military unification, see Millis, ed., *Forrestal Diaries,* 97, 167, 205, 223. Also, Forrestal sent Truman on 14 January 1947 a navy report entitled "The Hazards of Merger," Box 145, "Military: Army-Navy Unification," PSF, HSTL.

33. Robert Cuff, "Ferdinand Eberstadt, the National Security Resources Board, and the Search for Integrated Mobilization Planning, 1947–1948," *Public Historian* 7 (1985): 39n. 6. See also Dorwart, *Eberstadt and Forrestal,* 116, 119, 124, 132–33, 140–41. Eberstadt's report would in fact identify dangers of concentrated military authority. See "Summary of Report to Hon. James Forrestal," Eberstadt Papers, 4, 13, 14.

34. Barnet, *Roots of War,* quotation on 19. See also Hogan, *Cross of Iron,* 12–18. Eberstadt iterated the lessons he learned from the war to an interviewer many years later. See Eberstadt, "Interview with Christman," Eberstadt Papers.

35. In his report, Eberstadt identified the proactive and integrated approach he envisioned. See "Report on the Unification of the War and Navy Departments and Postwar National Security, September 1945," Box 9, "Armed Services Unification Files: Report to the Secretary of the Navy, James Forrestal," Eberstadt Papers, esp. 1:13; Forrestal to Clifford, quoted in Alfred D. Sander, "Truman and the National Security Council: 1945–1947," *Journal of American History* 59 (1972): 377. For Forrestal's views linking unification to the need for bringing coherence to U.S. national governance and to sustaining the wartime effort, see Millis, ed., *Forrestal Diaries,* 87, 141–42. See also Hammond, *Organizing for Defense,* 186–232; Dorwart, *Eberstadt and Forrestal,* 92–98, 119; Demetrios Caraley, *The Politics of Military Unification* (New York: Columbia University Press, 1966), 38–44.

36. First quotation and third set of quotations from prepared statement that follows very closely if not exactly the wording of the report itself ("For Release with Eberstadt Report of September 25, 1945 in Morning Papers, October 29, 1945," Box 9, "October 22, 1945," Eberstadt Papers). Second quotation (emphasis added) from "Summary of Report to Hon. James Forrestal," Eberstadt Papers, 3–4.

37. Forrestal in 1944 began the process of institutionalizing wartime military-corporate cooperation when he organized the National Security Industrial Association to ensure that "American business will remain close to the services" (Huntington, *Soldier and the State,* 365). Dorwart also makes it very clear that the "war planning, mobilization, military-industrial combinations, and extensive business-government cooperation" of World War II was crucial to bringing corporate elites into the government and crucial to establishing the state-class alliances that would in turn prove so important to the establishment of the postwar governance project (*Eberstadt and Forrestal,* 6–8, 69, 86, 97, 100–107, 124–25, quotations on 7, 104). See also Hogan, *Cross of Iron,* 67–68.

38. Smith to Truman, 22 May 1946, Box 145, "Military: Army-Navy Unification," PSF, HSTL.

39. Eberstadt and Forrestal, for example, were both concerned that George Marshall's army plan for unification would overcentralize military authority within the national state. Eberstadt worried about this from the perspective of the balance of power between state and society while Forrestal worried about the navy's place within a centralized military apparatus. Forrestal detailed his and the navy's concerns in a 4 June 1946 memorandum to Truman in which he raises the specter of militarism (Box 7, "Selected Correspondences—Armed Services Unification Files," "Miscellaneous," Eberstadt Papers). See also Dorwart, *Eberstadt and Forrestal,* 143; Hogan, *Cross of Iron,* 18, 49–50, 67.

40. Huntington, *Soldier and the State,* 345. See assessment by William Appleman Williams, "The Large Corporation and American Foreign Policy," in David Horowitz, ed., *Corporations and the Cold War* (New York: Monthly Review Press, 1969), 98.

41. Dorwart, *Eberstadt and Forrestal,* 108ff., esp. 145; Hogan, *Cross of Iron,* 49–57. Truman's eventual embrace of Eberstadt's plans is noted in Millis, ed., *Forrestal Diaries,* 162–63, 167–68, 230–31.

42. See "Summary of Report to Hon. James Forrestal," Eberstadt Papers, 5. Also see Millis, ed., *Forrestal Diaries,* 87.

43. The Navy Department produced a helpful review of the act for all its officers and bureaus. See Thomas H. Robbins Jr., Rear Admiral, U.S. Navy, memorandum of 1 August 1947, copy in Box 145, "Military: Army-Navy Unification," PSF, HSTL.

44. The NSC was little used by Truman until the Korean War, and the NSRB failed to attain the status Eberstadt hoped for and died as an organization in 1953. See Sander, "Truman and the National Security Council"; Cuff, "Ferdinand Eberstadt," 37–52.

45. See, for example, Williams, *Tragedy of American Diplomacy,* 270; Block, *Origins of International Economic Disorder,* 83.

46. See Block, *Origins of International Economic Disorder,* 92–97, 102–8, quotation on 103. See also Eden, "Capitalist Conflict," 241–42; Hogan, *Marshall Plan,* 337, 380–82, 388–89; Alan Wolfe, *America's Impasse: The Rise and Fall of the Politics of Growth* (Boston: South End Press, 1981), 62–63.

47. See Acheson to Truman, undated memorandum (soon after the NATO treaty was ratified), Box 145, "Military—Department of Defense," PSF, HSTL.

48. Myrdal, "Economic Developments and Prospects in America," address before the National Economic Society of Sweden, 9 March 1944, distributed in the U.S. by the National Planning Association, Box 7, "Government Files," Coy Papers; *Business Week* quoted in Hill, "Business Community and National Defense," 423. See Block, *Origins of International Economic Disorder,* 107. Kofsky actually traces the permanent war economy to 1948 since the war scare led to a 30 percent rise in military spending (*Truman and the War Scare of 1948,* 250–68).

Conclusion

1. Schattschneider, *Semisovereign People,* v–vi (emphasis added).

2. Skowronek, *Building a New American State,* 290.

Selected Bibliography

Archival Sources

National Archives
  RG 179: Records of the War Production Board
  WPB Policy Analysis and Records Branch
  Office Files of Bernard Gladieux
  James Knowlson Papers
  RG 250: Records of the Office of War Mobilization and Reconversion
  Robert Nathan Papers

Franklin D. Roosevelt Library
  Official File
  President's Secretary Files
  Wayne Coy Papers
  Leon Henderson Papers
  Harry Hopkins Papers
  Joseph Lash Papers
  Isador Lubin Papers
  William McReynolds Papers
  Gardiner Means Papers
  Donald Riddle Papers
  Harold Smith Papers

Harry S Truman Presidential Library
  Official File
  President's Secretary Files
  Thomas Blaisdell Papers
  Gerhard Colm Papers

Committee for the Marshall Plan Papers
Bernard Gladieux Papers
Paul Hoffman Papers
Joseph Jones Papers
Milton Katz Papers
J. Anthony Panuch Papers
Harry Price Papers
Sidney Souers Papers

Seeley G. Mudd Manuscript Library, Princeton University
Ferdinand Eberstadt Papers

University of Virginia Archives
Edward Stettinius Papers

Yale University Archives
James Fesler Papers

Published Government Sources

Baruch, Bernard M., and John Hancock. Office of War Mobilization. *Report on War and Post-War Adjustment Policies*. Washington, D.C.: Government Printing Office, 1944.

Cline, Ray S. U.S. Department of the Army, Office of the Chief of Military History. *Washington Command Post: The Operations Division*. Washington, D.C.: Government Printing Office, 1951.

Fairchild, Byron, and Jonathan Grossman. U.S. Department of the Army, Office of the Chief of Military History. *The Army and Industrial Manpower*. Washington, D.C.: Government Printing Office, 1959.

First, Edythe W. U.S. Civilian Production Administration. *Industry and Labor Advisory Committees in the National Defense Advisory Commission and Office of Production Management, May 1940 to January 1942*. Special Study No. 24. Washington, D.C.: Government Printing Office, 1946.

Holley, Irving Brinton, Jr. U.S. Department of the Army, Office of the Chief of Military History. *Buying Aircraft: Materiel Procurement for the Army Air Forces*. Washington, D.C.: Government Printing Office, 1964.

Jones, Drummond. U.S. Civilian Production Administration. *The Role of the Office of Civilian Requirements in the Office of Production Management and the War Production Board, January 1941 to November 1945*. Special Study No. 20. Washington, D.C.: Government Printing Office, 1946.

McAleer, James A. U.S. Civilian Production Administration. *Dollar-A-Year and Without Compensation Personnel Policies of the War Production Board and Predecessor Agencies, August 1939 to November 1945*. Special Study No. 27. Washington, D.C.: Government Printing Office, 1947.

McGrane, Reginald. U.S. Civilian Production Administration. *The Facilities and Construction Program of the War Production Board and Predecessor Agencies, May 1940 to May 1945*. Special Study No. 19. Washington, D.C.: Government Printing Office, 1946.

Millet, John D. U.S. Department of the Army, Office of the Chief of Military History. *The Organization and Role of the Army Service Forces*. Washington, D.C.: Government Printing Office, 1954.

Purcell, Richard J. U.S. Civilian Production Administration. *Labor Policies of the National Defense Advisory Commission and Office of Production Management, May 1940 to April 1942*. Special Study No. 23. Washington, D.C.: Government Printing Office, 1946.

Schuck, William J. "Industry and Labor Advisory Committees in the [WPB], January 1942 to November 1945," USCPA Special Study No. 34, unpublished typescript, National Archives, Washington, D.C.

Sitterson, J. Carlyle. U.S. Civilian Production Administration. *Aircraft Production Policies*. Special Study No. 21. Washington, D.C.: Government Printing Office, 1946.

———. U.S. Civilian Production Administration. *Development of the Reconversion Policies of the War Production Board, April 1943 to January 1945*. Special Study No. 15. Washington, D.C.: Government Printing Office, 1946.

Smith, R. Elberton. U.S. Department of the Army, Office of the Chief of Military History. *The Army and Economic Mobilization*. Washington, D.C.: Government Printing Office, 1959.

U.S. Bureau of the Budget. *The United States at War: Development and Administration of the War Program by the Federal Government*. Washington, D.C.: Government Printing Office, 1947.

U.S. Civilian Production Administration. *Industrial Mobilization for War*. Washington, D.C.: Government Printing Office, 1947.

U.S. Congress. House. Select Committee Investigating National Defense Migration. *Third Interim Report*. 77th Congress, 2d sess., 9 March 1942. Report No. 1879.

———. *Sixth Interim Report*. 77th Congress, 2d sess., 20 October 1942. Report No. 2589.

———. *Final Report*. 77th Congress, 2d sess., January 1943. Report No. 3.

U.S. Congress. Senate. Report of the Smaller War Plants Corporation to Special Committee to Study Problems of American Small Business. *Economic Concentration and World War II*. 79th Congress, 2d sess., 14 June 1946. S. Doc. 206. Washington, D.C.: Government Printing Office.

U.S. Congress. Senate. Special Committee Investigating the National Defense Program. *Hearings*. 77th Congress, 1st sess., Part 1, April 1941. "Progress of National Defense Program."

———. *Hearings*. 77th Congress, 1st sess., Part 3, May, June 1941. "Aluminum."

———. *Hearings*. 77th Congress, 1st sess., Part 5, June, July 1941. "Functions of the Office of Production Management."

———. *Hearings*. 77th Congress, 1st sess., Part 6, July, August 1941. "War Department's Accomplishments in fiscal year 1940," "Small Business in the Defense Program."

———. *Hearings*. 77th Congress, 1st sess., Part 7, August, September 1941. "Defense Contracts," "Aluminum."

———. *Hearings*. 77th Congress, 1st sess., Part 8, October 1941. "Defense Contracts."

———. *Hearings*. 77th Congress, 2d sess., Part 10, January, February 1942. "Dollar-a-year men," "Contract Review Branch, WPB."

———. *Hearings.* 77th Congress, 2d sess., Part 12, April, July 1942. "Conversion Program, WPB," "Procurement and Purchase Section, WPB."

———. *Hearings.* 77th Congress, 2d sess., Part 16, November, December 1942. "War Department Program for Procurement and Production of Munitions."

———. *Hearings.* 78th Congress, 2d sess., Part 21, September 1943–January 1944. "Reconversion Program."

———. *Hearings.* 78th Congress, 2d sess., Part 24, June 1944. "Reconversion."

———. *Aluminum.* 77th Congress, 1st sess., 26 June 1941. Report No. 480, Part 1.

———. *Report concerning Priorities and the Utilization of Existing Manufacturing Facilities.* 77th Congress, 1st sess., 17 November 1941. Report No. 480, Part 3.

———. *First Annual Report.* 77th Congress, 2d sess., 15 January 1942. Report No. 480, Part 5.

———. *Conversion to War Production Program of War Production Board.* 77th Congress, 2d sess., 18 June 1942. Report No. 480, Part 8, Appendix III.

———. *Interim Report on Steel.* 78th Congress, 1st sess., 4 February 1943. Report No. 10, Part 3.

———. *Additional Report—Second Annual Report.* 78th Congress, 1st sess., 11 March 1943. Report No. 10, Part 4.

———. *Additional Report—Renegotiation of War Contracts.* 78th Congress, 1st sess., 30 March 1943. Report No. 10, Part 5.

———. *Third Annual Report.* 78th Congress, 2d sess., 4 March 1944. Report No. 10, Part 16.

———. *Additional Report: Accumulation of Surpluses.* 78th Congress, 2d sess., 19 December 1944. Report No. 10, Part 20.

———. *Fourth Annual Report.* 79th Congress, 1st sess., 30 July 1945. Report No. 110, Part 4.

———. *Fifth Annual Report.* 79th Congress, 2d sess., 3 September 1946. Report No. 110, Part 7.

U.S. Congress. Senate. Special Committee on Post-war Economic Policy and Planning. *Post-War Economic Policy and Planning.* 78th Congress, 2d sess., 12 June 1944. Report No. 530, Part 4.

U.S. Congress. Senate. Special Committee to Study the Problems of American Small Business. *Additional Report.* 77th Congress, 2d sess., 5 February 1942. Report No. 479, Part 2.

———. *Additional Report.* 78th Congress, 1st sess., 18 January 1943. Report No. 12.

U.S. Department of State. *Foreign Relations of the United States: 1947.* Vol. 3. Washington, D.C.: Government Printing Office, 1972.

U.S. National Archives. *Federal Records of World War II.* Vol. 1, *Civilian Agencies.* Washington, D.C.: Government Printing Office, 1950.

Watson, Mark Skinner. U.S. Department of the Army, Office of the Chief of Military History. *Chief of Staff: Prewar Plans and Preparations.* Washington, D.C.: Government Printing Office, 1950.

Published and Unpublished Sources

Adams, Walter. *The Structure of American Industry: Some Case Studies.* 4th ed. New York: Macmillan, 1971.

Adams, Walter, and Horace M. Gray. *Monopoly in America: The Government as Promoter*. New York: Macmillan, 1955.

Albion, Robert, and Robert Connery. *Forrestal and the Navy*. New York: Columbia University Press, 1962.

Almond, Gabriel. "The Return to the State." *American Political Science Review* 82 (1988): 854–74.

Bailey, Steven Kemp. *Congress Makes a Law: The Story behind the Employment Act of 1946*. New York: Columbia University Press, 1950.

Baldanzi, George. "Organized Labor and the State." In *Postwar Economic Society*, edited by Arnold Zurcher and Raymond Page. New York: New York University Press, 1944.

Baldwin, David A. *Economic Development and American Foreign Policy, 1943–62*. Chicago: University of Chicago Press, 1966.

Baran, Paul, and Paul Sweezy. *Monopoly Capital*. New York: Monthly Review Press, 1966.

Barnet, Richard. *The Roots of War*. New York: Penguin, 1971.

Barrow, Clyde. *Critical Theories of the State*. Madison: University of Wisconsin Press, 1993.

Baruch, Bernard M. *American Industry in the War*. Paramus, N.J.: Prentice Hall, 1941.

Beaver, Daniel R. *Newton D. Baker and the American War Effort, 1917–1919*. Lincoln: University of Nebraska Press, 1966.

Bellush, Bernard. *The Failure of the NRA*. New York: W. W. Norton, 1975.

Belsley, G. Lyle. "Demobilization of Industry for the Peace." *Public Administration Review* 5 (1944): 263–70.

Berle, Adolf A., and Gardiner Means. *The Modern Corporation and Private Property*. Rev. ed. New York: Harcourt, Brace and World, 1968.

Bernstein, Barton J. "The Debate on Industrial Reconversion—The Protection of Oligopoly and Military Control of the Economy." *American Journal of Economics and Sociology* 26 (1967): 159–72.

———. "The Removal of War Production Board Controls on Business." *Business History Review* 39 (1965): 243–60.

Bernstein, Irving. *The Lean Years: A History of the American Worker, 1920–1933*. New York: Penguin, 1960.

———. *Turbulent Years: A History of the American Worker, 1933–1941*. Boston: Houghton Mifflin, 1970.

Bernstein, Michael A. *The Great Depression: Delayed Recovery and Economic Change in America, 1929–1939*. New York: Cambridge University Press, 1987.

Block, Fred L. *The Origins of International Economic Disorder: A Study of United States International Monetary Policy from World War II to the Present*. Berkeley: University of California Press, 1977.

———. *Revising State Theory: Essays in Politics and Postindustrialism*. Philadelphia: Temple University Press, 1987.

Blum, Albert A. "Birth and Death of the M-Day Plan." In *American Civil-Military Decisions: A Book of Case Studies*, edited by Harold Stein. University: University of Alabama Press, 1963.

Borosage, Robert. "The Making of the National Security State." In *The Pentagon Watchers*, edited by Leonard S. Rodberg and Derek Shearer. New York: Anchor, 1970.

Bowman, John R.. *Capitalist Collective Action*. New York: Cambridge University Press, 1989.

———. "The Politics of the Market: Economic Competition and the Organization of Capitalists." *Political Power and Social Theory* 5 (1985): 35–88.

Boyer, Richard O., and Herbert M. Morais. *Labor's Untold Story*. New York: United Electrical, Radio and Machine Workers of America, 1955.

Boylan, James. *The New Deal Coalition and the Election of 1946*. New York: Garland, 1981.

Brady, Robert. "The C.E.D.—What Is It and Why?" *Antioch Review* (spring 1944): 21–45.

Brand, Donald. *Corporatism and the Rule of Law*. Ithaca, N.Y.: Cornell University Press, 1988.

Brigante, John. *The Feasibility Dispute*. Washington, D.C.: Committee on Public Administration Cases, 1950.

Brinkley, Alan. *The End of Reform: New Deal Liberalism in Recession and War*. New York: Alfred A. Knopf, 1995.

Brody, David. "The New Deal and World War II." In *The New Deal: The National Level*, edited by John Braeman, Robert H. Bremner, and David Brody. Columbus: Ohio University Press, 1975.

———. *Workers in Industrial America: Essays on the Twentieth Century Struggle*. New York: Oxford University Press, 1980.

Brownlow, Louis. *A Passion for Anonymity: The Autobiography of Louis Brownlow*. Vol. 2. Chicago: University of Chicago Press, 1958.

Burch, Philip H., Jr. *Elites in American History*. Vol. 3, *The New Deal to the Carter Administration*. New York: Holmes and Meier, 1980.

Burns, James MacGregor. *The Lion and the Fox*. New York: Harcourt, Brace and World, 1956.

———. *Roosevelt: The Soldier of Freedom*. New York: Harcourt Brace Jovanovich, 1970.

Cammack, Paul. "Bringing the State Back In?" *British Journal of Political Science* 19 (1988): 261–90.

Caraley, Demetrios. *The Politics of Military Unification*. New York: Columbia University Press, 1966.

Carnoy, Martin. *The State and Political Theory*. Princeton, N.J.: Princeton University Press, 1984.

Catton, Bruce. *The War Lords of Washington*. New York: Harcourt, Brace, 1948.

Christman, Calvin Lee. "Ferdinand Eberstadt and Economic Mobilization for War, 1941–1943." Ph.D. diss., Ohio State University, 1971.

Clark, John Maurice. *Demobilization of Wartime Economic Controls*. New York: McGraw-Hill, 1944.

Clawson, Marion. *New Deal Planning: The National Resources Planning Board*. Baltimore: Johns Hopkins University Press, 1981.

Clifford, Clark. *Counsel to the President: A Memoir*. New York: Random House, 1991.

Collins, Robert M. *The Business Response to Keynes, 1929–1964*. New York: Columbia University Press, 1981.

Connery, Robert H. *The Navy and the Industrial Mobilization in World War II*. Princeton, N.J.: Princeton University Press, 1951.

Coulter, Matthew. "The Franklin D. Roosevelt Administration and the Special Committee on Investigation of the Munitions Industry." *Mid-America* 67 (1985): 23–35.

Crouch, Colin. "The State, Capital, and Liberal Democracy." In *State and Economy in Contemporary Capitalism,* edited by Colin Crouch. New York: St. Martin's Press, 1979.

Cuff, Robert D. "Ferdinand Eberstadt, the National Security Resources Board, and the Search for Integrated Mobilization Planning, 1947–1948." *Public Historian* 7 (1985): 37–52.

———. "An Organizational Perspective on the Military-Industrial Complex." *Business History Review* 52 (1978): 250–67.

———. *The War Industries Board: Business-Government Relations during World War I.* Baltimore: Johns Hopkins University Press, 1973.

Dallek, Robert. *Franklin D. Roosevelt and American Foreign Policy, 1932–1945.* New York: Oxford University Press, 1981.

Darilek, Richard E. *A Loyal Opposition in Time of War: The Republican Party and the Politics of Foreign Policy from Pearl Harbor to Yalta.* Westport, Conn.: Greenwood Press, 1976.

Davis, Mike. *Prisoners of the American Dream: Politics and Economy in the History of the U.S. Working Class.* London: Verso, 1986.

Domhoff, G. William. "American State Autonomy via the Military?: Another Counterattack on a Theoretical Delusion." *Critical Sociology* 18 (1992): 9–56.

———. *The Power Elite and the State.* New York: Aldine de Gruyter, 1990.

Donovan, Robert J. *Conflict and Crisis: The Presidency of Harry S Truman, 1945–1948.* New York: W. W. Norton, 1977.

Dorwart, Jeffrey. *Eberstadt and Forrestal: A National Security Partnership.* College Station: Texas A&M University Press, 1991.

Dubofsky, Melvyn. *The State and Labor in Modern America.* Chapel Hill: University of North Carolina Press, 1994.

Durr, Clifford. "The Defense Plant Corporation." In *Public Administration and Policy Development: A Case Book,* edited by Harold Stein. New York: Harcourt, Brace, 1952.

Eakins, David W. "Business Planners and America's Postwar Expansion." In *Corporations and the Cold War,* edited by David Horowitz. New York: Monthly Review Press, 1969.

———. "The Development of Corporate Liberal Policy Research in the United States, 1885–1965." Ph.D. diss., University of Wisconsin, 1966.

Eden, Lynn. "Capitalist Conflict and the State: The Making of United States Military Policy in 1948." In *Statemaking and Social Movements,* edited by Charles Bright and Susan Harding. Ann Arbor: University of Michigan Press, 1984.

Edwards, Richard. *Contested Terrain: The Transformation of the Workplace in the Twentieth Century.* New York: Basic, 1979.

Eiler, Keith. *Mobilizing America: Robert P. Patterson and the War Effort, 1940–1945.* Ithaca, N.Y.: Cornel University Press, 1997.

Eliot, Thomas, and Samuel Grafton. "The Meaning of the Elections." *New Republic* (16 November 1942): 623–42.

Engler, Robert. *The Politics of Oil.* New York: Macmillan, 1961.

Esping-Anderson, Gosta, Roger Friedland, and Erik Olin Wright. "Modes of Class Struggles and the Capitalist State." *Kapitalistate* 4–5 (1976): 186–220.

Fearon, Peter. *War, Prosperity, and Depression: The U.S. Economy, 1917–45.* Oxford: Philip Allan, 1987.

Ferguson, Thomas. "From Normalcy to New Deal: Industrial Structure, Party Competition, and American Public Policy in the Great Depression." *International Organization* 38 (1984): 41–94.

Ferguson, Thomas, and Joel Rogers. "How Business Saved the New Deal." *Nation* (8 December 1979): 589–92.

Fesler, James W. "Mobilization of Industry for the War." *Public Administration Review* 5 (1945): 257–62.

———. "Reflections of a Public Servant." *Bureaucrat* (summer 1987): 3–5.

———. "The State and Its Study: The Whole and the Parts." *PS* (fall 1988): 891–901.

———. Unpublished draft of autobiography, chapter 4, "The War Production Board."

Flynn, George Q. *The Mess in Washington: Manpower Mobilization in World War II.* Wesport, Conn.: Greenwood Press, 1979.

Fordham, Benjamin. *Building the Cold War Consensus: The Political Economy of U.S. National Security Policy, 1949–51.* Ann Arbor: University of Michigan Press, 1998.

Fossedal, Gregory A. *Our Finest Hour: Will Clayton, the Marshall Plan, and the Triumph of Democracy.* Stanford, Calif.: Hoover Institute, 1993.

Fraser, Steve. "The 'Labor Question'." In *The Rise and Fall of the New Deal Order, 1930–1980* edited by Gary Gerstle and Steve Fraser. Princeton, N.J.: Princeton University Press, 1989.

———. *Labor Will Rule: Sidney Hillman and the Rise of American Labor.* Ithaca, N.Y.: Cornell University Press, 1993.

Freeman, Joshua. "Delivering the Goods: Industrial Unionism during World War II." *Labor History* 19 (1978): 570–93.

Friedel, Frank. *Franklin D. Roosevelt: A Rendevous with Destiny.* Boston: Little, Brown, 1990.

Gardner, Lloyd C. "The New Deal, New Frontiers, and the Cold War: A Re-examination of American Expansionism, 1933–1945." In *Corporations and the Cold War,* edited by David Horowitz. New York: Monthly Review Press, 1969.

Gerth, H. H., and C. Wright Mills. *From Max Weber: Essays in Sociology.* New York: Oxford University Press, 1946.

Gilbert, Richard, et al. *An Economic Program for American Democracy.* New York: Vanguard, 1938.

Ginsburg, Benjamin. *The Captive Public: How Mass Opinion Promotes State Power.* New York: Basic, 1986.

Goldfield, Michael. "Worker Insurgency, Radical Organization, and New Deal Labor Legislation." *American Political Science Review* 83 (1989): 1257–82.

Goldman, Eric F. *The Crucial Decade—and After: America, 1945–1960.* New York: Vintage, 1960.

Gordon, Colin. *New Deals: Business, Labor, and Politics in America, 1920–1935.* New York: Cambridge University Press, 1994.

Graham, Otis. *Toward a Planned Society: From Roosevelt to Nixon.* New York: Oxford University Press, 1976.

Gulick, Luther. *Administrative Reflections from World War II.* University: University of Alabama Press, 1948.

Habermas, Jurgen. *Legitimation Crisis.* Boston: Beacon Press, 1975.

Hall, Peter A. "Policy Paradigms, Social Learning, and the State." *Comparative Politics* 25 (1993): 175–96.

Hamby, Alonzo. "The Mind and Character of Harry S. Truman." In *The Truman Presidency*, edited by Michael J. Lacey. New York: Cambridge University Press, 1989.

Hammond, Paul Y. *Organizing for Defense: The American Military Establishment in the Twentieth Century*. Princeton, N.J.: Princeton University Press, 1961.

Hansen, Alvin H. *The American Economy*. New York: McGraw-Hill, 1957.

———. *Full Recovery or Stagnation?* New York: W. W. Norton, 1938.

———. *The Postwar American Economy: Performance and Problems*. New York: W. W. Norton, 1964.

Harris, Howell John. *The Right to Manage: Industrial Relations Policies of American Business in the 1940s*. Madison: University of Wisconsin Press, 1982.

Hawley, Ellis W. *The Great War and the Search for a Modern Order*. New York: St. Martin's Press, 1977.

———. "Herbert Hoover, the Commerce Secretariat, and the Vision of an 'Associative State,' 1921–1928." *Journal of American History* 61 (1974): 116–40.

———. *The New Deal and the Problem of Monopoly*. Princeton, N.J.: Princeton University Press, 1966.

Hay, Colin. "Divided By a Common Language: Political Theory and the Concept of Power." *Politics* 17 (1997): 45–52.

———. "Political Time and the Temporality of Crisis." *Contemporary Political Studies* (1997): 1092–1102.

Hess, Stephen. *Organizing the Presidency*. Washington, D.C.: Brookings Institution, 1976.

Hill, William Steinert, Jr. "The Business Community and National Defense: Corporate Leaders and the Military, 1943–1950." Ph.D. diss., Stanford University, 1980.

Himmelberg, Robert. *The Origins of the National Recovery Administration: Business, Government, and the Trade Association Issue*. Bronx, N.Y.: Fordham University Press, 1976.

Hofstadter, Richard. *The American Political Tradition*. London: Jonathan Cape, 1971.

———. *The Age of Reform*. New York: Alfred A. Knopf, 1955.

———. *The American Political Tradition and the Men Who Made It*. New York: Vintage, 1954.

Hogan, Michael J. "American Marshall Planners and the Search for a European Neocapitalism." *American Historical Review* 90 (1985): 44–72.

———. *The Cross of Iron: Harry S. Truman and the Origins of the National Security State, 1945–1954*. New York: Cambridge University Press, 1998.

———. *The Marshall Plan: America, Britain, and the Reconstruction of Western Europe, 1947–1952*. New York: Cambridge University Press, 1987.

Hooks, Gregory. *Forging the Military-Industrial Complex: World War II's Battle of the Potomac*. Urbana: University of Illinois Press, 1991.

Hoopes, Townsend, and Douglas Brinkley. *Driven Patriot: The Life and Times of James Forrestal*. New York: Alfred A. Knopf, 1992.

Horowitz, David, ed. *Corporations and the Cold War*. New York: Monthly Review Press, 1969.

Huntington, Samuel. *The Soldier and the State*. New York: Vintage, 1957.

Huthmacher, J. Joseph. *Senator Robert F. Wagner and the Rise of Urban Liberalism.* New York: Atheneum, 1971.

Ickes, Harold L. *The Secret Diary of Harold Ickes.* Vol. 2, *The Inside Struggle, 1936–1939.* New York: Simon and Schuster, 1954.

———. *The Secret Diary of Harold Ickes.* Vol. 3, *The Lowering Clouds, 1939–1941.* New York: Simon and Schuster, 1955.

Isaac, Jeffrey. *Power and Marxist Theory: A Realist View.* Ithaca, N.Y.: Cornell University Press, 1987.

Isaacson, Walter, and Evan Thomas. *The Wise Men: Six Friends and the World They Made, Acheson, Bohlen, Harriman, Kennan, Lovett, McCloy.* New York: Simon and Schuster, 1986.

Janeway, Eliot. *The Struggle for Survival: A Chronicle of Economic Mobilization in World War II.* New Haven, Conn.: Yale University Press, 1951.

Jeffries, John W. "The 'New' New Deal: Franklin D. Roosevelt and American Liberalism, 1939–1945." *Political Science Quarterly* 105 (1990): 397–418.

Jessop, Bob. *The Capitalist State.* New York: New York University Press, 1982.

———. *Nicos Poulantzas.* New York: St. Martin's Press, 1985.

———. *State Theory: Putting the Capitalist State in Its Place.* University Park: Pennsylvania State University Press, 1990.

Kalecki, Michal. *The Last Phase in the Transformation of Capitalism.* New York: Monthly Review Press, 1972.

Kaplan, A. D. H. *The Liquidation of War Production: Cancellation of War Contracts and Disposal of Government-Owned Plants and Surpluses.* New York: McGraw-Hill, 1944.

Karl, Barry Dean. *Executive Reorganization and Reform in the New Deal: The Genesis of Administrative Management, 1900–1939.* Cambridge, Mass.: Harvard University Press, 1963.

———. *The Uneasy State: The United States from 1915 to 1945.* Chicago: University of Chicago Press, 1983.

Katznelson, Ira. "Rethinking the Silences of Social and Economic Policy." *Political Science Quarterly* 101 (1986): 307–25.

Kaufman, Allen, L. S. Zacharias, and Alfred Marcus (1990) "Managers United for Corporate Rivalry: A History of Managerial Collective Action." *Journal of Policy History* 2 (1990): 56–97.

Key, V. O., Jr. "The American Road to Peace, A Symposium: The Reconversion Phase of Demobilization." *American Political Science Review* 38 (1944): 1137–152.

Koenig, Louis William. *The Presidency and the Crisis: Powers of the Office from the Invasion of Poland to Pearl Harbor.* New York: King's Crown Press, 1944.

Koistinen, Paul A. C. *Beating Plowshares into Swords: The Political Economy of American Warfare, 1606–1865.* Lawrence: University Press of Kansas, 1996.

———. *The Hammer and the Sword: Labor, the Military, and Industrial Mobilization, 1920–1945.* New York: Arno Press, 1979.

———. *The Military-Industrial Complex: A Historical Perspective.* New York: Praeger, 1980.

———. *Mobilizing for Modern War: The Political Economy of American Warfare, 1865–1919.* Lawrence: University Press of Kansas, 1997.

———. *Planning War, Pursuing Peace: The Political Economy of American Warfare, 1920–1939.* Lawrence: University Press of Kansas, 1998.

———. "Warfare and Power Relations in America: Mobilizing the World War II Economy." In *The Home Front and War in the Twentieth Century,* edited by James Titus. Colorado Springs: U.S. Air Force Academy, 1984.

Kofsky, Frank. *Harry S. Truman and the War Scare of 1948: A Successful Campaign to Deceive the Nation.* New York: St. Martin's Press, 1993.

Kolko, Gabriel. *Main Currents in Modern American History.* New York: Pantheon, 1984.

———. *The Roots of American Foreign Policy: An Analysis of Power and Purpose.* Boston: Beacon Press, 1969.

———. *The Triumph of Conservatism: A Re-Interpretation of American History, 1900–1916.* Chicago: Quadrangle, 1963.

Krasner, Stephen D. "Approaches to the State: Alternative Conceptions and Historical Dynamics." *Comparative Politics* 16 (1984): 223–46.

Lacey, Michael J., ed. *The Truman Presidency.* New York: Cambridge University Press, 1989.

Leffler, Melvin P. *A Preponderance of Power: National Security, the Truman Administration, and the Cold War.* Stanford, Calif.: Stanford University Press, 1992.

Lekachman, Robert. *The Age of Keynes.* New York: Random House, 1966.

Leuchtenburg, William. *FDR and the New Deal.* New York: Harper and Row, 1963.

———. "The New Deal and the Analogue of War." In *Change and Continuity in Twentieth-Century America,* edited by J. Braeman, R. Bremner, and E. Walters. Columbus: Ohio State University, 1964.

Levi, Margaret. *Of Rule and Revenue.* Berkeley: University of California Press, 1988.

Levine, Rhonda. *Class Struggle and the New Deal: Industrial Labor, Industrial Capital, and the State.* Lawrence: University Press of Kansas, 1988.

Lichtenstein, Nelson. "From Corporatism to Collective Bargaining: Organized Labor and the Eclipse of Social Democracy in the Postwar Era." In *The Rise and Fall of the New Deal Order, 1930–1980,* edited by Steve Fraser and Gary Gerstle. Princeton, N.J.: Princeton University Press, 1989.

———. "Labor in the Truman Era." In *The Truman Presidency,* edited by Michael J. Lacey. New York: Cambridge University Press, 1989.

———. *Labor's War at Home: The CIO in World War II.* New York: Cambridge University Press, 1982.

———. *The Most Dangerous Man in Detroit.* New York: Basic, 1995.

Lindblom, Charles. *Politics and Markets: The World's Political Economic Systems.* New York: Basic, 1977.

Link, Arthur S. *Woodrow Wilson and the Progressive Era, 1910–1917.* New York: Harper and Row, 1954.

Luger, Stan. *Corporate Power, American Democracy, and the Automobile Industry.* New York: Cambridge University Press, 2000.

Lustig, R. Jeffrey. *Corporate Liberalism: The Origins of Modern American Political Theory, 1890–1920.* Berkeley: University of California Press, 1982.

Lynd, Robert. "Power in American Society as Resource and Problem." In *Problems of Power in American Democracy,* edited by Arthur Kornhauser. Detroit: Wayne State University Press, 1957.

McConnell, Grant. *Private Power and American Democracy.* New York: Vintage, 1966.

McEachern, Doug. *The Expanding State: Class and Economy in Europe since 1945.* New York: St. Martin's Press, 1990.

McQuaid, Kim. *Big Business and Presidential Power*. New York: William Morrow, 1982.

———. "Corporate Liberalism in the American Business Community." *Business History Review* 52 (1978): 342–68.

———. *Uneasy Partners: Big Business in American Politics, 1945–1990*. Baltimore: Johns Hopkins University Press, 1992.

Magdoff, Harry. *The Age of Imperialism: The Economics of U.S. Foreign Policy*. New York: Monthly Review Press, 1969.

Maier, Charles S. "The Politics of Productivity: Foundations of American International Economic Policy after World War II." *International Organization* 31 (1977): 607–33.

Manley, John. "Neo-Pluralism: A Class Analysis of Pluralist I and Pluralist II." *American Political Science Review* 77 (1983): 363–83.

Markowitz, Norman D. *The Rise and Fall of the People's Century: Henry A. Wallace and American Liberalism, 1941–1948*. New York: Free Press, 1973.

May, Dean L. *From New Deal to New Economics*. New York: Garland, 1981.

Melman, Seymour. *The Permanent War Economy: American Capitalism in Decline*. New York: Simon and Schuster, 1974.

Miliband, Ralph. *The State in Capitalist Society*. New York: Basic, 1969.

Millett, John D. *The Process and Organization of Government Planning*. New York: Columbia University Press, 1947.

Millis, Walter. *Arms and Men: A Study in American Military History*. New York: New American Library, 1956.

———, ed. *Forrestal Diaries*. New York: Viking, 1951.

Millis, Walter, with Harvey Mansfield and Harold Stein. *Arms and the State: Civil-Military Elements in National Policy*. New York: Twentieth Century Fund, 1958.

Mills, C. Wright. *The Power Elite*. New York: Oxford University Press, 1959.

Monsees, Carl Henry. *Industry-Government Cooperation: A Study of the Participation of Advisory Committees in Public Administration*. Washington, D.C.: Public Affairs Press, 1944.

Mosher, Frederick C. *"The President Needs Help": Proceedings of a Conference Held on January 15, 1987 . . .* Lanham, Md.: University Press of America, 1988.

Mucciaroni, Gary. "Political Learning and Economic Policy Innovation: The United States and Sweden in the Post-World War II Era." *Journal of Policy History* 1 (1989): 391–418.

Nash, Gerald D. "Experiments in Industrial Mobilization: WIB and NRA." *Mid-America* 45 (1963): 157–74.

Nelson, Anna Kasten. "National Security I: Inventing a Process (1945–1960)." In *The Illusion of Presidential Government*, edited by Hugh Heclo and Lester M. Salamon. Boulder, Colo.: Westview Press, 1981.

Nelson, Donald. *Arsenal of Democracy*. New York: Harcourt, Brace, 1946.

Neumann, Franz. *The Democratic and Authoritarian State*. New York: Free Press, 1957.

Novick, David, Melvin Anshen, and W. C. Truppner. *Wartime Production Controls*. New York: Columbia University Press, 1949.

O'Connor, James. *The Fiscal Crisis of the State*. New York: St. Martin's Press, 1974.

Offe, Claus. *Contradictions of the Welfare State*, edited by John Keane. Cambridge, Mass.: MIT Press, 1984.

————. "Structural Problems of the Capitalist State." *German Political Studies* 1 (1974): 31–57.

Offe, Claus, and Volker Ronge. "Theses on the Theory of the State." *New German Critique* 6 (1975): 137–47.

Ohl, John K. *Supplying the Troops: General Somervell and American Logistics in World War II.* DeKalb: Northern Illinois University Press, 1994.

Olson, James. *Herbert Hoover and the Reconstruction Finance Corporation, 1931–33.* Ames: Iowa University Press, 1977.

Paterson, Thomas G. "The Quest for Peace and Prosperity: International Trade, Communism, and the Marshall Plan." In *Politics and Policies of the Truman Administration,* edited by Barton J. Bernstein. Chicago: Quadrangle, 1970.

Patterson, James T. *Congressional Conservatism and the New Deal: The Growth of the Conservative Coalition in Congress, 1933–1939.* Lexington: University of Kentucky Press, 1967.

Peltason, Jack. "The Reconversion Controversy." In *Public Administration and Policy Development: A Case Book,* edited by Harold Stein. New York: Harcourt, Brace, 1952.

Piven, Frances Fox, ed. *Labor Parties in Postindustrial Societies.* London: Polity Press, 1991.

Piven, Frances Fox, and Richard Cloward. *The New Class War: Reagan's Attack on the Welfare State and Its Consequences.* New York: Pantheon, 1982.

————. *Poor People's Movements: Why They Succeed, How They Fail.* New York: Vintage, 1979.

Polenberg, Richard. *Reorganizing Roosevelt's Government: The Controversy over Executive Reorganization, 1936–1939.* Cambridge, Mass.: Harvard University Press, 1966.

————. *War and Society: The United States, 1941–1945.* Philadelphia: J. B. Lippincott, 1972.

————. "The Decline of the New Deal, 1937–1940." In *The New Deal: The National Level,* edited by John Braeman, Robert H. Bremner, and David Brody. Columbus: Ohio University Press, 1975.

Pollard, Robert A. *Economic Security and the Origins of the Cold War, 1945–1950.* New York: Columbia University Press, 1985.

Poulantzas, Nicos. "The Problem of the Capitalist State." *New Left Review* 58 (1969): 67–78.

————. *State, Power, Socialism.* London: New Left, 1978.

Prechel, Harland. "Conflict and Historical Variation in Steel Capital-State Relations: The Emergence of State Structures and a More Prominent, Less Autonomous State." *American Sociological Review* 56 (1991): 693–98.

————. "Steel and the State: Industry Politics and Business Policy Formation, 1940–1989." *American Sociological Review* 55 (1990): 648–68.

Riddle, Donald H. *The Truman Committee: A Study in Congressional Responsibility.* New Brunswick, N.J.: Rutgers University Press, 1964.

Robertson, David. *Sly and Able: A Political Biography of James F. Byrnes.* New York: W. W. Norton, 1994.

Romasco, Albert U. *The Politics of Recovery: Roosevelt's New Deal.* New York: Oxford University Press, 1983.

————. *The Poverty of Abundance: Hoover, the Nation, the Depression.* New York: Oxford University Press, 1965.

Romero, Federico. *The United States and the European Trade Union Movement, 1944–1951.* Chapel Hill: University of North Carolina Press, 1992.

Rosenof, Theodore. *The Failure to Develop a Democratic-Left Synthesis, 1933–1950.* New York: Garland, 1983.

Sander, Alfred D. "Truman and the National Security Council: 1945–1947." *Journal of American History* 59 (1972): 369–88.

Schattschneider, E. E. *The Semisovereign People: A Realist's View of Democracy in America.* 1960. Reprint, Hinsdale, Ill.: Dryden Press, 1975.

Scheuerman, William. "The Politics of Protest: The Great Steel Strike of 1919–20 in Lackawanna, New York." *International Review of Social History* 31 (1986): 121–46.

———. *The Steel Crisis: The Economics and Politics of a Declining Industry.* New York: Praeger, 1987.

Schlesinger, Arthur M. *The Coming of the New Deal.* Boston: Houghton Mifflin, 1958.

———. *The Crisis of the Old Order, 1919–1933.* Boston: Houghton Mifflin, 1957.

Schriftgiesser, Karl. *Business Comes of Age: The Story of the Committee for Economic Development and Its Impact upon the Economic Policies of the United States, 1942–1960.* New York: Harper and Brothers, 1960.

———. *Business and Public Policy: The Role of the Committee for Economic Development, 1942–1967.* Paramus, N.J.: Prentice Hall, 1967.

Schwarz, Jordan A. *The Interregnum of Despair: Hoover, Congress, and the Depression.* Chicago: University of Illinois Press, 1970.

———. *The Speculator: Bernard M. Baruch in Washington, 1917–1965.* Chapel Hill: University of North Carolina Press, 1981.

Sherry, Michael S. *In the Shadow of War: The United States since the 1930s.* New Haven, Conn.: Yale University Press, 1995.

———. *Preparing for the Next War: American Plans for Postwar Defense, 1941–45.* New Haven, Conn.: Yale University Press, 1977.

Shoup, Laurence H., and William Minter. *Imperial Brain Trust: The Council on Foreign Relations and United States Foreign Policy.* New York: Monthly Review Press, 1974.

Sirevag, Torbjorn, *The Eclipse of the New Deal and the Fall of Vice-President Wallace, 1944.* New York: Garland, 1985.

Sklar, Martin J. *The Corporate Reconstruction of American Capitalism, 1890–1916.* New York: Cambridge University Press, 1988.

———. *The United States as a Developing Country: Studies in U.S. History in the Progressive Era and the 1920s.* New York: Cambridge University Press, 1992.

Skocpol, Theda. "Bringing the State Back In: Strategies in Current Research." In *Bringing the State Back In,* edited by Peter B. Evans, Dietrich Reuschemeyer, and Theda Skocpol. New York: Cambridge University Press, 1985.

———. "Political Response to Capitalist Crisis: Neo-Marxist Theories of the State and the Case of the New Deal." *Politics and Society* 10 (1980): 155–201.

———. *States and Social Revolutions: A Comparative Analysis of France, Russia, and China.* New York: Cambridge University Press, 1979.

Skowronek, Stephen. *Building a New American State: The Expansion of National Administrative Capacities, 1877–1920.* New York: Cambridge University Press, 1982.

Smith, Jean Edward. *Lucius D. Clay: An American Life*. New York: Henry Holt, 1990.

Smith, Perry McCoy. *The Air Force Plans for Peace, 1943–1945*. Baltimore: Johns Hopkins University Press, 1970.

Somers, Herman Miles. *Presidential Agency: OWMR, the Office of War Mobilization and Reconversion*. Cambridge, Mass.: Harvard University Press, 1950.

Soule, George. *Prosperity Decade: From War to Depression, 1917–1929*. New York: Harper and Row, 1968.

Sparrow, Bartholomew. *From the Outside In: World War II and the American State*. Princeton, N.J.: Princeton University Press, 1996.

Speer, Albert. *Inside the Third Reich: Memoirs*. New York: Macmillan, 1970.

Stone, I. F. *Business as Usual: The First Year of Defense*. New York: Modern Age, 1941.

———. *The War Years, 1939–1945*. Boston: Little, Brown, 1988.

Sutton, Francis X., Seymour Harris, Carl Kaysen, and James Tobin. *The American Business Creed*. Cambridge, Mass.: Harvard University Press, 1956.

Tilly, Charles. "Reflections on the History of European State-Making." In *The Formation of the National States in Western Europe*, edited by Charles Tilly. Princeton, N.J.: Princeton University Press, 1975.

Tomlins, Christopher. *The State and the Unions: Labor Relations, Law, and the Organized Labor Movement in America, 1880–1960*. New York: Cambridge University Press, 1985.

Truman, David. *The Governmental Process: Political Interests and Public Opinion*. New York: Alfred A. Knopf, 1951.

Truman, Harry S. *Memoirs*. Vol. 2, *Years of Trial and Hope*. New York: Doubleday, 1956.

Tyson, James L. "The War Industries Board: 1917–18." *Fortune* 23 (1940): 2–16.

Vieux, Steve. "Containing the Class Struggle." *Studies in Political Economy* 27 (1988): 87–111.

Vittoz, Stanley. "The Economic Foundations of Industrial Politics in the U.S. and the Emerging Theory of the State in Capitalist Society: The Case of the New Deal Labor Policy." *Amerikastudien* 27 (1982): 362–412.

Vogel, David. "Why Businessmen Distrust Their State: The Political Consciousness of American Corporate Executives." *British Journal of Political Science* 8 (1978): 45–78.

Wann, A. J., *The President as Chief Administrator: A Study of Franklin D. Roosevelt*. Washington, D.C.: Public Affairs Press, 1968.

Weinstein, James. *The Corporate Ideal in the Liberal State, 1900–1918*. Boston: Beacon Press, 1968.

Weir, Margaret, Ann Schola Orloff, and Theda Skocpol. *The Politics of Social Policy in the United States*. Princeton, N.J.: Princeton University Press, 1988.

White, Gerald T. *Billions for Defense: Government Financing by the Defense Plant Corporation*. University: University of Alabama Press, 1980.

Williams, William Appleman. *The Contours of American History*. Cleveland: World Publishing, 1961.

———. *The Tragedy of American Diplomacy*. New York: Dell Publishing, 1962.

———. "The Large Corporation and American Foreign Policy." In *Corporations and the Cold War*, edited by David Horowitz. New York: Monthly Review Press, 1969.

Wilson, Theodore. *The First Summit: Roosevelt and Churchill at Placentia Bay, 1941.* Rev. ed. Lawrence: University Press of Kansas, 1991.

Wolfe, Alan. *America's Impasse: The Rise and Fall of the Politics of Growth.* Boston: South End Press, 1981.

Young, Roland. *Congressional Politics in the Second World War.* New York: Columbia University Press, 1956.

Zurcher, Arnold, and Raymond Page, eds. *Postwar Economic Society: Addresses Delivered at the Series of Conferences of the Institute on Postwar Reconstruction.* 4 vols. New York: New York University Press, 1944.

Index